ISSUES
IN BANKING
AND MONETARY
ANALYSIS

ISSUES
IN BANKING
AND MONETARY
ANALYSIS

Edited by

Giulio Pontecorvo
Robert P. Shay

Graduate School of Business
COLUMBIA UNIVERSITY

Albert G. Hart

Department of Economics
COLUMBIA UNIVERSITY

Holt, Rinehart and Winston, Inc.
New York, Chicago, San Francisco, Atlanta,
Dallas, Montreal, Toronto, London.

Preface

I n the fall semester of the 1965 – 1966 academic
year, the editors of this volume dedicated a
seminar on banking and monetary problems to
the long tradition of this subject at Columbia University. The authors of the papers in this book first
presented them at meetings of the seminar. Sub-
sequently comments on the papers were solicited
from other scholars throughout the United States.
While the seminar was sponsored by the Graduate
School of Business, members of the Department of
Economics at Columbia collaborated in its planning, preparation, and content.

The papers and comments are devoted to
topics involving policy decisions by banking and
monetary authorities. Ranging from proposals for

v

international monetary reform to appraisal of the performance of our banking and financial markets, the materials provide useful readings for courses in money and credit, central bank policy, and seminars devoted to monetary theory and policy. Executives and economists in financial institutions desiring to stay abreast of current academic thought will find policy recommendations that will stimulate and possibly challenge their current attitudes toward credit policy. We are fortunate to number among the contributors to this volume many leading proponents of change in our banking and monetary arrangements.

We would like to acknowledge our debt to Dean Courtney C. Brown for his encouragement of the seminar by making it possible to invite the participation of a wide range of scholars. We are also obligated to Mrs. Elizabeth B. Tang for her assistance in coordinating the preparation of this volume for publication. Finally, the participation of both M.B.A. and doctoral students in the seminar enlivened the discussions.

New York, N.Y.   G.P.
May 1967   R.P.
                                  A.G.

Contents

ISSUES
IN BANKING
AND MONETARY
ANALYSIS

General
Introduction

In the papers collected in this volume, nine
academic students of monetary problems
present analyses of many of the issues in banking
and monetary theory that are likely to influence
banking and monetary policy for years to come.
The authors appraise banking and monetary
markets with the hope of improving their functioning, drawing upon monetary and economic
theory to support their advocacy of criteria and
instruments needed to accomplish the goals of
economic stabilization. Their treatment of these
issues is essentially neo-Keynesian, and reflects
recent advances in theory within Keynes's basic
analytical framework.

1

The book begins with Almarin Phillips' strong attack upon currently accepted concepts of bank regulation and supervision, and ends with Peter M. Kenen's plea for rationality in the development of a supranational banking and monetary system. Both authors suggest that present official approaches to these problems take too narrow a view of the goals to be sought and of the policy instruments available for use, and thus evade important issues in a way that may impede progress.

Each of the seven other papers attempts to pierce the veil that for so long has obscured the way in which monetary policy can best contribute to economic growth and stability. Hyman P. Minsky and Marvin E. Rozen analyze flows of savings and money in the markets for loanable funds. Minsky analyzes the effects of the increased competition for savings on the elasticity of supply of loanable funds. Rozen augments Phillips' attack on existing concepts of regulation, citing as evidence the ways in which changes in Regulation Q have helped increase competition in the market for savings. Warren L. Smith investigates monetary-policy aspects of changes in the volume and composition of financial assets held in response to interest rate movements. Albert G. Hart presents evidence on the timing of private investment decisions in relation to monetary-policy actions — suggesting strongly that decision-makers react so promptly to monetary policy that hypotheses concerning the direct impact of monetary policy upon business expectations deserve closer study. Arthur Smithies presents a primer for the much needed coordination of fiscal and monetary policy in the spirit of what has come to be known, belatedly, as the "new economics."

In the last three papers, recognition is given to the importance of international monetary arrangements. George N. Halm notes the burden placed by fixed exchange rates upon adjustment of balance-of-payments deficits among countries with convertible currencies. He urges adoption of the "band proposal," which is a widening of the range within which exchange rates are free to fluctuate. Ira O. Scott, Jr. analyzes recent innovations affecting international capital markets in Europe that represent the beginnings of the capital mobility needed to integrate the financial markets of these nations. Yet it is painfully evident that with current impediments to the mobility of goods and the factors of production, including capital, there can be no easy solution to international-payment problems. As Kenen points out, the major problem confronting trading nations today is not the problem of international liquidity, but rather the provision of an international monetary system that permits payments disturbances to be adjusted by discretionary policies designed to treat the type of disturbance according to the common interests of member nations.

The rationale of the book is that banking and monetary authorities face challenges that call for marked changes in the administration of monetary policy—both within individual countries and at the level of international coordination. Both the authors and editors urge changes in banking and monetary arrangements beyond the scope of those presently envisioned.

Chapter 1

Introduction

In the 1890s, from the eminence of Victorian Britain, Alfred Marshall was able to say that the foundations of economic analysis were firmly rooted in the solid rock of historical development. Yet less than thirty years later, looking at the fragmentation of the nineteenth century world economy, Marshall's pupil, J. M. Keynes, began his essay on *The Economic Consequences of the Peace* by asserting that our knowledge of economic affairs stood on shifting sands. The elements of truth and the psychological attitudes inherent in these two contradictory statements are suggestive of the recent history of monetary analysis.

Before the middle 1950s, monetary theorists generally considered such basic concepts as the standard definition of money (cash and demand deposits) to be reasonably workable tools for analysis. At the same time, most persons who thought objectively about monetary affairs felt that although the structural organization of the banking system was inefficient, it was, at least after 1935, reasonably stable; in addition, it worked. Therefore, structure was largely ignored, a convenience permitting analysts to concentrate on theory and policy problems.

More recently, our ability to rely comfortably on the traditional monetary assumptions has been destroyed. External competitive pressures from nonbank financial institutions, accompanied by internal technological advances, have already caused significant changes in the structure of American banking, and even greater shifts are expected in the future. There is increasing pressure for greater branching privileges, and mergers and consolidation among banks. Various regulatory bodies, both state and national, struggle for control of the situation, and the well-advertised differences of opinion between James J. Saxon, then Comptroller of the Currency, on one side, and the Federal Reserve Board and the Federal Deposit Insurance Corporation on the other, point up the disagreements present even on the same level. The internal tensions in the structure of American banking have also been reflected in a series of laws, especially the Banking Holding Company Act of 1956 and the 1966 merger legislation.

The authorities' unrest and the general public uneasiness over the adequacy of the banking structure have led to the development of a substantial literature directed at improving our understanding of banking as an industry. In his paper, Professor Almarin Phillips draws together much of this literature and uses broad conclusions about it to present a well-articulated argument for major revisions in the current organization of our banking system.

We would add that the current organization of federal regulatory agencies is obviously in need of change. The burden of much criticism of the Federal Reserve System has been that it tries to do too much. This criticism should be considered in any attempt to think through to an optimal structure. Phillips correctly points to the need for basic structural change, and stresses the subversion of the regulatory process to the interests represented by today's structure. If Phillips' argument is accepted, we could move vigorously toward a free market in banking services, a market protected primarily, as in other industries, by the antitrust statutes. The users of bank services have borne the cost of the protection that historically banking regulation has attempted to provide.

STRUCTURAL AND REGULATORY REFORM FOR COMMERCIAL BANKING

Almarin Phillips

"Change," Carlyle long ago observed, "indeed, is painful, yet ever needful; and if memory have its force and worth, so also has hope."

I shall argue in this paper that there is need for what would necessarily be a painful reexamination of the question of banking structure and regulation in the United States. The current worries about bank mergers, bank holding companies, overlapping jurisdictions of regulatory agencies, and proposals for modifications of the federal and state banking codes are symptomatic of an underlying need for change; however, those concerned have not attacked some obvious and fundamental problems, the cure of which lies in a major reform of the entire industry.

To an outsider—that is, one who is neither a monetary economist nor a banker—commercial banking in the United States seems to be an enormously confusing and confused industry. Although two-thirds of the twentieth century is gone, commercial banking retains strong vestiges of a remote past. Some of these vestiges are public regulatory features that arose in response to a variety of crises in banking performance. Others are private organizational characteristics that developed for similar reasons, but which presumably reflect the interests of banks and bankers more than do the public regulations. Both, however, affect performance and the structure of the industry.

Through use of an analogy between milk markets and banking markets, I will argue that banking organization and regulation have been and continue to be the dominant factors which, through their effect on performance, tend to preserve the present general structure of banking markets. These public and private constraints on the market process have permitted the retention of a structure that is quite different from that which would otherwise be obtained and, moreover, be quite different from that which is the most efficient with today's technologies. From this I argue that the public interest can best be served by altering regulations so a structure and an organization consistent with that interest will tend to emerge. In conclusion, I indicate the general nature of structural and regulatory reforms that would almost certainly lead to improved market performance.

REGULATION
AND THE STRUCTURE OF MARKETS

A cursory examination of relationships between the structure, organization, and performance of milk markets over the past several decades makes clear the forces that have led to attempts to regulate industries and, where the latter have succeeded, the effect of regulations on market structure. These forces can be illustrated by reference to Figure 1, a simple schematic representation of the market process.

Static theories of the market stipulate by assumption a market structure, a given technology, and the goals and modes of behavior of firms. From these, given the market demand, market performance characteristics are deduced. In Figure 1, such a system is shown by the solid lines connecting the structural variables (number, sizes, and locations of firms), technology, and the behavior of firms with supply, indicating the interaction of supply and demand which produces market performance. Except for the "feedback" to entry and exit and to investment in plant and equipment involved in the definition of static positions of long-run equilibrium, these theories do not ordinarily include feedbacks from market performance. In particular, dynamic feedbacks which might significantly alter the initial structural conditions and modes of behavior are not incorporated in the theories. Figure 1 specifically includes such feedback relationships in the pattern of broken lines running from market performance to structure and behavior.

The operation of these other feedbacks is crucial to the present analysis. In milk production, for example, their influence is reasonably clear. There have in the past been notable changes in milk production technology—changes which originated largely exogenous to the milk industry—the effects of which have been to increase the size of the most efficient milk farms, to reduce the costs of transporting fresh milk over long distances, to increase the size of the most efficient distribution network for packaged milk, and to open new distribution outlets. These changes have permitted a broadening of markets or, more precisely, have created opportunities for persons and firms which were previously not in competition with one another to enter one another's markets. The sudden eclipse of market demand after 1929 was the proximate cause of a shift in market performance which led to the use of these opportunities.

In these developments, new technologies had the effect of altering the structure of markets, increasing the degree of competition and, in turn, lowering the profits and the market power of particular firms. The feedback from market performance centered on collective action by private, interfirm groups, and, abetted by an alleged "public interest" in the provision of "clean, wholesome milk," on government regulation of milk markets. The feedback tended to extend the scope and size of private organizations and to foster the development of public regulations, which would together mitigate or eliminate the effects of increased competition.

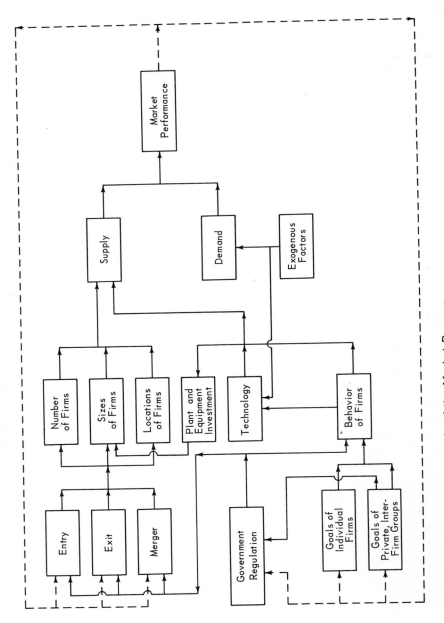

FIGURE 1. Simple Schematic of the Market Process.

Public regulations at the state level are particularly relevant here. In general, those states that regulated milk were those in which imports of "foreign" milk from other states posed strong threats to established firms. While the details of regulation varied widely among the states, the critical control device was one which prevented or made prohibitively more costly the distribution of fluid milk products made from imported milk. In addition, internal markets were often allocated to particular groups of producers, with those closest to consuming markets having *de jure* or *de facto* preference. Entry of new producers from within the state was limited by licensing, a form of production control was instituted, and restrictions were placed on mergers through control of the transfer of licenses. Distributors might also be licensed more or less restrictively and, through use of this device in conjunction with the requirements that local milk be used, many innovations in distribution that might have injured historic distributors were stifled. Price controls at producer and sometimes at the wholesale and retail levels capped the control mechanism but, given the protection afforded by the other regulations, private controls often resulted in actual prices that were above the established legal minimums.

The effects of regulations such as these on the structure of markets are often unnoticed because they take the form of preserving an existing structure that without the regulations would have disappeared. In the case of milk, it is clear that the effects, by preventing the operation of the feedback from performance to market structure via entry, exit, and merger, included the preservation of a larger number of smaller producing and distributing firms, a less efficient geographic distribution of supply, lower rates of innovation and diffusion of new technologies, and higher prices than would otherwise have occurred. The best supporting evidence for these conclusions is not found in statistical studies, but in the constant attempts of the regulatory agencies to fashion means to prevent the encroachment of larger firms on smaller, the inflow of less expensive milk from new areas, and the introduction of new products and processes.

It may be asked, however, what relevance this narrative has to banking markets. Why should the milk industry be considered in a volume on commercial banking? The principal reason is that conclusions that seem obvious in a discussion of milk markets are resisted when applied to banking. In the former, it is clear that regulations have resulted in the preservation of an inefficient structure, because constraints have led to patterns of market performance yielding adequate rewards to firms to preserve inefficiency. The same situation occurs—though less obviously so—in commercial banking. In both regulated milk markets and in banking, there is little possibility of attaining socially preferable market performance by altering the market structure. Unless the regulation and organization of the market is changed, market performance will be largely unaffected by, for example, preventing mergers. Indeed, the effects on performance of such policies may be perverse.

It is quite certain that there are economies of scale in commercial banking.[1] In terms of total operating costs per unit measure of size, or in terms of direct costs per unit measure of a particular bank activity, average costs tend to decrease as the size of the bank or level of activity increases. It is not clear just how far these economies extend, but available evidence indicates a significant decline in costs up to sizes between $5 million and $10 million in deposits; some evidence suggests that costs continue to decline as size increases well beyond this range. It has not been determined whether these economies are due to technical factors associated with the production of bank services or to the possibly better quality of management available to larger banks.

In 1963, 5.6 percent of insured commercial banks in the United States had deposits of less than $1 million. More than half of all insured banks had deposits of less than $5 million. Of the total of 12,984 such banks, 76.3 percent—9904—had deposits of less than $10 million.[2] To a considerable extent, these data reflect unit banks operating in towns which constitute so small a market that neither a more efficient nor an additional bank could be

[1]See David A. Alhadeff, *Monopoly and Competition in Banking*, Berkeley: University of California Press, 1954, pp. 77–80; Paul M. Horvitz, "Economies of Scale in Banking," *Private Financial Institutions*, Englewood Cliffs, N.J.: Prentice-Hall, Inc., pp. 1–54, 1963; Irving Schweiger and John S. McGee, "Chicago Banking," *Journal of Business*, Vol. 34, No. 3, July 1961, pp. 203–366; Lyle E. Gramley, *A Study of Scale Economics in Banking*, Kansas City, Mo. Federal Reserve Bank of Kansas City, 1962; Stuart Greenbaum, *Banking Structure and Costs: A Statistical Study of the Cost-Output Relationship in Commercial Banking* (unpublished Ph.D. dissertation, Johns Hopkins, 1964); George Benston, *The Cost of Bank Operations* (unpublished Ph.D. dissertation, University of Chicago, 1964).

[2]*Annual Report,* Federal Deposit Insurance Corporation, Washington D.C.: Government Printing Office, 1963.

supported. In 1959, for example, 6390 unit banks operated the only office in the population centers in which they were located, and all except 244 of these banks were in centers with fewer than 5000 persons. On the other hand, 1674 unit banks operated in centers of less than 5000 persons in which there were two or more banking offices.[3] In the latter cases, an inefficient structure quite certainly exists; without some regulatory or organizational influence preventing the feedback to the structural variables, the market structure would be unstable.

At the opposite extreme, 385 unit banks operated in 1959 in population centers of 100,000 or more persons in which there were 20 or more banking offices. Many of these banks, too, are of less than the apparent minimum efficient size; for example, the 170 unit banks in the 12 Standard Statistical Metropolitan Areas of Pennsylvania in 1964 had an average of $7.6 million of deposits. Again, with the indicated scale economies, this structure would appear unstable over time in the absence of some restraints on behavior.

Structural inefficiency is also evident from the patterns of branch banking in the United States, though conclusions on this point rest more on observations of the way in which markets operate than on statistical studies. There are, of course, costs associated with branching. If two banks are of equal deposit size, and one is a unit bank and the other operates two or more offices, the latter will typically have higher total costs than will the former.[4] For some sizes and types of operations, however, market phenomena indicate that the costs of operating a branch office are less than those of conducting a unit bank of the same size at the same location. Branch offices have been established *de novo* in locations and in sizes in which unit banks, while not prohibited, do not in fact tend to be established. The frequent occurrence of small branch offices in shopping centers, transportation terminals, universities and office buildings, and the rarity, if not absence, of unit banks in similar locations suggest cost advantages for branch operations in some activities.

The existence of at least limited advantages for branches over unit banks may partially underlie recent changes in the number of bank offices. Between 1953 and 1962, only 768 of the net change

[3]*Annual Report,* Federal Deposit Insurance Corporation, Washington D.C.: Government Printing Office, 1959.

[4]George Benston, "Branch Banking and Economies of Scale," *Journal of Finance,* Vol. 20, No. 2, May 1965, pp. 312–331.

of 6091 offices occurred in the 18 states that prohibited branching. The 32 branching states and the District of Columbia accounted for the other 5323 net new offices.[5] Thus, the requirement that bank offices must operate as independent units is associated with fewer offices being opened. While differences in chartering policies are undoubtedly important in the full explanation of this association, it is not unreasonable to conjecture that the relatively greater chartering of branches reflects also the possibility of operating branches profitably in locations and sizes for which unit operations would be unprofitable.

Likewise, the tendency for unit banks to be absorbed as branches through mergers, where this action is permitted, lends credence to the conclusion that branching is sometimes less costly than unit operations. The absorption of unit banks into the branching system requires in each instance that the acquiring bank be willing to pay an amount equal to, or more than, the minimum expected value of continuing the independent operations of the acquired bank. While factors such as stock market imperfections, tax advantages, and noneconomic growth goals may also be involved, the bank merger movement itself is consistent with, though not conclusive proof of, the contention that branches are more economical than unit banks in some conditions.

The tendencies toward branching and mergers imply, of course, that market regulations have not totally prevented market structure from changing. To admit this is far from arguing that structural inefficiency does not exist, however. Indeed, the search for features of public regulation which have lessened the impact of the feedbacks to structure are not difficult to find, though they are somewhat less obvious than those governing milk markets.

It is of signal importance that state regulatory agencies are typically controlled by persons who have or have had direct association with the industry. This is required by legislative mandate in states such as Alabama, Colorado, Kansas, New Jersey, New York, North Dakota, Oklahoma, Pennsylvania, South Dakota, Texas, and Wisconsin. It is permitted in most other states. While few would wish to impugn either the honesty or good motives of the members of such agencies, no one should fail to recognize

---

[5]"Changes in Banking Structures, 1953–1962," *Federal Reserve Bulletin*, Vol. 49, No. 9, 1963, p. 1320.

that considerable value is bound to attach to the preservation of
the existing order for those whose own incomes and prestige
depend on its maintenance.

The influence of regulations on structure are demonstrated
most clearly in state laws dealing with branching. The prohibition
of branching by eighteen states is only a small indication of the
full effect. The discretionary authority of the regulatory agencies
in approving branches in some other states undoubtedly operates
in a protective way when the "adequacy" of existing banking
facilities is considered. Even in the statewide branching states,
many regulations have clear protective aspects. In Connecticut,
for example, *de novo* branching outside of the home office town is
restricted to those "in which the head office of no state
bank . . . or national banking association is located."[6] The Idaho
code prohibits *de novo* branching outside of the home office locale
if in the proposed location "there is located a bank or banks, state
or national, . . . unless the corporation establishing such branch
banking office shall . . . obtain consent of all banks there located."[7] North Carolina law requires that branching approval
not be given until it is ascertained that the probable level of demand "is sufficient to assure and maintain the solvency . . . of
the existing bank or banks. . . ."[8]

The regulations of the limited branching states are restrictive
in particulars other than broadly defined areas. The Georgia code
provides that in municipalities of less than 80,000 persons—all
municipalities other than Atlanta and Savannah for the 1950
Census relevant at the time of the passage of the statute—"not
more than one of either a bank office or bank facility for each
population unit of 40,000 or fraction thereof"[9] can be established.
In Indiana, the number of permissible branches varies with the
population of counties and cities and the size of the bank. In some
cities, branches may be "not nearer than one . . . mile to any

[6]*Compilation of Federal, State and Territorial Statutes Relating to Branch Banking,*
Legal Division of the Board of Governors of the Federal Reserve System (mimeo,
1961), p. 22.

[7]Legal Division of the Board of Governors of the Federal Reserve System,
p. 33.

[8]Legal Division of the Board of Governors of the Federal Reserve System,
p. 101.

[9]Legal Division of the Board of Governors of the Federal Reserve System,
p. 28.

existing bank. . . ."[10] For cities in excess of 50,000 persons, the banking department must determine "that the welfare of any other bank already established in such city will not be jeopardized"[11] before a branch can be established. Mississippi does not allow branching in towns and cities of less than 3100 population if "such town or city has one or more banks in operation."[12] Pennsylvania, which has had a greater number of banks than any other state permitting any form of branching, until 1965 required approval by its banker-dominated banking board in addition to that of the Department of Banking for branching outside of the city, borough, or village of the home office. In these cases, "each other institution whose principal place of business is in the county in which the proposed branch is to be located" must be notified "by registered mail, return receipt requested."[13] If the applicant bank has its home office outside the county of the proposed branch, the application may be denied "if an incorporated institution having its principal place of business in the county . . . has, in good faith, notified the department of its intention to establish a branch in the same city, borough, or village."[14]

These details, which are illustrative rather than exhaustive of the restrictions on branching imposed by state codes, are recited to emphasize the contention that the classification of states into unit banking, limited branching, and statewide branching categories does little towards explaining differences among states in the strength of the tendency for structure to change when more efficient and more profitable alternatives exist. The fact is that in virtually all states there are regulations that either nullify or mitigate the feedbacks to structure. And, just as it can be argued that the best evidence of the influence of milk control agencies on structure comes from their activities in preventing structure from changing, so it can be argued that the best evidence of the same phenomena in banking is the complex array of state law govern-

[10]Legal Division of the Board of Governors of the Federal Reserve System, p. 38.

[11]Legal Division of the Board of Governors of the Federal Reserve System, p. 39.

[12]Legal Division of the Board of Governors of the Federal Reserve System, p. 64.

[13]Legal Division of the Board of Governors of the Federal Reserve System, p. 118.

[14]Legal Division of the Board of Governors of the Federal Reserve System, p. 118.

ing structure. That is, it is difficult to imagine that the laws were not passed, and are not executed, to prevent structure from changing in the proscribed ways. Without them—and based more on the fact that the laws exist than on empirical observations of what has happened to structure when such laws have been relaxed—it is clear that structure would radically change.

The obvious purpose, as well as the effect, of branching laws is to control and preserve banking structure. Other aspects of banking regulation, with ostensibly different purposes, have similar effects. In the past, banks have engaged in loan, investment, and interest rate behavior which have induced forms of market performance that have posed threats to bank earnings. Through the effects on earnings, the behavior has also threatened the viability of the basic structure of banking markets. The policy response has not typically been one which considered a "trade-off" between regulation and structure—even though this approach is necessary to attain efficiency—but rather one which developed regulatory machinery adequate to prevent the feedback to structure from becoming strong. The preservation of structure, that is, has implicitly—and sometimes explicitly—been a primary policy objective.

Restrictions of interest rates on time deposits, the prohibition of interest on demand deposits, limitations on the amount and terms of mortgage loans, and other investment restrictions have had the effect of preventing individual banks from behaving in ways that, if made general for the system through competitive forces, might lower bank earnings or increase the risk associated with these earnings. The objective of these forms of regulations, as well as of bank supervision and examination, may indeed be "the maintenance of a sound banking system."[15] But the soundness of the system and the preservation of liquidity for the payments mechanism has, in the United States, meant "strong individual units with sound assets and adequate capital, operated in accordance with banking principles and applicable banking laws and regulations; in short, a system composed of individual banks in strong financial condition, under proper management."[16] The fact that virtually all existing banks must, according to this approach, be "sound" has meant that regulation has developed only

[15]R. F. Leonard, "Supervision of the Commercial Banking System," *Banking Studies*, Washington, D.C.: Board of Governors of the Federal Reserve System, 1941, pp. 191–192.

[16]Leonard, pp. 191–192.

with reference to the present and past structure. No obvious consideration has been given to the creation of a combination of new structure and new regulations that would be consistent with both efficiency and the liquidity of the payments mechanism.

In addition to public regulations, there has historically been a community of interests among bankers that has operated to emphasize common problems and the dependence of individual banks on the joint resolution of such problems.[17] That is, the influence of private, interfirm groups on banking behavior has also been significant. These groups have tended to perpetuate the existing structure, partly because the joint resolution of problems necessarily constrains competition among firms, and partly because jointly conceived actions often incorporate protection for the weakest members of the relevant group. The extent of collective private actions in 1966 is impossible to assess. Both antitrust suits and revisions of examining procedures have made overt cooperation more difficult than in former years. Nonetheless, we must remember that not many years ago it was openly admitted that "the local clearing-house association frequently serves as a medium for united action on problems affecting the common welfare of the associated bank, such as the regulation of interest payments on deposits, adoption of schedules of service charges, and fixing of business hours."[18] Furthermore, lest it be concluded that banking legislation and supervision arose external to the industry and solely out of social concern, it was also acknowledged that bankers' associations "not only provide a forum for the discussion of problems of common interest, but they afford bankers a means of giving effective expression to their views on banking legislation and other matters of similar nature." Interfirm groups affect the nature of government regulation. Even the Graduate School of Banking and other educational programs, it has been said, provide "an opportunity for bringing about a considerable degree of uniformity in the banker's approach to his problems and a generally higher standard of banking practices."[19]

[17]Bankers are not, of course, unique in this respect. But while it has usually been recognized that when people of other trades "meet together, even for merriment and diversion, . . . the conversation ends in a conspiracy against the public," this stigma has not until recently attached to the joint activities of bankers.

[18]John E. Horbett, "Banking Structure of United States," *Banking Studies,* 1941, p. 107. See also "Commercial Bank Competition for Savings," *Journal of the American Bankers Association,* Vol. 23, October 1930 pp. 350 ff., Dan V. Stephens, "Nine Pictures of Clearing Houses in Action," *Journal of the American Bankers Association,* Vol. 24, April 1932, pp. 624 ff.

[19]Horbett, p. 107.

To these aspects of public and private regulation should be added to the so-called "prime-rate convention,"[20] tacit or overt arrangements between city correspondent banks and their suburban and country customer banks which keep the former from invading the geographic market of the latter,[21] and the expressed aversion of bankers to direct price competition.[22] No one of these characteristics makes commercial banking unique among American industries. However, it is as clear for banking markets as it is for milk markets that a combination of regulatory and organizational characteristics has sustained the industry structure. To suggest the existence of large numbers of banks is indicative of competitive conditions—at least as market theorists would use that term—is to ignore the most fundamental truths about banking markets. As competition or opposition among banks has occurred in types and to degrees which have threatened bank earnings and the banking structure, regulations—private and public—have been devised which have mitigated and prevented behavior which produces important structural consequences. Given existing evidence of scale economies and the benefits of branching, no other conclusion except that which gives regulations credit for having such effects is at all tenable.

RECENT DEVELOPMENTS: STABILITY OF BANKING STRUCTURE AND REGULATIONS

There have been no major changes in banking regulation and supervision in recent years. There is, however, evidence that the present array is no longer adequate to preserve the structure now

[20]Donald R. Hodgman, *Commercial Bank Loan and Investment Policy*, Urbana: University of Illinois, 1963, pp. 120–135; Albert M. Wojnilower and Richard E. Speagle, "The Prime Rate," *Essays in Money and Credit*, Federal Reserve Bank of New York, 1964; J. S. G. Wilson, "Keener Competition in Commercial Banking," *The Banker*, Vol. 112, 1962, pp. 592–594.

[21]*Correspondent Relations: A Survey of Banker Opinion*, Committee on Banking and Currency, 88th Congress, 2d Session, Washington, D.C., 1964; Roland Robinson, "Unit Banking Evaluated," *Banking and Monetary Studies*, D. Carson, ed., Homewood, Illinois: Richard D. Irwin, Inc., 1964, p. 302.

[22]Lester V. Chandler, "Monopolistic Elements in Commercial Banking." *Journal of Political Economy*, Vol. 46, No. 2, 1938, pp. 1–22; Alhadeff, *Monopoly and Competition in Banking*, 1954, 120 ff.; Hodgman, *Commercial Loan and Investment Policy*, 1963, Chaps. 10–11.

in existence, and some evidence that conditions facing banking are such as to create a schism within the industry, with the interest of large metropolitan banks at variance with those of the smaller banks in suburban and rural areas.

The mergers already mentioned are themselves indicative of a degree of instability in the present structure. Between 1953 and 1962, 1669 bank mergers and absorptions occurred from an initial population of 14,073 commercial banks.[23] These mergers have affected the structure of metropolitan banking markets, where banks tend to be larger and to have more branches, relatively more than they have affected the structures of banking markets in smaller towns and cities. In Pennsylvania, for example, the 12 largest metropolitan areas, comprising 22 counties, had 442 banks in 1956, while the remainder of the state had 365. By mid-1964, these numbers were 229 and 310, respectively. Thus, 143 of the net reduction of 198 banks occurred in 22 metropolitan area counties, and only 55 in the remaining 45 counties in the state. Without ignoring the possible differential effects of that state's "contiguous county" branching law, it is still suggested that the structure of banking markets in smaller towns and cities is more stable with existing regulatory constraints than is the structure for metropolitan banking markets. Rivalry in the latter may be creating merger-inducing factors to which the rural banks are more immune.

Witness, too, the more than usual interest at state levels in revising banking codes as they pertain to branching. New York and Virginia have both made changes—hardly ideal ones—in recent years. In Pennsylvania, Illinois, and Wisconsin, there are strong pressures for revision, primarily from the larger city banks that favor less restrictive branching provisions. In these states, resistance to change comes, among other sources, from the smaller, nonmetropolitan banks.

At the federal level, the same forces and schisms are apparent. The Bank Merger Act of 1960 reflects the compromise of a variety of interests, none of which is well served by the Act. Additional control over mergers was sought by the smaller banks to prevent or to slow down the process of their absorption by larger banks. This control was abetted by historical, antitrust-type biases favoring the maintenance of atomistic structures. However, control

[23]"Changes in Banking Structure," *Federal Reserve Bulletin*, Vol. 49, No. 9 September, 1963, p. 1320.

over mergers was not given to the Department of Justice. Instead, it was apportioned among the federal bank regulatory agencies so that each had some share of the work and, furthermore, so that each could use its particular expertise and familiarity with the industry in the consideration of "banking factors." The problem of how far this apportionment removes federal merger policy from self-regulation by the industry can hardly be resolved, but mergers among large city banks have not, by means of this legislation alone, been greatly retarded. The passage in 1966 of H. R. 12173, amending the 1960 Bank Merger Act, reduces still further the power of the Department of Justice to intervene in mergers.

Recent Federal Reserve action on ceiling interest rates for time deposits and the spreading use of certificates of deposits and bank savings bonds have allowed banks to compete among themselves and with other institutions for savings. It is no longer true that the maximum time deposit rate is the effective rate for most banks, and no longer true that this regulation affords substantial protection for the present banking structure.

Finally, it should be noted that the trend of technological developments in data processing, information transfer, and information retrieval may progressively add to the importance of scale and branching economies. In particular, geographic distances among operating locations of single information systems may become of negligible importance, permitting efficient branching at locations remote from home offices. The same developments may mean that size and complexity of the most efficient information networks are increased, leading to pressures to "internalize" via bank mergers decisions relating to the design of efficient account-clearing mechanisms.[24]

This development sounds remote, of course, but it could be argued that signs portending these changes are now apparent. Consider, for example, the interests of banks in the credit card field. Credit cards operated by nonbanking institutions have a degree of "money-ness" associated with them because of the additional liquidity provided to card users. But the final settling of accounts permits very little clearing equivalent to that accomplished among banks. Check payments representing gross ac-

[24]See George W. Mitchell, "Effects of Automation on the Structure and Functioning of Banking," *American Economic Review*, Vol. 56, No. 2, May 1966, pp. 159 ff.

counts payable move from the card issuer to businesses and from card users to the card issuer.

Suppose that the credit-card concept of approved lines of credit becomes more commonplace, that banks become the issuers of this credit, and that both business and individual accounts are "computerized." One can conceive, as an extreme development, of the supplanting of both check writing and currency in many transactions. Furthermore, depending on the scale economies associated with the transactions networks of the system, one can conceive of the need for regional or national clearing and accounting institutions developed for this purpose. Whether the latter should themselves be credit-creating institutions is not clear, but were they to assume such a function, their strategic position for both monetary policy and credit rationing would argue against private operation and ownership. In any case, the role of individual banks in the exhange process would be quite different from their current role, and possibilities would be created for new types of lending institutions.

STRUCTURAL AND REGULATORY REFORM

It has been difficult to effect reforms in the banking system of the United States except in times of crisis.[25] The preceding discussion is not intended to portend such a crisis, but it is intended to point to the accumulation of factors that are creating pressures for change; ideally, their early recognition could lead to a gradual, orderly, and rational reorganization of the system. Changes made in times of crisis are often of a "second-best" character and, judging by the experience in banking, tend to provide symptomatic relief rather than fundamental cures.

The changes suggested in the following comments should be considered rather as topics deserving additional study than as obviously correct solutions. Indeed, it is likely that the role of an economist in most questions of public policy is most valuable when it is restricted to criticism and to evaluating the costs of existing conditions. The task of selecting from a number of alternatives

[25]See Paul Horvitz, "Stimulating Bank Competition through Regulatory Action," *Journal of Finance* Vol. 20, No. 1, March 1965, p. 1.

the one which is socially preferable is not one which by training the economist is well-equipped to handle.

With these caveats, however, it seems clear that several changes deserve serious consideration. Their consideration here does not, of course, imply that one should be sanguine concerning the probability of their adoption. First, the present "dual banking system" should be abolished in favor of uniform regulation of all banks at the national level. Without this change, it seems impossible to eliminate in many states the use of public regulation and private organizational arrangements that give primacy to the maintenance of the existing and inefficient structure of banking, or to eliminate from banking markets the impediments of economically meaningless state boundaries. Uniform regulation would mean that all banks would be nationally chartered and subject to regulations which take no cognizance of the state in which the bank is located.

Second, within the framework of national regulations and law, improved policies towards branching should be developed. This policy, rather than providing protection to existing individual banks and to arbitrarily defined geographical groups of banks, should be aimed at developing as efficient a banking structure as is possible and at providing a number of alternative banks to customers within this structure. It is clear that this would eventually mean far fewer banks than currently exist. Without a breaking up of the hundred or so largest banks, the efficient system would have only a small fraction of the number of banks now in existence.[26] And it is quite conceivable that this number will become smaller through time.

It is quite possible to have this drastic reduction without having anticompetitive effects. Properly instituted, the new structure should, in fact, have the effect of increasing competition. Despite the difficulties involved in the product and geographic definition of markets, enough precision can be given to the concepts to prohibit the merger of two or more banks in the same market when either is of such size that no significant economies can be shown to result from the merger. Mergers that would be instrumental in reducing the number of banks and, hence, in eliminating inefficiency would be those between banks of inefficient

[26]This implies an *average* bank size well above the figures mentioned for minimum efficient size. What is required, however, is that *all* banks be of efficient size, with efficient branch structures.

scales in the same markets, and between banks of inefficient scales in one market and efficient scales in another. Without the current artifical geographic limitations, this would permit intermetropolitan area as well as metropolitan-nonmetropolitan area branching, except for cases in which, because of the market size for the banks proposing merger, substantial anticompetitive effects might be demonstrated. The pressure of actual or potential entry by the efficient banks of one market into other markets would have a strong *procompetitive* influence which does not now exist in most bank markets.

The branching rule being proposed would, then, prohibit the merger of two banks in the same geographic and product markets where the probable effect was substantially anticompetitive. This would include not only the giant banks in the largest cities, whose markets are regional *and* national, but also banks of small scales which are large relative to the markets in which they operate. For the latter, independent absorption into separate branching banks would preserve customer alternatives as well as provide the advantages of efficiency.[27]

Branching *de novo* and growth by internal expansion are not likely to cause serious anticompetitive problems in banking. Many small markets would, of course, be occupied by one or a small number of banks or branches of banks, but as long as entry is unimpeded, their market power would not be commensurate with their small number. So far as the largest banks now existing are concerned, none has more than 4 percent of the nation's deposits, the markets of each might be entered by other banks, mergers among them would be largely prohibited, and internal expansion and *de novo* branching, without obviously prohibited predatory or exclusionary behavior, is not likely to change their relative status rapidly. In other words, no need is seen for seeking their dissolution.

In the revisions being suggested, market entry is likely to

---

[27]For example, the merger of two large New York City banks increases concentration and reduces the number of customer alternatives at the local, regional, and national levels. The merger of a large and a small bank, both in New York, would have similar effects at the local level. The merger of a large New York bank with a large Chicago bank would have these effects at the national level. But the merger of a large New York bank and a small Chicago bank has, by itself, none of these effects and could tend to increase the degree of competition between New York and Chicago banks at all levels.

result primarily from the expansion of existing banks rather than from the establishment of new ones, not because chartering would be barred, but because of the lack of structural protection in the system. Currently, entry needs to be restricted because regulations minimize risks of failure, tending to induce entry and compounding the regulations required to prevent failure. A better alternative would be to permit new charters if minimum capital requirements are met, if the organizers have the legitimate purpose of attempting profitably to operate a commercial bank, and if there are reasonable prospects of success. Charters are likely to be sought only where no existing banking facilities exist, where existing banks are inefficient, or where some monopoly power is being exercised. The possibility that new banks might, in the latter circumstances, injure or even cause the demise of some existing banks should not be used as an argument against charter issuance. Since mergers would be possible, banks could disappear without public crises and with losses occurring only to the owners of inefficient enterprises.

Unless it can be demonstrated that bank holding companies have real advantages to the public which are thus far undiscovered, bank holding companies could be totally forbidden. The problem here is simply that common control of two or more banks may have anticompetitive effects without efficiency gains. Hence, in addition to the prohibition of control by stock ownership or other means of two or more banks by a single bank or nonbank institution, common directorates and noncommon directors with common interests should be forbidden.

This package of essentially antitrust provisions should be administered not by a banking agency but by the Antitrust Division of the Department of Justice. The competitive policies could, with the abolition of state controls, be effected by the repeal of the Bank Holding Company Act of 1956 and the Bank Merger Act of 1960, as recently amended. The former would be replaced by new legislation prohibiting bank holding companies and other means of common control of two or more banks, with enforcement by the Justice Department. The latter would be replaced by an amendment to Section 7 of the Clayton Act giving the Department specific authority to act in bank merger cases. The amendment would require premerger notification, with pertinent information for the banks involved and also require that the department seek injunctive relief within, for example, 120 days of notification, or be stopped from acting against the merger.[28] Because of possible scale economies and other "banking factors" of which the Department might be unaware or to which it might give inadequate weight, an advisory opinion by a federal bank regulatory agency dealing with the relevance of the special banking factors to competition would be required prior to the seeking of injunctive relief. Furthermore, that agency might be permitted to enter legal proceedings either as *amicus curiae* or by joining the Department or the defendant banks.[29]

Additional legislation would also be necessary with respect to national charters. Such legislation should provide for minimum capital requirements—probably above those now required for national banks, in order to discourage inefficient scales—for all new banks other than those required to shift from state to national charters. It should also require "blue law" type of information to prevent fraud, and adequate market information to assess the probable success of the venture. To assure nondiscriminatory chartering, provisions for judicial review of denials of charter applications should be expressly permitted.

Some may object to these suggestions because they fear the power that would attend a national system of a few hundred relatively large banks. Such an argument is not without foundation. It should, however, be advanced in a comparison between the power structure now existing and one with the proposed changes. The fact that there are now many thousands of banks, fifty state regulatory agencies, and three primary federal agencies does not indicate an absence of power. Many of the suggested changes are designed to reduce local and state blocks of private economic and political power and to lodge power in federal agencies which would at the same time be less responsive to the interests of the industry and more responsive to public needs. These agencies would, of course, have enormous power, but the use and the abuse of this power should be more obvious and, hopefully,

---

[28]Premerger notification rather than premerger approval is suggested in order to relieve the administrative burden of handling each case in detail.

[29]The regulatory agency might similarly be permitted to appear as a party in Sherman Act cases. Because of the need for loan participations and other forms of exchanges of reserves, loans, and investments among banks, some horizontal and vertical agreements should be permitted to continue. Note, however, that the suggested structural changes should lessen these agreements. What is currently done by contractual arrangements among banks would to some extent become interbranch, intrabank relationships.

more amenable to checks from representative government than is the present private and public regulatory structure.

"Change, indeed, is painful, yet ever needful; and if memory have its force and worth, so also has hope."

Commentary

Giulio Pontecorvo
and
Robert Shay

The essay by Professor Phillips challenges the present organization and regulation of our banking structure in relation to the goals of a competitive society. We applaud the vigor of his attack on the "conventional wisdom" in banking and concur with much of his argument.

Phillips argues that our present banking structure is inefficient because historically it has been shaped under the joint influence of public and private constraints upon competition. The procedures of regulatory agencies, which act to maintain the soundness of banks and to protect existing competitors, inhibits effective competition in banking. Under such conditions, Phillips cannot see how nominal changes in the number and size distribution of banks can materially improve bank performance. Accordingly, he urges that reforms be considered which would liberalize banks from regulatory constraints so that competitive forces can develop and maintain an efficient bank structure—efficient, that is, in the sense of having a socially optimum allocation of resources in banking that would result in lower costs and prices for banking services.

Because we are at present a long way from free enterprise in the banking sector, Phillips does not propose unrestricted entry into banking markets at this time. He would allow a national chartering authority to judge when the decision to enter a market is legitimate—that is, when a bank could operate with "reasonable prospects of success." He would expect most new market entrants to come from existing banking units through *de novo* branching and mergers. These would be subject to antitrust standards in order to prevent the abuses of market power that he has carefully outlined. The obvious result of his suggested reforms, assuming the existence of economies of scale, is that a large proportion —possibly 95 per cent—of today's 13,000 banks would probably disappear if forced to compete in Phillips' competitive society. This awesome prospect reveals the hidden tax paid by users of bank services in the United States because of the misallocation of resources in banking.

Phillips' analogy between banking regulation and the regulated milk industry clarifies the forces at work to impair productivity, restrict output, and raise prices. In addition to the milk industry, we would cite another example which illuminates the tangle of bank structure and the interrelationship of structure with state and federal regulatory agencies—the salmon fisheries of the Pacific, which employ thousands of fishermen. Regulations ostensibly for "conservation" prevent the utilization of the most efficient techniques of capture. In order to further "protect" the resource, the Oregon legislature prohibited the use of a monofilament gill net, a more efficient device for catching fish than the present ones, within forty-eight hours after its introduction in a fishery. This analogy illustrates the tendency of regulations to perpetuate inefficiency and to preserve the number of competitors. On the other hand, there is the dilemma faced by the banking authorities in New York State. They were forced to request more liberal legislation in order to permit the state banking units to meet competition from national banks and, at the same time, accommodate the diverse interests of large money market banks, relatively large urban upstate banks, small rural banks, and other financial institutions. Not only is resolution of the dilemma difficult, but, as Phillips suggests, any compromise will only alleviate the present problem and delay ultimate competitive adjustments. Forced solutions detract from efficiency in the use of resources and cannot materially improve competition in the banking industry.

While we agree with Phillips' diagnosis of the problem of bank structure, we are not nearly as ready to accept his prescriptions for a cure. First, concerning abolition of the dual banking system, what assurance do we have that the elimination of competition between state and national chartering authorities will not supplant one set of anticompetitive constraints with another set of constraints designed to improve the present, but ill-suited for longer-run considerations in a changing world? For example, if the emergence and recent departure of a vital, controversial Comptroller of the Currency were viewed as a historical accident, what guarantee would we have that shifting all of the lobbying pressures from the fifty states to future Comptrollers would insure that competition would prevail with reasonable checks and balances between the Department of Justice and the banking authorities?

Second, with fifty state governments, there always remains the possibility of greater experimentation and more innovation resulting in legislation than would be true at the federal level — barring the solution of national crises. After all, deposit insurance, which is social legislation of great merit, was pioneered in the states between 1908 and 1930, providing an example for federal legislation to adopt during the banking crisis.

Despite the merit in Phillips' argument that the dual banking system, local clearing house associations, correspondent banking arrangements, and bank association activities all tend to limit competition, we would prefer that these restraints be allowed to disintegrate under the pressures of national competition rather than be abolished as a prerequisite to such competition. Observers may be surprised how viable the correspondent banking system becomes under competition as a means of permitting local groups to offer local services efficiently alongside of branches of truly national banks. To assume that these present arrangements cannot become competitive may be plausible, and possibly correct, but why not find out?

We believe that any realistic prospect of change, in the absence of crisis, is more likely to be achieved by indirect means such as the Hoover Commission studies than by wholesale reorganization through bank legislation. It may also be easier to legislate the necessary competitive reforms if states rights (and privileges) are not directly assaulted.

We support the position that would permit banks with national charters to be immune from state legislation. We accept branching rules designed to increase competition and decrease market power, and we endorse the application of the branching rules to merger applications. However, we would recommend that holding company acquisitions be subjected to similar standards. We would further support the priority given the Justice Department over the banking agencies in bank merger cases. Finally, we would like to see the overlapping responsibilities of the Comptroller of the Currency, the FDIC, and the Federal Reserve authorities eliminated, with the Comptroller determining the charter and scope of bank activities under existing law, the FDIC determining bank examination procedures consistent with insurance requirements, and the Federal Reserve Board limiting its activities to monetary policy questions and severing its direct connection with the supervisory aspects of the banking system. If these reforms were enacted, competition in banking could become workable, and should result in lower cost to the users of bank services.

Chapter 2

Introduction

The preceding paper by Professor Phillips analyzed some of the tensions in our banking system. As he pointed out, the problems of structural organization are only one source of concern in the investigation of monetary problems. The following two papers by Professors Hyman P. Minsky and Marvin E. Rozen take up some other major issues, those surrounding the question of so-called financial intermediation.

Some insight into what is meant by intermediation in relation to the definition of the money supply can be obtained by a historical analogy. From 1718 to 1720, both France and England experienced a "South Sea Bubble." The French bubble, largely organized by John Law, involved direct expansion of the money supply. The English experience was more complex and did not involve, as part of the scheme, any inflation in the money supply; instead, it involved the substitution of one set of liabilities for another. A private corporation, in one sense analogous to today's mutual funds, was given the right to try to convince the public to exchange or trade government bonds, then selling at substantial discounts, for shares in the South Sea company. A necessary condition for achieving this type of voluntary conversion was the creation of positive expectations in the public's mind of capital gains in South Sea shares. Although this scheme did not require an increase in the money supply, it did increase the number of claims available in the market place. And in fulfilling the necessary condition with respect to the public's expectations, the claims were rendered highly liquid.

The South Sea experience raises several questions about the traditional definition of the money supply as cash plus the liabilities of the banking system. Was the South Sea Company a bank? How should we regard the claims that were created?

In the papers that follow, Minsky and Rozen deal with different aspects of the intermediation issue. Minsky develops an interrelationship between the money and capital markets. According to him, the principal contribution of the money market is to facilitate the use of monetary resources in the savings-investment process that takes place in the capital market; it also provides links between the money sector and neo-Keynesian models of income determination.

Rozen is concerned with the flows of savings through the financial sector. In his thoughtful paper, he suggests that much of the question of intermediation turns on the observed rate of growth in various financial institutions. His evidence on Regulation Q suggests that the growth of commercial banks has been retarded in past years, but that commercial banks basically remain the strongest competitors in the market place for the increasing flow of savings out of our rising income. Recent events appear to have supported this viewpoint.

FINANCIAL INTERMEDIATION IN THE MONEY AND CAPITAL MARKETS

Hyman P. Minsky

Capitalism is essentially a financial system, and the peculiar behavioral attributes of a capitalist economy center around the impact of finance upon system behavior. The behavior of the financial system in turn depends upon the behavior of its component parts; and a complex set of financial intermediaries is central to the financial system of an advanced capitalist economy. It is my aim in this paper to explore the impact of the layered set of financial intermediaries upon system behavior.

This paper is an exercise in economic theory. The documentation of the argument by evidence—including the evidence of specifying the meaning of a concept by identifying examples—is neglected. Although much evidence on the growth and evolution of financial intermediation has been accumulated, we will not refer to it here.[1] What we will do is more model-building, using as building blocks concepts that seem natural for the analysis of finance.

The argument that follows seems to indicate that the term "money" means different things in different contexts. Occasionally, the terms "inside money" and "outside money" will be used. The distinction depends upon the extent to which the consolidation of the accounts of units is carried and upon the purpose for which the distinction between types of money is being made. If, for example, the effect of wealth on consumption is under consideration, the negative impact upon private wealth of taxes that may be levied to service and repay government debt may offset the financial asset, government debt, in private portfolios.[2] It is clear that state and municipal debt is not a net addition to wealth even if the consolidation excludes these units. The extent to which federal debt is included in wealth depends upon a view as to how a larger debt affects taxes. Thus, for the operation of a real balance effect, monetized state and local debt is not outside money, and the "outsidedness" of the federal debt depends upon the extent to which taxes are related to the size of the debt.

On the other hand, if the definition of money that is of interest emphasizes that money is a default-free asset, and that *no* inside unit is constrained to make payments to the monetary system because of the existence of this asset, then federal debt certainly is money and a good argument can be made for including all or part of state and municipal debt.

The argument that follows identifies two "classes" of financial intermediaries — savings and money market intermediaries. As is

[1]The various writings of Raymond Goldsmith document the growth of financial intermediaries. See in particular R. W. Goldsmith, *Financial Intermediaries in the American Economy since 1900*, National Bureau of Economic Research, Princeton, N. J.: Princeton University Press, 1958.

J. Gurley and E. Shaw's major work,. *Money in a Theory of Finance*, Washington, D.C.: The Brookings Institution, 1960, is almost entirely abstract. In other pieces some institutional considerations were introduced. See J. Gurley and E. Shaw, "Financial Aspects of Economic Development," *American Economic Review*, Vol. 45, No. 4 September 1955, pp. 515 ff. "Financial Intermediaries and the Saving-Investment Process," *Journal of Finance*, Vol. 11, No. 2, May 1956, pp. 257 ff.; and "The Growth of Debt and Money in the United States 1800–1950," *Review of Economics and Statistics*, Vol. 39, No. 3, August 1957, pp. 250 ff.

[2]See Franco Modigliani, "The Monetary Mechanism and Its Interaction with Real Phenomena," *Review of Economics and Statistics*, Vol. 45, No. 1, Part 2, Supplement, February 1963, pp. 93–97.

true of much of economics, the real world institutions often do not fit into the abstract classes of theory. Many institutions — especially commercial banks — are simultaneously savings and money market intermediaries. Nevertheless, within a given view as to the over-all stability of the economy, savings intermediation affects the determination of aggregate demand. Money market intermediation affects the stability of the financial system and thus the view of the over-all stability of the economy.

Conceptually, savings intermediation can be identified with the process by which the flow of savings is allocated to finance investment. The asset preferences of households, the ultimate savings units, are brought into consistency with the liability preferences of business firms, the fundamental investing units, as a result of the ability of these intermediaries to emit liabilities with risk attributes that households prefer to absorb, while absorbing as assets instruments with risk attributes that business firms prefer to emit. Inasmuch as risk is involved, the ability of price differentials to offset these inconsistent preferences is limited. As a result of savings intermediation, both sets of units earn higher returns, if the returns are defined to include income in kind in the form of a decrease in uncertainty.

Money market intermediation cannot be interpreted in terms of risk absorption for households and firms. The primary domain of the money market consists of financial intermediaries: the major participants in the short-term financing of the money market are large scale nonfinancial units and financial units. The major function that can be imputed to the money market is the facilitation of the operation of savings intermediation. The extent to which savings intermediaries can safely economize on cash depends upon the scope of the money market. In this sense, money market intermediation indirectly facilitates savings intermediation. However, the major impact of money market intermediation upon system behavior centers around a rare event — financial instability. Even though the way financial instability arises is of major importance in analyzing money market intermediation, we will not emphasize this aspect here.[3]

Some authors in writing about financial intermediation postulate the existence of a diversification demand for money and other financial intermediary liabilities. In order to understand

[3]See H. P. Minsky, "Can 'It' Happen Again," in *Banking and Monetary Studies*, edited by D. Carson, Homewood, Illinois: Richard D. Irwin, 1963, pp. 101–111.

fully why such a demand exists, it is necessary to explicitly introduce uncertainty. Once introduced, uncertainty not only helps explain the behavior of asset holders, but it also helps explain the behavior of liability emitters.

The view of uncertainity that seems most appropriate to an analysis of finance centers around the likelihood of specific "events" and the implications of these events for the unit. The absorption of risks by financial intermediaries will often take the form of changing what an event means for the unit rather than changing the likelihood of the event.[4]

The discussion of the definition and significance of money market and savings intermediation is continued in the next part of this paper, and is followed by an integration of savings into the standard presentation of the Keynesian system. The relation between money market intermediation and financial stability is then touched upon, but in the space available, only the briefest of introductions to this aspect of the problem is possible. In the conclusion, brief comments on policy implications are put forth.

MONEY MARKET
AND SAVINGS INTERMEDIATION

The category, financial institutions, consists of those business organizations and government agencies whose assets are almost entirely financial. As this broad category covers many types of economic units with a wide variety of behavioral characteristics, it has little if any analytical significance. To understand how financial institutions affect system behavior, it is necessary to break this broad category down into classes that have similar properties with respect to at least some systemic characteristics. The major impact that any particular set of financial institutions has upon system behavior depends upon how it affects the environment within which nonfinancial units make their decisions.

In order to understand the behavior of an enterprise econ-

---

[4]The basic view of uncertainty put forth here seems close to that of K. Arrow, especially in "Uncertainty and the Welfare Economics of Medical Care," *American Economic Review*, Vol. 53, No. 5, December 1963, pp. 941 ff. Certainly a view of "uncertainty" which looks at the "likelihood" of an event and the implications of the event for the unit is most natural for a portfolio decision-maker.

omy, it is necessary to deal explicitly with uncertainty. The financial structure distributes and attenuates the uncertainty that is inherent in any decentralized economy and is a marked attribute of an enterprise economy. In addition, the financial system is important because it does at times lead what seems to be a life of its own. In particular, the possibility of financial instability and crisis introduces into the economy an element of uncertainty that is a result of the structure of the financial system.

Several different kinds of uncertainty that are inherent in an enterprise economy can be identified. The various financial institutions offer options that affect the impact that these types of uncertainty have in quite different ways. A complete catalogue of how each class of financial institution affects the likelihood and distribution of each particular type of contingent event is beyond the scope of this paper. However, the broad distinction that is usually made between the capital and the money markets roughly corresponds to the distinction between savings and money market intermediation. A specification of the relation between these classes of financial intermediation and specific types of uncertainty is relevant: it will help make precise some differences between the money and capital markets.

Usually a distinction is made between monetary and nonmonetary financial institutions. The banking or monetary system is customarily treated as a distinct group of financial institutions, because commercial banks are protected by special government agencies, make payments among themselves in a "unique" money, and their ability to acquire assets is in good part exogeneously determined. In terms of behavior, commercial banks are a heterogeneous class: they range from institutions whose major impact is upon the saving and investment process to institutions whose prime focus is upon the money market. Perhaps breaking commercial banks into "money market" and "local" banks would be a useful analytical device, and certainly central bank behavior which recognizes this distinction would be desirable. However, because the payments mechanism plays a central role in maintaining financial stability, it seems best to recognize banks and the monetary system as a separate class.

It is worth noting that the typical "giant" commercial bank is a conglomerate institution that has its fingers in almost every class of money and capital market. This is especially so when the trust functions of banks are taken into account. Thus, a considerable amount of the arbitrage among financial markets can take the form of internal decision-making within the giant banks.

The term "financial intermediary" almost always refers to nonmonetary financial institutions, and quite often the term seems to mean specifically those units that mediate in the savings and investment process. This emphasis virtually ignores the intermediation among intermediaries that is carried out in the money market. Money market intermediation, by absorbing and distributing risks among intermediaries, defines the conditions under which savings intermediation is carried out. An essential characteristic of money market intermediation is that it facilitates financial layering.

Government units not only deal as financial intermediaries in particular assets but also endorse, either explicitly or implicitly, the liabilities of various classes of financial institutions. Government endorsement sets an effective limit on the nominal losses that are possible on some assets. This government protection is an important determinant of the uncertainty that various units carry. Note that if the government contingent liability becomes actual, the government debt increases but simultaneously an inside financial liability to the government arises. Unless bankruptcy of the private party or a government amnesty wipes out this private debt to the government, this increase in government debt is not outside money. Nevertheless, risk has been absorbed, for the government in meeting its contingent liability minimized the impact upon other private units of whatever event activated the contingent liability.

The distinction between the money and the capital market corresponds to a classification of financial intermediaries that distinguishes between money market and savings intermediation. In the capital market, users of real resources gain command over necessary financial resources. If refinancing and trading in second-hand real resources are ignored, activity in the capital market can be closely related to the saving-investment process. As asset holders cannot distinguish between legally equivalent "new" and "second-hand" claims in particular financial units, it is in the capital market that consistency is achieved between prices attached to the stock of existing real assets and the flow of new real assets. Monetary policy is effective to the extent that by varying the price of the stock of existing real and financial assets it can affect the flow of new real assets.[5] Monetary policy is inherently imprecise because it operates on the flow indirectly—its first impact is upon the price attached to the stock. Essentially, savings intermediaries emit household assets and hold the liabilities of households and business firms. The complex layering of financial institutions, by expediting velocity changes, may be a part of the savings intermediation process.[6] However, the most significant aspect of layering among intermediaries is not directly related to the process which finances investment; rather, it sets the framework within which savings intermediaries function.

The money market is where financial institutions and other large-scale financial units (giant nonfinancial corporations) adjust their balance sheets and finance positions. There are three facets to money market dealings. One centers around the need to refinance positions due to both "normal" and "unexpected" cash drains. A second relates to how financial intermediaries and other firms acquire assets. The third is due to short-run, surplus cash positions of financial and nonfinancial units. Such short-run cash positions, which exist as a result of imperfect synchronization in the payment process, are an essential raw material in the present money market.

Savings intermediaries characteristically emit liabilities that commit the intermediary to make cash payments at the initiative of the liability holder or upon the occurrence of some specified contingency. These cash payments are usually not well synchronized with the cash flow which results from the intermediary's assets. If an intermediary is to acquire, with safety, a portfolio which generates a cash flow that is not synchronized with the most unfavorable possible cash requirement, it must be able, upon its own initiative, to generate a large cash flow in its favor. Such a favorable cash flow can be achieved by selling assets or borrowing. At any particular date, the set of institutions that exist in the

[5] See J. Tobin and W. C. Brainard, "Financial Intermediaries and the Effectiveness of Monetary Controls," *American Economic Review,* Vol. 53, No. 2, May 1963, pp. 383–400.

[6] See H. P. Minsky, "Central Banking and Money Market Changes," *Quarterly Journal of Economics,* Vol. 71, No. 2, May 1957, pp. 171–187.

money market determines the assets that can be used for such operations and the extent to which any particular intermediary can rely upon such operations.

In much of the literature on commercial banks and other financial intermediaries, it appears as if these institutions first acquire resources and then dispose of them by lending or investing. In fact, lending and investing may very well be the initial step, and the emission of liabilities takes place in order to finance a position already taken. The contention that commercial banks acquire resources by actively marketing their liabilities is supported by evidence from the market for certificates of deposits, in addition sales and consumer finance organizations actively marketed their liabilities during past periods in which commercial banks were more passive than at present. In a large-scale, decentralized financial institution, such as a giant commercial bank or insurance company, asset acquisition and liability emission processes are obviously carried out quite independently in the short run.

As financial institutions often finance a position by emitting liabilities which individually may be volatile, every such institution will plan on having standby sources for refinancing. This refinancing can take the form of selling assets or of the *de novo* emission of liabilities. The money market is that set of institutions and usages which provides standby financing for financial and large-scale nonfinancial organizations that do not have direct access to the central bank—that is, it is the institutional framework for refinancing positions.

If we view liability emission as taking place to cover payment commitments that arise as assets are acquired, the fact is emphasized that all units must have some source of temporary financing available if for any reason their normal or preferred source of financing is not available. For many units, the money market is both a temporary abode for excess liquidity and a source of temporary financing. Money market transactions are mainly portfolio adjustments and no planned or recently achieved savings need be involved. On the other hand, as money market adjustments enable investment to be financed, so to speak, out of excess liquidity, they can set into motion forces which result in actual saving and income exceeding their expected or planned values.

The existence of a sophisticated money market facilitates the development of financial intermediation and the economizing of cash. A recent study indicates that the income elasticity of demand for money is inversely related to the state of development of the money market in the respective economies. The findings are that in the postwar period, the income elasticity of the demand for narrow money (demand deposits and currency) for the United States and the United Kingdom was about .4, for Sweden, Canada, Netherlands, and Belgium between .8 and 1.0, and for France, Japan, and Italy from 1.1 to 1.3.[7] This means that in countries with poor money markets, or, rather, a poor structure of financial intermediaries, money is more important as a repository of wealth than in countries with a richer financial structure. It also means that the money-income relation is sensitive to changes in the sophistication of the money market.

A savings or capital market intermediary finances a position in particular assets by emitting its own liabilities. However, the extent to which the intermediary can safely emit redeemable or callable liabilities for a given asset structure depends upon the availability of refinancing. Refinancing can take place either by the sale of an asset or the emission of a liability. The existence of a broad, deep and resilient market in which financial intermediary liabilities—or assets—can be negotiated is a necessary ingredient in an efficient capital market.

Underlying the above is the view that financial intermediation affects uncertainty in two ways. The first is that savings intermediaries, because of the distribution of assets in their portfolios, and a specialization or partitioning of risk, make possible an attenuation of uncertainty by broadening the spectrum of assets available to households and liabilities available to real resource owners. The second is that the meaning of various possible events for financial intermediaries is determined by the money market. A smoothly functioning money market can transform what would, under other circumstances, be a disaster into a minor inconvenience; that is, it can attenuate the effects of uncertainty. Thus, the willingness of saving intermediaries to acquire assets with specified characteristics depends upon the extent to which the money market attenuates the effect of the uncertainty as to the value of the assets that savings intermediaries must carry.

[7]G. C. Kaufman and Cynthia M. Latta, The Demand for Money: Preliminary Evidence from Industrial Countries, *Journal of Financial and Quantitative Analysis*, Vol. 1, No. 3, September 1966, pp. 75–89.

INTEGRATION OF SAVINGS INTERMEDIATION INTO STATIC MACRO-THEORY

General Theory

The jumping-off point for an integration of savings intermediation into an explanation of system behavior is the realization that
we are dealing with an urban capitalist economy in a world in
which uncertainty is a fact of life. The significance of the emphasis upon *capitalist* is that private net worths exist, which reflect the
nonhuman capital in the economy. Hence, units must make portfolio choices. The urban attribute means that wealth holdings for
the most part will take the form of holding financial rather than
tangible assets. The pervasiveness of uncertainty is important
because market failure with respect to the absorption or transfer
of uncertainty is widespread. Even though the public would
purchase many types of insurance which do not exist, it is not
feasible for private organizations to underwrite such risks. Much
government intervention into finance, as well as much noncom-
petitive market behavior, can be interpreted as surrogates for
nonexistent insurance policies.

With market failures, institutional arrangements that prevent,
decrease the possibility, or ameliorate the consequences of particular contingencies develop. To urban households, savings intermediary liabilities afford protection against some events and ease
the burdens imposed by others. To a business firm, its liability
structure specifies the consequences of various contingencies. The
likelihood of various contingencies and the weight of their consequences feed back upon both households and business firms and
affect their decisions.

The way in which financial institutions and usages constrain
and modify the uncertainty a unit faces can be illustrated. Fixed
exchanges lead to relatively narrow limits to changes in the domestic currency value of debt instruments denominated in a
foreign currency. It is an institutional device that acts as a substitute for the protection that would be available from a broad,
deep, and resilient futures market. A well-operating money market enables financial institutions that hold "eligible" assets to
generate, on their own initiative, a large cash flow in their favor.

The relation between the Central Bank as a lender of last resort and the money market delimits the extent and the conditions under which the market value of specified assets is pegged. There are many other insurance surrogate attributes of financial insitutions.

The proposition about financial intermediaries that is relevant for the determination of system behavior is that "dealer" intermediaries are not just more efficient "brokers," but that the liabilities that dealer-financial intermediaries emit to finance their position have different distributions of possible values than the assets they acquire. In general, financial intermediaries produce risk absorption, and perhaps more important, the attenuation of the range of possible outcomes.

A world with uncertainty cannot be analyzed by first ignoring uncertainty and then "correcting" the result. This proposition underlies recent work by Arrow and is essential to much of Galbraith's work.[8] Even more important, it is an essential postulate of Keynesian economics.[9] Liquidity preference is best interpreted as a relation describing portfolio choice in a world with uncertainty.[10] As will be argued in what follows, the marginal efficiency of capital schedule is not simply a transformation of a productivity of capital relation; it also takes into account both how the investment is to be financed and the liability structure of investing units. That is, the marginal efficiency of investment schedule allows for the impact upon the firm of various contingencies, and it is the financial structure of the firm that determines the effect of such contingencies upon the firm.

In what follows, the Hicksian *IS-LM* framework will be used, even though the use of a static framework for what is essentially a dynamic problem is a doubtful procedure.[11] This will be done in order to introduce what may be novel by starting from a well-known framework. Both the IS and LM function will be reinter-

[8]K. J. Arrow, "Uncertainty and the Welfare Economics of Medical Care," *American Economic Review*, Vol. 53, No. 5, December 1963, pp. 914 ff.; K. Galbraith, *The Affluent Society*, Boston: Houghton Mifflin Co., 1958.

[9]J. M. Keynes, *The General Theory of Employment Interest and Money*, London: Macmillan and Co., 1936.

[10]J. Tobin, "Liquidity Preference as Behavior Toward Risk," *Review of Economic Studies*, Vol. 25 (2), No. 67, February 1958, p. 65.

[11]J. R. Hicks, "Mr. Keynes and the 'Classics': A Suggested Interpretation," *Econometrica*, Vol. 5, No. 2, April 1937, pp. 147 ff.

preted so as to allow for both the essential uncertainty within which investment and portfolio decisions are made and the central role of financial relations in apportioning uncertainty. The proposition that will be argued is that any development that decreases the adverse effects of various contingencies without increasing the adverse effects of other contingencies will swing one or both of the IS and LM curves to the right. In particular, any improvement in financial intermediation will swing one or both functions to the right, thus increasing income over what it otherwise would have been.

Primary deficit units that emit liabilities and use the funds so acquired to finance tangible investment are one starting point for monetary economics. Typically, these units are business firms, so that for want of a better term this starting point can be called "corporate finance." However, the primary deficit unit can very well be a household; governments as deficit units have quite different effects than private units.

In this paper, the impact of financial intermediation upon the investment and liquidity preference relations will be emphasized. The impact of uncertainty and financial intermediation upon the savings and consumption relation will not be discussed. Nevertheless, it is worth noting that consistent with the view expounded here is the postulate that households attempt to maximize utility in a world where insurance is a commodity. Net worth and a protected portfolio provide insurance. The returns from thrift are not measured solely by market returns on wealth, but a portion of the returns are in the form of "certainty." As the various returns from an existing stock of wealth need not always move in the same direction, "perverse" reactions of desired savings to a change in measured market returns may take place.

A spending decision is simultaneously a real and a financial decision. For consumption, the Keynesian assumption is trivial: consumption is financed by income determined cash flows to households. The proposition that consumption is a function of disposable income is a straightforward conclusion of this premise. Of course, this proposition is not strictly true, and its validity decreases as both the proportion of households with significant net worth and the sophistication of financial usages increase: that is, as the ability to average over time increases. It is obvious that once households can go into debt to finance the acquisition of homes and consumer durables, the relation between household disposable income and spending decisions is attenuated. In a complex financial environment, there will be many unexploited financing opportunities for households. A change in view as to the necessary amount and type of protection against contingencies will affect spending decisions.

For the savings intermediation portion of financial intermediation, the interesting questions center around housing and business investment. We will next consider business investment — taking it as the general case.

Investment

Investment can be conceived of as resulting from portfolio adjustment by "firms." The asset acquired is the tangible investment good. The change in liabilities — including net worth — states how the investment, together with the acquisition of any other financial or second-hand tangible assets, was financed. The ex-post balance sheet changes are quite clear. The ex-ante or decision relation must be derived.[12]

An investment decision is a decision both to acquire tangible assets and to emit financial liabilities (including the implicit emission of liabilities by way of retained earnings). For a business organization, a financing plan is as vital as a facilities plan. The scenario for a corporate board meeting that adopts an investment program includes a discussion of how the planned program is to be financed. Among the elements in a firm's financial position that will affect the investment program are:

1. The existing liability structure;
2. the expected cash flow from operations, net of the contractual commitments as stated in the existing balance sheet and after allowance for "regular" dividends has been made;
3. the terms upon which external financing is available.

In a sophisticated financial environment, there is no need for a firm to "acquire money" first and then carry out an investment program. The acquisition of cash, either from operations or by the emission of liabilities need not precede the spending. By using

---

[12]A. G. Hart, "Capital Appropriations and the Acceleration," *Review of Economics and Statistics,* Vol. 47, No. 2, May 1965, pp. 123 ff.

bank lines of credit, the actual liability emission and the spending become simultaneous events. Whether to borrow short and then fund, or to borrow long and invest excess cash short, depends upon the firm's "speculative" view of how the money and capital market will behave rather than on any fundamental financial characteristic of an investment process. A firm will finance long before spending if it holds that long term rates may rise; the speculative demand for cash includes units seeking a capital gain as well as units seeking to avoid a capital loss. To the extent that risk aversion is a dominant trait of financial managers, a tendency to fund the planned external portion of any financing program immediately after the decision is made exists. By doing this, the financing conditions will almost always closely approximate those used in making the investment decision, whereas if funding is delayed the possibility that more adverse circumstances will exist at the funding date increases.

It may be true that the transactions demand for money depends upon the composition of transactions. However, it does not seem to be true that a demand for finance is necessarily an independent factor that shifts the demand for money upward with an expected increase in the investment component of output. There is no a priori way of determining whether investment spending is or is not better coordinated with cash receipts than consumption spending.

What "finance" properly means is that the decision to invest is also a decision to emit particular liabilities.[13] As no necessary connection exists between the "investment" and the financial instruments used, the decision to invest is based upon some view about the conditions that will rule in particular financial markets and the firm's evaluation of the implications of various balance sheet positions.

External financing conditions depend upon the structure of financial institutions and the terms upon which financing is available from each institution.

Thus, the investment decision envisages a "planned" balance sheet over some horizon. This planned balance sheet may include some expected emission of liabilities for external finance. Each liability emitted by a firm carries with it an explicit contractual or a contingent payment commitment. To the decision-maker, the

[13]P. Davidson, "Keynes' Financial Motive," *Oxford Economic Papers*, Vol. 17, No. 1, March 1965, pp. 47 ff.

price for not meeting these commitments, the cost of default or of a forced reduction in dividends, is high. The "probability" that an event will occur which will lead to default is an important determinant of an investment decision. The set of events that will lead to default depends upon the balance sheet structure of the firm at the time the event occurs. Thus the acceptance or rejection of a particular investment opportunity depends upon the balance sheet change that would accompany the investment.

The scenario for a corporate investment decision can be made a bit more precise. Assume that the engineering and marketing people come into the corporate board meeting with a ladder of projects ranked according to gross-after-taxes return. Going down the ladder, the financial manager will state the expected balance sheet for the firm as a function of the projects that are accepted. For each project, the increment to firm returns will be compared to the costs associated with the change in the balance sheet. The costs include the penalties associated with default on obligations. As the firm proceeds down the ladder, the balance sheet changes so that both the probability of and the penalty associated with financial stringency increases: that is, the set of events that would lead to default and the probability of some event that would lead to default occurring with sufficient intensity both increase.

The decision to undertake an investment program is simultaneously a decision to acquire some assets and to emit some specified set of liabilities. There are liability supply functions in financial markets which reflect investment programs. It is impossible to draw a meaningful investment demand function without simultaneously specifying the liabilities that will be emitted.

Within a given set of financing options, each increment of external financing, given the initial balance sheet, the flow of internal resources, and general financial market conditions, raises market terms to the firm as well as the likelihood that unfavorable contingent events will lead to a default. That is, there is a "monopsonistic" element in the financing of any firm.[14] However, the rising supply price of external funds relates not only to the new financing but also to the entire liability structure of the firm, as in time the initial balance sheet requires refinancing. Any short period investment program of a firm is limited by the fact that the

[14]M. Kalecki, "The Principal of Increasing Risk," *Economica*, N.S. Vol. 4, No. 16, 1937, pp. 440 ff. Reprinted in his *Essays in the Theory of Economic Fluctuations*, London: Allen and Unwin, 1939.

cost of large-scale external financing may include rising refinancing costs. A rise in refinancing costs increases the likelihood that the occurrence of an unfavorable contingent event will lead to default. Often it is the need for refinancing of a debt that triggers a firm's financial crisis.

A firm will have the maximum flexibility in exploiting investment opportunities if the initial balance sheet includes a minimum of constraints. One constraint, the amount of refinancing that is to take place over the life of an investment, can be minimized by having no balance sheet liabilities that will require refinancing. (This is a virtue of equity financing in general and retained earnings financing in particular.) One way of minimizing the expected need to refinance is by tying the payments on liabilities acquired to finance an investment to the expected cash flow from the investment. By treating the investing firm as a unit, and by recognizing that the firm is a monopsonist in acquiring financial resources and that future flexibility is an asset to the firm, the rule-of-thumb that ties incremental liabilities to incremental expected cash flows becomes a sensible way of doing things.

An important implication of the above is that for a going concern investment decisions are made on an evaluation of the impact on the operations of the firm as a whole, rather than by treating each project in isolation. Let us assume, in our continuing scenario, that we are at the second board meeting that has investment on its agenda and that, in the interval, the cash flow from operations fell short of what had been forecast. As an investment program once started is not quickly nor easily reversed, the financial manager met the firm's cash needs by resorting to unplanned external financing; for example, he engaged in some unplanned bank borrowing. As a result of the short fall of cash flows, the balance sheet is "inferior" to what had been forecast. The determination of a new investment program, and the extent to which the firm will go down the ladder of projects presented by the engineering and marketing people, will be affected by the inferior balance sheet; it is one of the effective initial conditions for new decisions. A downward shift in the marginal efficiency of investment schedule for this firm will take place not because of any deterioration in the payoffs expected from investment but because the balance sheet has deteriorated. Constraining investment and using cash flows to clean up the balance sheet is an alternative to tangible investment.

The marginal efficiency of investment schedule is a financial as well as a real relation. Any set of events that (a) improves the initial balance sheet or (b) improves the liabilities that firms can emit will shift upward the efficiency of investment schedule associated with any technological and market conditions. A broadening set of financial institutions, which make available new and improved financing terms, will effectively shift investment schedules.

Although we have emphasized firms' investment decisions, it is obvious that the improvement in the financing conditions for owner-occupied homes has been a factor increasing the effective demand for investment in housing. Similarly, the great improvement in household financing has broadened the spectrum of financing terms available to households and raised the consumption-disposable income relation. The erratic $\Delta c/\Delta y$ relation, of which much has been made, may not be due to the effect of nominal money upon demand, but to the fact that consumption decisions are being made in an ever-changing financial environment which effectively changes both the opportunities and the risks.[15]

Liquidity Preference

The liquidity preference function of Keynesian theory is an ambiguous relation. For each income level, it not only states the interest rate at which an existing stock of real and financial earning assets will be held, given the quantity of money (whatever that may mean), but it also states that at this interest rate, the liabilities emitted by investing units in order to finance a related level of investment will be assimilated into portfolios. The ambiguity is due to the attempt to deal with stock flow relations without paying sufficient attention to tedious details. However, the main proposition of the Keynesian approach, that aggregate demand is affected if the market for the stock of outstanding earning assets is affected, is valid. The point of view that follows from this proposition is that the significance of monetary, debt management, and fiscal policies is in their ability to generate a desired disequilibrium in the market for the stock of earning assets.

In discussing portfolio balance, two types of assets can be

[15]M. Freidman and D. Meiselman, "Relative Stability of Monetary Velocity and the Investment Multiplier in the United States, 1897–1958," in *Commission on Money and Credit Stabilization Policies,* Englewood Cliffs, N.J.: Prentice-Hall, Inc., 1963, p. 170.

identified: those whose nominal value is uncertain because it depends upon system behavior, and those whose nominal value at some date is independent of system behavior.[16] For our purposes, dated government interest-bearing debt, government currency, and the gold stock are the assets whose nominal value at some date is independent of system behavior and the state of the system at that date. The ambiguity of how government interest-bearing debt affects consumption via a real balance effect does not enter into the fact that government debt is in nominal terms a default-free asset..

A risk-averter balances default-free debt and debt which may be defaulted in his portfolio. Since the assets of the liquidity preference function carry default risk, the money of the liquidity preference relation must be default-free assets — that is, government debt (ex consuls), and gold.[17] If over a period of time the money supply so defined remains constant, and by accumulation the stock of assets that must be held increases, then, ignoring various price deflation possibilities which are unstable because unit elasticity of expectations is not a very sensible assumption, the liquidity preference function shifts upward; that is, the interest rate for each quantity of money-level of income pair will increase.

However, in a world with financial intermediaries, the household does not have to balance a portfolio by combining money and primary default-sensitive assets. The spectrum of assets available includes not only liabilities of business firms, households, and governments, but also liabilities of financial intermediaries. Financial intermediaries make available earning assets that represent a piece of a large, perhaps, diversified and professionally managed portfolio. The behavior of the liabilities of financial intermediaries under specified contingencies will be quite different than the behavior of some of their assets. Given the prevalence of risk aversion, the ability of financial intermediation to absorb risk tends to increase the ratio of nonmonetary to monetary assets that is compatible with any given over-all willingness to accept risk by households. This also means that the amount of primary liabilities emitted to finance investment that will be ab-

[16]J. Tobin, "An Essay in Principles of Debt — Management" in *Fiscal Policy and Debt Management Policies*, Commission on Money and Credit, Englewood Cliffs, N.J.: Prentice-Hall, Inc. 1964 pp. 143 ff.

[17]H. P. Minsky, "Money, Other Financial Variables, and Aggregate Demand in the Short Run." Forthcoming in G. Horwich, ed. *Monetary Process and Policy*, Homewood, Illinois: Richard D. Irwin, 1967.

sorbed directly or indirectly into portfolios at any interest rate increases as the range of financial intermediation available increases.

Financial innovation—in the sense of an increase in the range of financial options open to households and firms—is a vital part of the mechanism by which growth is financed. However, it is not necessary for financial invention to be especially rapid during a period of rapid growth—the diffusion or more intensive use of a past invention may suffice. All that is needed for financial intermediation to enable portfolios to adjust to changing proportions of ultimate default susceptible to default-free assets without a rise in interest rates is an increase in the weight of financial intermediation in the total financial structure.

Whereas real investment cannot be easily shifted from one location or industry to another, because of layering and refinancing possibilities the structure of assets made available to households by financial intermediaries can change rapidly. In a period of rapid financial adaptation, the financing terms for specific sectors and contracts can improve even though the relevant default-free asset concept of money is decreasing relative to income and net worth.

The extent of uncertainty that is absorbed by any set of financial institutions is partly a matter of the structure of the money market and of the responsibilities undertaken by the central bank. However, the subjective view of how these assets will affect the value of a portfolio if any one of the various alternative contingencies occurs is also a determinant of the extent to which the effect of changing ratios among primary assets can be offset by intermediation. The belief in the validity of the savings intermediaries commitment depends upon how they have been honored in the past—and a run of good times in a generally myoptic world will increase the willingness to absorb, directly or indirectly, the liabilities emitted by investing units.

In other words, in a world with financial intermediation, the LM curve will reflect not only the structure of financial options open to households but also the past of the system.

The Determination of Aggregate Demand

From the preceding discussion, it follows that the position of the LM and IS curves that make up a common diagram drawn to illustrate the simultaneous achievement of equilibrium in the money and output markets is conditional. Their position depends upon the recent past of the economy and the structure of financial intermediation. It follows also that a stable or even downward shifting LM curve is possible even though the money-other assets ratio has decreased, if the exploitation of financial intermediation increases or the range of alternatives offered portfolio holders by financial intermediaries increases.[18]

Because of the conditional nature of the LM and IS relations, the articulation between money and aggregate demand is not close. Even though a persuasive case can be made that the concept of money that is relevant for income determination is government debt (ex consuls) and gold, money, defined as demand deposits and currency, is not without significance in determining aggregate demand. Traditionally, commercial and central banks are the most powerful uncertainty absorbers among financial intermediaries. The rise in commercial-bank liabilities in portfolios will be a closer approximation to a rise in "properly defined" money than an increase in the other intermediary liabilities. Thus, if commercial banking is just one type of financial intermediary, in essence no different than the others, it nevertheless is the first, perhaps by far, among equals.

MONEY MARKET INTERMEDIATION: GROWTH AND FINANCIAL STABILITY

In the process of capitalist growth, financial innovation has played as large a role as real innovation. Real innovation serves to sustain the "efficiency of investment" schedule. Financial innovation serves to offset what can be considered as income-elastic demand for liquidity, which reflects an underlying income-elastic demand for security.

Growth in real income, if the wide spectrum of financial options, including many with specified contingent liabilities that offset computable uncertainties, had been absent would have been accompanied by a larger demand for "outside" money assets than in fact existed. In the absence of a growth of savings intermediaries,

[18]R. Turvey, "Does the Rate of Interest Rule the Roost?" in F. Hahn and F. Brechling, *The Theory of Interest Rates*, London and New York: Macmillan and St. Martins, 1965, pp. 164–172.

with their ability to absorb risk, large-scale deflationary pressures would have existed. With the growth and the exploitation of savings intermediation, income is higher and the interest rate is lower for any given money base (defined either as outside money or as a means of payment), than they would have been in the absence of savings institutions.

The existence of financial institutions that offset household and business firms' risk-aversion by properly designed assets has generated risks relating to system performance that center around the ability of financial intermediaries to fulfill the commitments they have undertaken. A change in the willingness to believe that financial intermediaries offer a good substitute for money can cause a sharp shift in the IS and LM curves.[19]

Savings intermediaries emit liabilities that commit the unit to make cash payments under stated conditions. These conditions almost always are such that it is possible for the payments to be greater than the receipts that the assets are expected to generate over a short period; however, this flow of funds can fall short of expectations. For an organization to operate successfully in such circumstances, some sources of funds that it can tap on its own initiative are needed. The money market and the financial institutions that operate there make it possible for savings intermediaries to survive under these conditions.

In addition, financial intermediaries and nonfinancial firms often make payment commitments without having the cash on hand. Almost always, the expectation is that the cash flow from operations will be large enough to cover the commitment. However, if operations do not generate a sufficiently large cash flow, then the survival of the unit—or at least the avoidance of embarrassment—requires that the unit be able to borrow or sell assets to obtain the necessary cash.

The extent to which savings intermediaries can be liquid, and to which firms can make commitments in advance of funding, depends upon the scope and strength of money market intermediation. The money market enables organizations to be safely illiquid—provided they have assets which are eligible for this market.

The basic raw material for the money market is the existence

---

[19]J. R. Hicks, *A Contribution to the Theory of the Trade Cycle*, Oxford: Clarendon Press, 1949, Chap. 11.

of pools of excess liquidity. Even in a tight money period, such as the last part of 1965, the annual rate gross national product was only slightly greater than four times the money stock, defined as demand deposits and currency. A large part of the money supply is held in balances which, while related to expected transactions, are expected not to be used in the very near future. The emission of appropriate liabilities enables money market institution to tap these cash pools. The funds made available from these pools will be somewhat responsive to variations in interest rates, the responsiveness being greater for short- than for long-term funds.

The money market basically is the locus for the refinancing of savings intermediaries individually, and in the short period, it can provide some flexibility in the total amount available to finance positions. In the normal functioning of any financial institution, days occur in which there is a net cash loss. As we can assume the institution to be nearly fully invested at all times, any significant cash drain will require a replenishment of its cash position. To a large extent, the set of financial institutions is a closed system, so that a normal functioning cash drain to some units will imply a cash surplus for other units: the funds to finance the deficit unit exist within the set of intermediaries. In a smoothly working money market, the surpluses and deficits will be matched.

The money market intermediaries emit liabilities that require them to manage their cash position efficiently — and in turn they need a standby source which will refinance their position if needed. For although the funds available from cash pools are sensitive to interest-rate changes, in the very short run this elasticity is not very great, and any mild doubts as to the riskiness of committing funds to the money market will lead to a sharp shift of funds out of this market.

A viable money market therefore requires a lender of last resort. However, in our ever-evolving complex set of financial institutions, the relevant money market institutions and the financial instruments used in the money market change rapidly. Any attempt to settle finally upon a mode of operation and a domain of responsibility of the central bank runs the risk that actual change will make the agreed-upon rules obsolete.

Note that the cash needs of financial institutions and their customers are satisfied by nominal money — demand deposits and currency for most units, reserve bank deposits for others. Whereas outside money has a deep significance in offsetting uncertainty, and the over-all riskiness of the situation is in part determined by the ratio of outside money to income and to transactions, the pure liquidity problems centering around payment commitments can be satisfied by whatever is commonly used to make payments. A flexible central bank that stands ready to acquire any type of asset it feels is necessary to avoid instability is a major requirement for the successful operation of a complex financial system. The central bank must follow, and in crisis ratify, what has taken place in the market. Only in times of stagnation or tranquillity can the economy afford a central bank that stands on principal.[20]

CONCLUSION

Apparently there are elements in a complex financial system that are inherently unstable. Savings intermediation is a substitute for the growth of outside money in sustaining an expanding economy, but an increase in the weight of savings intermediation implies a money market that is growing in size and complexity. This means that the domain of the central bank should be expanding to meet the evolving situation. Historically, central banks have not been adventurous in expanding the scope of their operations, and the Federal Reserve System is bound by a legislative mandate.

There is another element of instability in the system that might be of special interest. The current expansion is, in 1966, in its sixth year. Pronouncements that we are in a new era of permanent prosperity are plentiful. The willingness to finance investment by emitting liabilities and the willingness to shift to portfolios that are more heavily weighted with inside assets both depend upon this evaluation of how the system is going to behave.

There is a tremendous potential for an investment boom in the belief that the business cycle is no longer a threat. However, a private investment boom will eliminate the government deficit, and it may even result in a surplus. Such a private enterprise boom will lead to a rapid rise in the ratio of inside to outside

[20]I have dealt at length with the generation of financial instability in "Financial Crisis, Financial Systems, and the Performance of the Economy" in Commission on Money and Credit, *Private Capital Markets,* Englewood Cliffs, N.J.: Prentice-Hall, 1964.

money. The secure financial positions and the real risk-avoidance that exists in outside money will decrease. That is, as expansionary fiscal policy, by prompting a rapid increase in private investment, proves to be a down payment on future surpluses, one foundation of a stable financial system is undermined. In addition, as monetary policy is used in an attempt to constrain inflationary pressures, the payoff from economizing on cash balances increases and undermines another basis of a stable financial system.

From the perspective of finance, the lesson of the recent past is that a rapidly evolving financial system has been part of the mechanism that has sustained the expansion. Given this characteristic of the economy, the question as to whether or not the business cycle is now a thing of the past must be held open. The answer will depend in good part upon the flexibility and perceptiveness of our central bank in preventing any large shock from the financial system to the determinants of real demand.

Commentary

Roger F. Murray

In his conclusion, Professor Minsky points to the "expanding domain" required of the central bank in its key role as lender of last resort in the money market. In turn, the facilities of the money market are essential to enable nonbank financial intermediaries to adjust their inflows of funds to their outflows. If the intermediaries hold money market instruments for this purpose, as a kind of secondary reserve, the central bank need only see to the maintenance of orderly markets for such instruments. However, the present policies of financial intermediaries are to maximize the scale of their activities by reducing or eliminating the types of assets having widespread acceptance as liquid instruments.

For example, the leading home-financing institutions, such as member savings and loan associations, obtain advances from the Federal Home Loan Bank System in order to adjust their positions. Only as the Home Loan Banks seek to raise funds in the money market through the sale of short-term notes do the central bank's operations impinge upon their major sector of the capital market. In the case of mutual savings banks and life insurance companies, it is often the practice to borrow from commercial banks to meet commitments either for short periods or for longer periods by mortgage warehousing arrangements. The cost and availability of such credit is, of course, under central-bank influence. Nevertheless, the trend of these savings institutions toward reliance upon their ability to borrow instead of on carrying secondary reserves in the form of money market instruments is changing the pattern of their adjustments in financial position.

An illustration of current practices is found in the operations of Savings Banks Trust Company, owned by New York mutual savings banks and chartered to serve their needs. At the end of 1965, the bank held almost $145 million of mortgages under repurchase agreements, having secured the funds largely through the sale of short-term collateral trust notes in the money market. In effect, a new instrument was created to meet savings banks' needs as they had developed since early 1963. The alchemy of financial intermediation changes mortgages into a form of short-term commercial paper commanding a good market among similar instruments. A companion illustration is found when a commercial bank sells negotiable certificates of deposit to a non-financial corporation and advances the proceeds to a life insurance company to meet loan commitments.

The money market, broadly conceived, has had to expand its range of activities to deal in a wider range of instruments than the traditional mix of government securities, federal funds, bankers' acceptances, day loans, and commercial paper. The need for innovation is equally important in the area of corporate finance. Minsky does well to emphasize the importance of financing conditions in reaching an investment decision. "External financing conditions," he concludes, "depend upon the structure of financial institutions and the terms upon which financing is available from each institution." In addition, "a broadening set of financial institutions, which make available new and improved financing terms, will effectively shift investment schedules." The importance of these characteristics of financial intermediaries in facilitating a high level of investment which contributes to economic growth is seldom adequately recognized in public policymaking.

Implicit in Minsky's analysis are two points worthy of further elaboration. The first concerns the contribution of more effective methods of financing to economic growth resulting from a high level of investment. Although the tendency of conventional instruments and arrangements to dominate the capital markets is reinforced by questions of legal status and by the statutes and regulations applicable to financial institutions, the postwar years have witnessed the widespread use of techniques seldom seen in prior years. Some examples are the issuance of subordinated debentures and capital notes, sale-and-leaseback transactions, take-or-pay contracts and charters as collateral, third-party agreements, incentive financing arrangements, equipment leasing, and a variety of ingenious devices for the indirect use of a business firm's credit standing.

This type of innovation in the design of terms to facilitate special types of financing requires the participation of financial intermediaries who have enough at stake to incur the expense of staffing for complex negotiations. The public market is not only hostile to the unconventional; it also has developed as a wholesale market to distribute standardized securities at narrow spreads. The direct placement of securities with institutions has become almost the only field for experimentation and innovation.

The second important element in the availability of new and improved financing terms is the extent of competition, both within and between groups of intermediaries. When the lending and investing powers are restrained to traditional activities, the full play of competitive forces is inhibited. Usually the case for such limitations is based on some vague notion of the advantages of specialization. In reality, circumscribing the range and variety of activities can be justified only when a case can be made for allowing uneconomic units to survive in protected markets.

Public policy in the chartering and regulating of financial intermediaries should weigh Minsky's analysis against customary compromises with pressures generated by the holders of existing franchises. Those who are concerned over the number of alternative sources of funds in a community or trading area ignore the advances in communication and the flexibility developed by national suppliers of funds in meeting emerging needs for financial conditions geared to particular investment opportunities.

In summary, the liabilities that a firm emits should be closely geared to the characteristics of the investment. As the type of investment changes to keep pace with scientific and technological progress, the form and terms of such liabilities should be subject to continuous revision. A structure of financial intermediaries that is efficient and effective in maximizing the level of productive investment must be characterized by flexibility and innovation. Those who make public policy on chartering, regulation, and competition must recognize that disturbances in traditional concepts of specialization cannot be permitted to impede progress.

COMPETITION FOR FUNDS BETWEEN COMMERCIAL BANKS AND SAVINGS INSTITUTIONS

Marvin E. Rozen

Increased competition for savings has been one of the more significant developments in recent financial history. In this paper, I will discuss recent trends in savings flows and the resulting effects on savings institutions. I shall then explore some of the wider consequences and implications of these important changes as they affect the evolution of savings markets, the operation of monetary policy, and the techniques and goals of financial regulation.

SAVINGS FLOWS AND THE PERFORMANCE OF THRIFT DEPOSITARIES

Because the term "savings" can mean different things, a precise statement of what is included is essential. I am using the Flow-of-Funds data on savings which consist of time and savings deposits held by households and nonprofit organizations. Several issues arise with respect to these data. Obviously, savings held as currency or demand deposits are excluded. The inclusion of nonprofit organizations makes the aggregates grosser than is desirable but by a relatively small magnitude. Distinctions must be made between time and savings deposits; businesses, for instance, are prohibited from holding ordinary passbook savings accounts in commercial banks, but can hold similar accounts in other thrift depositaries, and these accounts must be excluded from the savings totals. Households, on the other hand, can and do hold their savings in the form of nonpassbook savings certificates which are lumped with time deposits in the over-all figures, and therefore some estimate of this component of savings must be made. Savings certificates are of considerable current interest since the 1966 increase and rollback in the Regulation Q ceiling on these savings certificates, and their use as a competitive weapon is becoming increasingly important. Finally, there is some small change included in time accounts, such as Christmas Club accounts and open-end accounts devoted to loan repayment, which also enter into the household savings total.

An Over-all View of Savings Flows from 1956–1966

As Figure 1 indicates, the predominant feature of savings flows over the past decade has been the see-saw behavior of the shares of savings and loan associations and commercial banks. This behavior clearly reflects the timing of rate increases by the commercial banks. Bank shares fall until a rate increase, usually associated with a permissive increase in the Regulation Q ceiling, brings a sharp rise. Numerous studies, especially those concerned with local savings markets, have shown a high degree of share sensitivity to rates paid by alternative savings media, although other factors—cyclical impact, lags, and diversity within financial institution populations—are also at work. Within the period 1965–1966, the strong performance of the commercial banks has been most noteworthy.

Indeed, what seems to be the resurgence of the commercial banks as vigorous intermediaries during the 1960s is the most striking trend in recent savings flows. (If, of course, all time deposits were included, this result is even more spectacular.) Considering that not too long ago, scholarly treatises were written on the declining importance of commercial banks among financial institutions and numerous academicians were counseling banks on the inadvisability and unprofitability of competing for savings, this resurgence is all the more remarkable.

Several interconnected factors account for the expanded intermediation and its likely continuance. First, the continued strong pull of profitable lending opportunities throughout the current expansion coupled with the disequilibrium situation implied by the low Regulation Q ceiling of 3 percent until January 1, 1962 have been of major significance. Given the underlying strong loan demand, raising ceilings allowed banks to bid aggressively for funds with which to service these loans. Sometimes this argument is reversed, and it is asserted that banks were forced by the higher costs of attracting savings (and time) deposits to reach

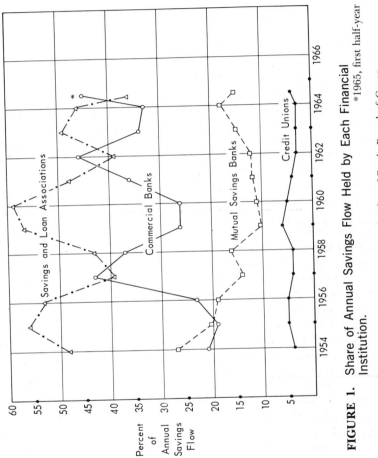

FIGURE 1. Share of Annual Savings Flow Held by Each Financial Institution.   *1965, first half-year

Source Federal Reserve Board, *Flow of Funds*, Board of Governors of the Federal Reserve System.

out for higher yielding and more remunerative instruments. This "recoupment thesis," however, must face the fundamental difficulty of its implication that banks were not maximizing previously; after all, if riper plums were there to be picked all the time, what prevented banks from doing so? A simpler and more persuasive explanation is that prior to the raising of the Q ceiling, banks were limited in their aggressiveness. After the ceiling was lifted, they were able to bid for funds as long as attractive lending opportunities made bidding worthwhile. For this reason, because profitable lending opportunities could not be fully exploited, one can characterize the previous situation as one of disequilibrium.

Second, as bank holdings of government securities became a smaller percentage of total assets, their ability to shift out of governments into loans—so marked a feature of past cyclical expansions—was greatly impaired. Thus, their intermediary role could be implemented only through greater reliance on liability creation. Third, compared with previous experience, the Federal Reserve System has been remarkably permissive with respect to reserves availability and rate ceilings. Indeed, the monetary authorities have, for several reasons, looked with favor on expanded intermediation. (I shall deal more fully with this point later.)

Fourth, the changes in the operating behavior and environment of commercial banks (and bankers) deserves great emphasis. There is a greater commitment to retail banking and an obvious complementarity between consumer lending and aggressive savings competition. Traditionally, banks have been clever imitators: they have indulged a conservative preference for letting other financial institutions pioneer and establish a going market (automobile paper, consumer installment loans, longer term mortgages), and then hopped on the bandwagon. Thus, banks are now following the trail blazed by the savings and loan associations, with the added advantages of being able to offer full-service, one-stop facilities, having more offices, and having done more branching. A final factor which will be of increasing value is the emergence of highly sophisticated electronic data-processing which can greatly lower the marginal costs of account expansion and servicing.

For all of these reasons, the lively interest in savings flows by banks is not likely to be a transient phenomenon. All signs in both the economic environment and in banking behavior indicates that banks will be more, rather than less, interested in savings in the future.

Diversity in Commercial Banking

One feature of commercial banking that has far-reaching ramifications and has received remarkably little recognition is the diversity among commercial banks. In the context of savings competition, it is very important to distinguish those banks which consciously and deliberately choose not to compete. In some cases, tacit understandings and a division of labor with pure thrift intermediaries reflect long standing deposit relationships, mutuality of interest, and, occasionally, common control. These arrangements seem most relevant in New England because of the long tradition of mutual savings banking, and in rural areas and small towns because of the over-all fewness of financial institutions. Another class of noncompeting banks are the business and trade banks, which largely do a wholesale and commercial business, especially in unit banking states where location may prohibit pursuing savings and where specialization by function is more common. Because of the substantial number of noncompeting banks, evaluation of rivalry between banks and pure savings institutions utilizing data for the respective total populations must be handled carefully to eliminate the inherent bias.

Diversity—in a somewhat wider sense than simply the existence of noncompeting banks—has a tremendous impact on competitive relationships among banks. When one reads accounts of banking rivalry in the trade press, especially in more recent periods, there is a recurrent theme: competition is usually initiated by a new, small, or outlying bank. This phenomenon has long been recognized in oligopoly theory as the impact of the "competitive fringe." Its rationale is both simple and persuasive: these banks are seriously disadvantaged by their aforementioned characteristics, and since deposit insurance greatly inhibits product differentiation, the rate weapon becomes the great equalizer.

The last point is significant because it has been argued that as long as a great many banks were not hitting the Regulation Q ceiling, competition was not being seriously affected. Yet the very existence of rate ceilings stifles competition by not permitting the use of the most important competitive technique by a strategically placed group of banks. (A fortiori, the same argument applies to entry barriers.) Vigorous action by some competitors sets the pace for all; if Regulation Q affected some, it must have affected all.

Pure Thrift Depositaries

The other notable aspect of commercial bank resurgence is the growth slowdown, especially since 1965, of savings and loan associations (SLA). In part this slowdown reflects the inevitable impact of a softening in the mortgage market on highly specialized lenders, and a consequent conscious choice by SLA to compete less aggressively by stabilizing rates and reducing promotional expenditure. One can thus discern a shift in managerial attention towards problems of internal efficiency and operational economies. Likewise, there is a trend towards greater portfolio diversification: an increase in industrial and business mortgage financing and residential income properties, educational loans, and the promotion of open-end mortgages. As might be expected, diversification is bound to be more attractive when residential housing markets weaken, but a crucial dependence upon legislative goodwill insures that changes in this direction must be made cautiously and warily.

An aspect of growth slowdown that may take on more significance is the extent to which SLA fortunes and performance are overly growth-sensitive. Directly, turnover is of major consequences since fees, commissions, and premiums are dependent upon generating new business, and SLA have come to rely on these revenues as an important source of income. Indirectly, many SLA officers may be affiliated with various ancillary home financing operations (insurance, legal title, and so forth), and the income therefrom is also related to turnover. Finally, as predominantly mutual institutions, managerial rewards must undoubtedly lean more heavily on the prestige and glory associated with large size as a surrogate for an equity interest. If growth- rather than profit-maximization models have any application, it is likely to be found in the area of mutual enterprise.

Another highly significant feature of recent years has been the expanded role of the regulatory authorities. Prompted by concern over the soundness of associations in periods of rapid expansion, the Federal Savings and Loan Insurance Corporation in 1964 prescribed required additions, out of current income, to reserves based essentially on the growth in risk assets and delinquent and foreclosed mortgages and real estate owned. Failure to meet these reserve requirements will lead to review of an association's dividend policy and the possible imposition of a reduction in dividend rates. Even more relevant in this connection have been a series of actions through which the Federal Home Loan Bank Board during 1965 has sought to establish what may be termed the "prevailing rate" doctrine. That is, associations raising their dividend rates above that prevailing in their area would be penalized, chiefly by being denied advances at their District Federal Home Loan Bank if the board thought that such rate increases were not warranted by local mortgage market conditions. Other recently proposed restrictions would deny such associations the authority to sell participation loans, make nationwide loans within the 5 percent limit allowable in metropolitan areas, and make mortgages within the 50–100 mile lending radius. Such expanded regulation raises broader issues which will be discussed later.

SOME CONSEQUENCES OF HEIGHTENED SAVINGS COMPETITION

The Evolution of Savings Institutions and Markets

The most striking trend in savings markets has been the narrowing of differences among savings institutions. Convergence has come from both sides, but the historically more decisive movement has been the apparently irreversible commitment by commercial banks to compete actively for savings. In the past, banks have had an off-again, on-again attitude towards savings, and doubtlessly, there will be some variation in their intensity of interest in the future. But the permanence of expanded intermediation, the increased emphasis on retail banking, the reduced portfolio flexibility, and the economies of large-scale data processing all point towards an irrevocable commitment. Likewise, the pure thrift depositaries will find the balance of advantage in further diversification. The logic of convergence rests, after all, on the basic similarity of function. No appreciable cost advantages seem to exist in either direction, and over time historic differences will matter less and less. The pace of convergence, however, will be strongly influenced by the attitudes of regulators and legislators.

One important factor affecting convergence will be its impact on entrepreneurial behavior and internal operating efficiency. Paradoxically, because banks have more accounts with a smaller average size and greater deposit turnover, more scope for improvement in internal operations should be possible. In any case, the trend toward sharper calculation and cost analysis should accelerate. Charges on excessive account activity, minimum balance requirements before payment of interest, differential rates, and bonus savings plans, rewarding the long-term saver and paying marginally higher returns to the most easily shiftable accounts—in sum, a more discriminating and complex system of rewards and charges will be seen. In addition, greater discernment and sophistication on the part of savers, and increasingly liberal regulatory action permitting more ingenious pricing will also work in this direction. In a sense, we will be leaving the Model T period for savings, and more options will emerge for the saver.

Savings Competition and Monetary Policy

It seems clear that, at least until 1966, monetary policy in the 1960s has differed from policy in the preceding decade. One reason is that the money supply has been allowed to expand more rapidly. Another is that the monetary authorities have taken a permissive attitude on the growth of time and savings deposits by supplying reserves to support such growth and by adjusting the rate ceiling when it tended to curtail expansion. What can be called the central bank's natural propensity for restraint has been held in check. Populist pressure from the White House has undoubtedly been the most important factor in this expansion, but memories of previous premature tightening episodes, a remarkable price stability record and, perhaps, responsiveness to academic criticism may also have been supplementary reasons.

Savings competition, then, must be analyzed within the framework of this new monetary dispensation which allows greater scope for intensified intermediation. Federal Reserve System permissiveness on this score has been strongly influenced by several other factors: 1) intensified intermediation means an increase in borrowing short and lending long, and, hence, to the extent that rate patterns can be affected, fits in nicely with the interest rate structure objectives of "Operation Twist"; 2) the belief that time and savings growth represents "real savings flows" and, hence, reserve provision, simply validates freely expressed market preferences and is not tainted as "inflationary money creation"; and 3) there is an awareness of the competitive equity arguments with respect to the absence of rate ceilings on rival financial intermediaries.

Expanded intermediation by commercial banks within the new monetary dispensation raises the fundamental issue of whether the rising velocity implied seriously impairs monetary control by making the link between money and expenditure too elastic. The same issue appeared in the late 1950s when the specter of the alleged effects of the growth of nonbank financial intermediaries on velocity was haunting monetary economists. The evidence, on the whole, exorcised this specter by showing that the most active portfolio switchers were commercial banks. How much more than in the latter case does intensified intermediation through liability creation enhance the scope for counter-cyclical velocity movements, especially if the monetary authorities remain motivated as I suggest? For instance, a large part of compensating balances could be switched to noninterest-bearing time accounts, and, given Federal Reserve System passivity, this action would represent a tremendous potential for expansion.

Such "slippage" in monetary policy could in principle be offset by a further tightening turn of the monetary screw. Yet one should consider this argument very carefully, because there are distinct limits on the pace of monetary policy. The dangers of upsetting financial markets and creating great uncertainty, both of which cannot as easily be undone, the uneven impact of monetary policy both within the economy and on financial institutions, the problems of debt-management coordination—all conspire to limit greatly the actual maneuverability of the monetary authorities. Furthermore, to the extent that banks are dependent upon liability creation for liquidity, the monetary authorities are even more circumscribed. It is one thing, and part of the accepted rules of the game, to impose asset sales at a loss on banks, but it is quite another matter to adjust to what must seem an arbitrary and capricious rate ceiling. In that event, as suggested earlier (and as the actions taken in December 1965 confirm), the rate ceiling will give way.

The problem of slippage brings up a related and more general difficulty that has beset monetary policy: a belief in "control by stickiness." This may be defined as a reliance by central banks on the notion that commercial banks will be rigidly bound by certain operating conventions and traditional behavior patterns (liquidity ratios, capital-risk asset ratios, reluctance to rediscount, and so forth) which can then be taken as parameters for purposes of monetary policy. Yet again and again, these supposed rigidities in the environment have crumbled, and usually for the very good (and foreseeable) reason that they stand in the way of profit-maximizing behavior.

If, as I suggest, the Federal Reserve System has "lost" the availability weapon, leaving the main influence to be borne by rate considerations, this loss is not necessarily an unmitigated evil. In a world of second-best arrangements, it might be a very desirable offset to central-bank conservatism, especially if, as I am inclined to believe, our economic problems derive more from a deficiency than from a surfeit of aggregate demand. Those who fear that inflation is always just around the corner will not, of course, share my diffidence. Much depends on the future course of international relations in general, and, as of 1966, on what will happen in Southeast Asia in particular.

Savings Competition
and Problems of Regulation

Heightened competition has led to greater awareness of the effects of regulation, and this greater sensitivity has merged with a wider concern evident in recent years over the possible harm done by regulation. There is a growing disenchantment with rate ceilings, portfolio controls, capital adequacy tests, reserve requirements against nondemand deposits, merger policies, entry and branching restrictions, and so forth. A consensus seems to be emerging that regulations are harmful or inappropriate or both. This judgment is based on several considerations. First, much regulation, it is argued, arose largely as a result of the misreading of the reasons for the financial debacle of the 1930s. Unwise central bank policy, rather than excessive competiton or unsound bank practices, was primarily at fault, and the form of regulation was heavily influenced by the general New Deal philosophy of government-sponsored private cartels. In any case, subsequent improvements in the economy and in policy formation suggest a reconsideration of rules devised for a previous era and with a particular crisis in mind.

Second, regulatory restrictions interfere in obvious and generally recognized ways with allocative efficiency, and stifle competition. Third, alternative ways of accomplishing the goals of regulation, involving different kinds of regulatory techniques and/or a different mix of regulation and competition, can be found. Fourth, given tremendous variation and nonuniformity within the regulated population, inequities and inconsistencies abound. Thus, as shown in a previous example, a uniform rate ceiling will have a differential impact on banks because of fundamental differences in their underlying position. Finally, given the multiplicity of regulatory authority, difficult problems of coordination are bound to arise. A Federal Interagency Committee, such as has been established recently, is not likely to be effective in resolving deep-seated differences unless it is granted greater powers.

The regulatory counterarguments against this line of attack emphasize the need to avoid financial failures because of the externalities associated with absolute confidence in the means of payment and in thrift deposits. (The disruption of long-standing financial ties is also mentioned sometimes.) In the absence of competition-inhibiting devices, such as rate ceilings or portfolio controls, the arguments continue, financial institutions would reach out for riskier assets. Partly they would be taking advantage of the immense leverage provided by a very thin capital margin—they are, after all, gambling with other people's money, and they stand to gain very much at the risk of losing very little of their own. Partly they would inevitably follow the easy path of credit quality deterioration, as "unrestrained rivalry" would coerce the weak to follow the lead of the strong, and thus, in the end, make everybody worse off as failure spreads. It should be emphasized that this argument does not rest on the lesser wisdom of bankers nor on their urge for self-destruction, but rather on the attractions of gambling with other people's money and the fact that ascending the escalation ladder of credit-quality deterioration is likely to prove irresistible. The failure of financial institutions which will result will lead to great social loss. The Federal Deposit Insurance Corporation institutionalizes this concern over failure by charging fixed premiums and controlling the level of portfolio risk.

Is a synthesis of the regulatory and antiregulatory points of view possible? Can we safeguard the economy against the social cost of failure and at the same time allow greater freedom to financial institutions? I believe we can certainly move in this direction, if we shift our objective from failure prevention to third-party compensation. There are many ways in which this change could be carried out. The most elegant, perhaps, would be to charge variable premiums, roughly adjusted for degree or risk, and allow freer asset choice. Thus, at a price, lenders could indulge their desires for risk, and their liabilities would be covered by an adequate insurance fund. A second way would be to shift toward more intensive supervisory treatment in lieu of relying on standardized ratios and rules of thumb. Such a development could be made manageable by developing reliable sampling techniques on a continuous audit basis rather than through periodic and individual item-by-item investigation. A third way might be to develop and publicize a risk-classification categorization, a sort of grade labeling, to provide information for depositors. As long as a completely riskless option would always be maintained to meet the absolute confidence criterion, a more variegated liability structure might allow more depositors to choose more intelligently in matching options with preferences. A final (and atavistic) alternative would be to deny financial institutions the privileges of limited liability.

Obviously, these options need not be mutually exclusive. Nor are they panaceas. At best, they would be exceedingly difficult to implement, and, given the importance of confidence in financial arrangements, the pace would have to be slow and acceptance forthcoming each step of the way. Some options would be used, perhaps, on a stand-by basis, to be invoked as needed. The first option – variable premiums – has many practical problems relating to the establishment of actuarial criteria for devising premiums, the applicability of insurance principles when high risk interdependence is present, and the choice of public or private insurance. Despite these difficulties, some cautious experimentation might be in order so that we will have more information with which to make a decision.

When all is said and done, the problem of failure in financial institutions is a true dilemma. An increase in the failure rate would be desirable because total risk aversion cannot be socially optimal, and the process of economic natural selection working to weed out the inefficient and keep all concerned alert would be continuously at work. But an increase in the failure rate would be undesirable because of its confidence-disturbing impact and the possible breakdown of a smoothly functioning payments-thrift mechanism. Attention must be paid to both horns of this dilemma; perhaps it might prove comforting to remember that it is the nature of both horns and dilemmas that they can never be straddled with complete comfort. In any case, it is doubtful whether existing arrangements are suboptimizing.

CONCLUSION

One cannot write this type of paper without at least testifying to the vivid impression that the process of financial innovation so unmistakably leaves. Since the evolution of savings markets and marked behavior shifts by savings institutions occur in bewilderingly rapid fashion, I find it difficult to have faith in simple predictive models, presumptively based on institutional and behavioral stability, which could encompass such complex phenomena. I have in mind a statement by James Duesenberry on some models of financial markets which is very appropriate:[1]

> "Before concluding, I would like to draw your attention to an important methodological problem posed by these papers. Mr. DeLeeuw's model is based on the empirical regularities connecting the short-run movements of financial variables in a given institutional setting. Professor Minsky emphasizes the importance of the evolution of financial institutions and markets. He also emphasizes the importance of slowly moving processes like debt accumulation, which reveal their effects only in a response to a shock whose timing may be accidental. Professor Minsky's fears cannot be readily reflected in a model like Mr. DeLeeuw's. One of the most important and vexing methodological problems is that of finding ways to construct empirical models which do full justice to both kinds of consideration."

This paper has been qualitative and, I hope, heuristic. Incorporating the considerations with which it was concerned within a more complicated and quantitative model of savings market behavior remains a job for the future.

[1]*American Economic Review*, Vol. 54, No. 3, May 1964, pp. 337–338.

Commentary

Lawrence S. Ritter

Professor Rozen has given us a comprehensive and thought-provoking assessment of recent competitive relationships in the market for household savings. As he indicates, these relationships contain significant implications for public policy, particularly with respect to the appropriateness of many of the regulations under which financial institutions currently operate.

Financial institutions do business within a framework of federal deposit insurance and traditional central banking controls. *In addition,* they are also subject to a vast and intricate network of legal specifications regarding almost every aspect of their asset and liability structure—a finely spun cobweb of detailed requirements, restrictions, and prohibitions which specify permissible prices, terms, conditions, and dollar amounts of almost every conceivable source and use of their funds.

These regulations are intended to strengthen the liquidity, the solvency, and the safety of financial institutions. They are the product of the periodic distress that has afflicted these institutions over the past century and a half, always with disastrous consequences. Innocent victims have lost their life savings, and the repercussions have precipitated or aggravated over-all economic contraction, including widespread bankruptcy and unemployment. The present network of regulations represents society's means of avoiding a similar calamity in the future.

Given the desirability of these ends—the maintenance of safe repositories for savings, and the avoidance of financially induced economic instability—one may nevertheless question the effectiveness and the efficiency of detailed regulation of specific sources and uses of funds as a means of achieving them. Such regulation involves implicit and largely unrecognized costs. For the individual financial institution, it sharply curtails management flexibility, innovation, and risk-taking. For financial institutions taken as a group, it also curtails competition. And for society at large, it bypasses the market in the allocation of financial resources and thereby tends to misallocate the real resources they reflect.

Is there any economic reason, for example, why mutual savings banks should be forbidden to make consumer loans? Why should commercial banks be free to purchase any amount of municipals, but be forbidden the purchase of any equities? Why should savings and loan portfolios to all intents and purposes be confined by law to mortgages and Governments? The implications of such regulations for the allocation of real resources are extensive and pervasive.

Presumably, all of these regulations are necessary to safeguard depositors' funds and to prevent the mass failure of banks and other financial institutions, with consequent deleterious effects on the economy as a whole. But are they *really* necessary?

There are two alternative ways to prevent the emanation of undesirable consequences from given activities. One way is to prohibit the activity, because if there is no activity, there are no consequences. The other way is to insulate the activity, to contain it, permitting it to take place but erecting barriers at the same time so that undesirable consequences will be negligible or at least limited.

The first course — prohibition — is always preferable where no social benefit is discernible in the activity itself, and where it would be difficult or impossible to compensate innocent parties adequately for damages suffered. Thus pure food and drug legislation is primarily prohibitive. The adulteration of food, the sale of harmful drugs, and the mislabeling of products are of no social value, have harmful consequences, and are therefore prohibited.

The second course — insulation or containment — is always preferable when there is some social benefit discernible in the activity, and when, in addition, it is possible to compensate innocent parties adequately for damages suffered. Indeed, society often prefers to use insulation as a control device even when the assessment of such compensation is difficult or practically impossible. Thus, we permit the driving of automobiles despite the tremendous cost in lives lost, and try to contain the damage via freeways, pedestrian overpasses, and speed limits.

The detailed network of regulation governing the sources and uses of funds by financial institutions appears to be based on the assumption that the only *one* way to prevent the undesirable consequences of bank failure is by prohibition. By limiting risk-taking, curbing flexibility, and inhibiting competition in financial markets, we are evidently trying to make it practically impossible for any financial institution to close its doors. If no financial institution ever fails, there can be no undesirable consequences.

However, insofar as social values are served by risk-taking, freedom to innovate, flexibility, and competition in financial markets, the proper social policy for financial institutions is insulation, not prohibition. What we should do is permit the activity to take place, and at the same time see to it that such undesirable consequences as may occur are contained to negligible proportions.

This can be done in two ways. The first way is by making sure that if a few banks fail, the savings of the individuals held therein remain undisturbed. This promptly breaks what was formerly a primary transmission mechanism infecting other financial institutions, and through them, the economy at large. The second way is by making sure that if aggregate spending, whether due to financial or nonfinancial causes, threatens to rise above or fall below tolerable limits, total expenditure is promptly adjusted down or up by appropriate governmental action. Only in this way can confidence in future business conditions — the ultimate foundation on which all asset values are based — be reinforced and strengthened. In so doing, the second transmission mechanism from bank failure to over-all economic contraction is broken.

Not surprisingly, instruments for accomplishing these purposes are already available — federal deposit insurance and monetary-fiscal policy. Because of the existence of deposit insurance, some banks *can* fail without the distress being communicated in shock waves to others. And because of monetary-fiscal policy, even if that distress does start to have ramifications, they can be promptly counteracted.

However, unlike federal deposit insurance and monetary-fiscal policy, the vast labyrinth of regulations about specific assets and liabilities is unsuccessful in forestalling the consequences of financial institution failure. These regulations appear to have been enacted as though federal deposit insurance did not exist, as though orthodox monetary policy was completely powerless, and as though compensatory fiscal policy had never been conceived. If these policies actually did not exist, I venture to suggest that our present cumbersome network of financial regulation would be no more effective in the 1960s in insuring bank safety and economic stability than the commercial loan theory was in the 1920s.

The now discredited commercial loan theory (or the real bills doctrine) — which held that commercial banks should make only short-term, self-liquidating, productive loans — was supposed to assure safety for the individual bank and stability for the economy as a whole. At its core, however, the real bills doctrine contained a fundamental fallacy: that the safety of the individual bank and the solvency of the financial system could be maintained by specifying the types of loans permissible for individual lenders to extend. It was assumed that if each *individual* loan and investment taken by itself appeared to be liquid and safe, then *all* loans and investments taken in the aggregate would thereby be liquid and safe.

The safety and liquidity of all loans and investments taken in the aggregate, however, depends on factors that are to a large extent *outside* the financial system, on factors that are beyond the control of an individual financial institution as well as of all financial institutions taken together. The main outside factor is confidence on the part of the general public that savings are really safe, and that business conditions will continue prosperous. To maintain this confidence is the function of deposit insurance and monetary-fiscal policy.

At the present time, we are making too much use of detailed regulation with respect to what financial institutions can and cannot do. If more energy were devoted to improving the efficiency of federal deposit insurance and over-all monetary-fiscal policy—both of which can use imaginative improvement—we could really insure against the undesirable consequences of bank failure, improve the allocation of resources, and probably realize a greater rate of economic growth. I do not know how to measure the value of these private and social benefits in money terms, but I suspect that they would be far from negligible.

Chapter 3

Introduction

Analysis of the direction and rate of money flows has revealed some interesting cyclical patterns. During the later stages of cyclical expansions in the economy, a smaller proportion of the savings invested by individuals has been directed to financial intermediaries while a larger proportion has been going into direct investment in the money and capital market. These proportions have been reversed during periods of recession. Similarly, during cyclical expansions, the velocity (the rate at which money turns over) of money has increased. This latter phenomenon raises questions about the effectiveness of monetary policy; that is, if a given stock of money turns over faster, the result may be similar to an increase in the money supply. Disagreements among monetary theorists in interpreting these developments reflect our incomplete state of knowledge about the interest-elasticities of alternative types of financial assets held by individuals.

In the selection that follows, Professor Warren L. Smith provides a theoretical basis for decisions by monetary authorities in order to increase the effectiveness of monetary policy. His analysis depends on relative interest-elasticities of substitution among money, time deposits, and securities. Assuming that the willingness of the market to substitute these types of assets for each other can be estimated or anticipated, Smith's analysis offers a logical basis for selecting which of the various instruments of credit policy should be chosen to obtain the desired effects with greater precision. A wide range of interesting alternatives are considered: Should reserve requirements on time deposits be set at zero or at levels equivalent to those set for demand deposits? Should the discount rate be adjusted regularly in relation to some market rate, for example, the Treasury bill rate, or should it be changed infrequently for discretionary purposes? What are the effects of interest rate ceilings on time deposits? Do commercial banks differ from nonbank financial intermediaries in determining the supply of loanable funds? Are there automatic monetary stabilizers at work which supplement the automatic fiscal stabilizers in counteracting disequilibrating surges of economic activity? These questions, and others, receive rigorous attention in the context of post-Keynesian monetary theory.

In view of the importance of the ability to estimate the interest-elasticity of substitution among financial assets in reaching policy decisions, we would caution the nontechnically trained reader from assuming that monetary policy will become an exact science on the basis of propositions derived from abstract theory. Smith's analysis will force policy makers to consider a wider range of alternatives with respect to the instruments of credit policy. His logic requires examination of assumptions about the use of reserve requirements, the discount rate, Regulation Q, and the relationship of these variables to the money supply and economic activity.

TIME DEPOSITS,
FREE RESERVES,
AND MONETARY POLICY

Warren L. Smith

The primary objective of this paper is the development of a theoretical framework that will show how substitutions involving money, time deposits, and securities may influence the effectiveness of monetary policy. I hope that this framework will contribute to an improved understanding of the role of free reserves in the functioning of the monetary mechanism. I shall also demonstrate that all of the elements I have mentioned can be incorporated without serious difficulty into the corpus of post-Keynesian monetary theory.

The method employed will be that of comparative statics applied to the financial sector of the economy. That is, the links and feedbacks that connect the financial and real sectors of the economy will be neglected except at a few points where I cannot avoid taking them into account in developing my argument.

SUBSTITUTION BETWEEN
TIME DEPOSITS AND SECURITIES

To provide a realistic basis for the analysis in terms of U.S. monetary institutions, it is necessary to take account of the factors determining the supply of member bank reserves available to serve as the basis for creation of money and time deposits. The sources and uses of member bank reserves are summarized in sufficient detail for present purposes in the following table:

Table 1

SOURCES	USES
P = F.R. portfolio of U.S. Government securities	R_q^d = Required reserves for demand deposits
R_b = Bank borrowing from F.R.	R_q^t = Required reserves for time deposits
A = Other sources and uses, net	R_e = Excess reserves
	N = Currency outside banks

From this table of sources and uses, we have the identity,

$$P + R_b + A = R_q^d + R_q^t + R_e + N$$

Let $W = P + A$ (unborrowed reserves + currency). Assuming that the Federal Reserve uses Roosa-type "defensive" open-market operations to offset undesired changes in "other" factors (such as float, gold stock, foreign deposits, and Treasury deposits) affecting reserves, W may be treated as the exogenous variable that is controlled by the Federal Reserve through open-market operations.[1] Thus, we have

$$W + R_b = R_q^d + R_q^t + R_e + N$$

or

$$W - F = R_q^d + R_q^t + N \tag{1}$$

where $F = R_e - R_b$ = free reserves.

Suppose, for simplicity, that currency is a fixed proportion (c) of the money supply [demand deposits (D) plus currency (N)] and that the reserve requirements are k for demand deposits and t for

---

[1] In order to avoid complicating the analysis without adding appreciably to its usefulness, I shall neglect the operations of nonmember banks, assuming, in effect, that all banks are members of the Federal Reserve System.

time deposits (T).[2] Then the money supply (M) is

$$M = D + N$$

and

$$R_q{}^d = kD$$
$$D = (1 - c)M$$
$$R_q{}^d = k(1 - c)M \tag{2}$$
$$N = cM \tag{3}$$
$$R_q{}^t = tT \tag{4}$$

Substituting (2), (3), and (4) into (1), we have

$$W - F = k(1 - c)M + tT + cM \tag{5}$$

There is considerable evidence that the demand for free reserves varies inversely with the interest rate on primary securities (r) and directly with the Federal Reserve discount rate (i).[3] That is, a rise in the market rate of interest with a constant discount rate will increase the incentives of member banks to borrow at the Federal Reserve and may also cause some banks to reduce their holdings of noninterest-earning excess reserves, thereby bringing about a decline in free reserves. On the other hand, an increase in the discount rate with a constant market rate will cause free reserves to increase by inducing member banks to repay borrowings at the Federal Reserve and perhaps by inducing some of them to hold greater excess reserves in order to reduce the probability of having to borrow.[4] Thus, we have

$$F = F(r, i)$$
$$\left(\frac{\delta F}{\delta r} < 0; \frac{\delta F}{\delta i} > 0 \right) \tag{6}$$

[2]The handling of the demand for currency in this paper is considerably oversimplified. However, I have seen no very convincing analysis of the demand for currency, and I believe the subject is very poorly understood. Accordingly, I can see little justification for attempting to handle it in a more sophisticated way. Moreover, the present simple method of dealing with it avoids complications that might stand in the way of clear analysis of the matters that primarily concern me.

[3]For simplicity, I shall assume throughout this paper (except in the Appendix) that there is only one interest rate on securities.

[4]This line of reasoning is developed in W. G. Dewald, "Free Reserves, Total Reserves, and Monetary Control," *Journal of Political Economy*, 71, April 1963, pp. 141–153. Empirical evidence in support of the view that the demand for free reserves depends inversely on the short-term market rate of interest and directly on the Federal Reserve discount rate is presented in A. J. Meigs, *Free Reserves and the Money Supply*, Chicago: University of Chicago Press, 1962. The response of free reserves to relative changes in the market rate and the discount rate underlies the response of the money supply to interest rates that is measured by R. L. Teigen in "Demand and Supply Functions for Money in the United States: Some Structural Estimates," *Econometrica*, Vol. 32, October 1964, pp. 476–509.

For convenience, let m be the reserve requirement applicable to money [the average of the reserve requirement for demand deposits (k) and the reserve requirement for currency (unity) weighted by the proportions of demand deposits $(1 - c)$ and currency (c) in the money supply]. That is,

$$m = k(1 - c) + c \tag{7}$$

Substituting (6) and (7) into (5), we have

$$W - F(r,i) = mM + tT \tag{8}$$

Now suppose that the demand equations for money and time deposits are as follows:[5]

$$M = L(r, \bar{p}, \bar{Y}, \bar{K}) \tag{9}$$
$$T = T(r, \bar{p}, \bar{Y}, \bar{K}) \tag{10}$$

For the present, we shall assume that the interest rate on time deposits (p) is fixed and that GNP (Y) and wealth (K) do not change because the analysis is short-run in character and the links and feedbacks connecting the monetary and real sectors of the economy involve such long lags that they can be neglected. (These assumptions are reflected in the bars over p, Y, and K.)

Collecting the last three equations, we have

$$W - F(r, i) = mM + tT \tag{8}$$
$$M = L(r, \bar{p}, \bar{Y}, \bar{K}) \tag{9}$$
$$T = T(r, \bar{p}, \bar{Y}, \bar{K}) \tag{10}$$

These equations contain three endogenous variables: M, T, and r. There are four exogenous policy parameters: W (for open-market operations), i (the discount rate), k (the reserve requirement for demand deposits), and t (the reserve requirement for time deposits). We assume, of course, that $\delta L/\delta r < 0$ and $\delta T/\delta r < 0$.

Measures of the Effectiveness of Monetary Policy

In this paper, I shall take open-market operations (changes in W) as the instrument by which monetary policy is conducted, and I

[5]There are three markets involved in this model: the money market, the time-deposits market, and the securities market. By Walras' Law, if two of the market are equilibrated, the third must be also. Accordingly, it is necessary to take only two of the markets explicitly into account. I have chosen to deal with the markets for money and time deposits.

shall use the magnitude of the response of the interest rate on securities to open-market operations as a measure of the effectiveness of monetary policy.[6] That is, the larger the absolute value of dr/dW, the more effective is monetary policy. Of course, one may question this measure, since a smaller value of dr/dW simply means that it will require a larger volume of open-market operations to produce a given change in the interest rate on securities than would be needed if dr/dW were larger. Unless there is some limit on the magnitude of open-market operations per unit of time, it might be argued that the size of dr/dW is a matter of little importance. I believe that, as a practical matter, there is some such limit (especially for open-market sales), but I will not debate the matter here. The effectiveness of monetary policy in the sense in which I am using the term is surely of interest to monetary economists.

A better measure of the effectiveness of monetary policy (in the sense of the potency of open-market operations) would be dY/dW rather than dr/dW, since the objective of monetary policy is to control aggregate demand for goods and services in order to achieve optimal combinations of employment and price stability. Moreover, dr/dW as used in this paper takes account only of responses within the monetary sector of the economy, neglecting the links and feedbacks connecting the monetary and real sectors. However, for models of the Keynesian variety and under what may probably be regarded as normal conditions, an increase in the absolute value of dr/dW, in the sense in which we are using that measure, must necessarily be accompanied, *ceteris paribus*, by an increase in dY/dW.[7]

---

[6] A similar definition of the effectiveness of monetary policy is used in L. E. Gramley and S. B. Chase, Jr., "Time Deposits in Monetary Analysis," *Federal Reserve Bulletin*, October 1965, pp. 1380–1406.

[7] It is shown in the first part of the Appendix that if the marginal propensity to spend out of income is less than unity, an increase in the absolute value of dr/dW must be associated with an increase in dY/dW. (The model employed in the Appendix incorporates the more elaborate formulation of the financial sector taken up in the section titled "Both Substitution Effects Present.") It is also shown, however, that if the propensity to spend is greater than unity, the relation is reversed—that is, an increase in dr/dW is associated with a decrease in dY/dW. (This is the case of the upward-sloping IS curve referred to in footnote 25.) While a marginal propensity to spend of less than unity appears to be normal, the possibility that this condition will be violated certainly cannot be completely ruled out. Under such conditions, some of the conclusions derived in this paper might need to be changed rather drastically.

Since a great deal of emphasis has traditionally been given to movements of the money supply as an index of monetary policy, I shall also pay some attention to the effect of open-market operations on the money supply (again neglecting the links and feedbacks connecting the monetary and real sectors), as measured by dM/dW. It turns out that, for the kinds of effects I am concerned with, most structural changes that increase the absolute value of dr/dW will also increase dM/dW. Consequently, dM/dW rather than dr/dW could generally be used as an index of the effectiveness of monetary policy. Nevertheless, I prefer to use dr/dW.

Effect of Open-Market Operations on r and M

The effects of open-market operations on the interest rate on securities (r) and on the money supply (M) can be found by differentiating equations (8) through (10) with respect to W, treating i as a constant, and solving for dr/dW and dM/dW. This yields the following result:

$$\frac{dr}{dW} = \frac{1}{m\frac{\delta L}{\delta r} + t\frac{\delta T}{\delta r} + \frac{\delta F}{\delta r}} \tag{11}$$

$$\frac{dM}{dW} = \frac{\frac{\delta L}{\delta r}}{m\frac{\delta L}{\delta r} + t\frac{\delta T}{\delta r} + \frac{\delta F}{\delta r}} \tag{12}$$

Since $\delta L/\delta r < 0$, $\delta T/\delta r < 0$, and $\delta F/\delta r < 0$, it follows that $dr/dW < 0$ and $dM/dW > 0$. We shall also assume that the reserve requirement for money is greater than that for time deposits (that is, $m > t$).

Two effects are taken into account here that have traditionally been overlooked: (1) the interest-sensitivity of free reserves, measured by $\delta F/\delta r$, and (2) interest-induced substitution between time deposits and securities, measured by $\delta T/\delta r$. These effects reduce the size of both dr/dW and dM/dW. If both effects are absent — that is, if $\delta F/\delta r = \delta T/\delta r = 0$ — we have

$$\frac{dM}{dW} = \frac{1}{m} = \frac{1}{k(1 - c) + c}$$

This is the standard "textbook" version of the credit expansion multiplier when account is taken of cash drain. Thus, if either or both of the effects referred to are present, they will reduce the "money multiplier" below its textbook level.[8]

The Money-Supply Function

The analysis presented above can be placed in the framework of a money supply function. Substituting (10) into (8), we have

$$W - F(r, i) = mM + tT(r, \bar{p}, \bar{Y}, \bar{K})$$

Solving for M, we obtain

$$M = \frac{1}{m} [W - F(r, i) - tT(r, \bar{p}, \bar{Y}, \bar{K})]$$

This is the money supply function, to which (9) is the corresponding money demand function. Differentiating with respect to r, we have

$$\frac{dM}{dr} = -\frac{1}{m} \frac{\delta F}{\delta r} - \frac{t}{m} \frac{\delta T}{\delta r} \qquad (13)$$

Since $\delta F/\delta r < 0$ and $\delta T/\delta r < 0$, it follows that $dM/dr > 0$.[9] Thus, the money supply responds positively to the rate of interest on securities for two reasons: (1) the response of free reserves to the rate of interest, and (2) substitution between securities and time deposits due to changes in the rate of interest. The first term on the right-hand side of equation (13) reflects the first of these effects—the tendency for banks to increase their free reserves as the market interest rate falls by repaying borrowings at the Federal Reserve and perhaps also by increasing their holdings of excess reserves. This reduces the amount of reserves available to support deposits and currency, thereby causing a decline in the money supply.

[8]Empirical estimates of short-run "money multipliers" taking account of the "free reserves effect" (measured above by $\delta F/\delta r$) are made by R. L. Teigen in "A Structural Approach to the Impact of Monetary Policy," *Journal of Finance*, Vol. 19, May 1964, pp. 284–308.

[9]The reader may be puzzled by the fact that dM/dr [equation (13)] is not equal to dM/dW [equation (12)] divided by dr/dW [equation (11)]. However, it should be noted that dM/dW and dr/dW are derived from all three of the equations (8), (9), and (10), while, in deriving dM/dr, we used only equations (8) and (10). That is, dM/dW and dr/dW measure the responses of the quantity of money and the interest rate on securities to Federal Reserve open-market operations, taking account of both money supply and money demand relationships, whereas dM/dr measures the response of the *supply* of money to a change in the interest rate on securities.

The second term on the right-hand side of (13) reflects the second effect—the tendency of investors to shift funds from securities to time deposits as the interest rate on securities declines.[10] Perhaps the best way to explain this second effect is by means of a numerical example. Suppose a decline in the interest rate on securities causes investors to sell 100 of securities and deposit these funds in time accounts. If we assume that reserve requirements are 15 percent for demand deposits and 4 percent for time deposits and that currency holdings change by 20 percent of the change in money balances, the results will be as follows:[11]

Table 2   COMMERCIAL BANKS

(1) Currency	+20.0	(1) Time deposits	+100.0
(2) Loans and investments	+87.5	(1) Demand deposits	− 80.0
(2) Currency	−17.5	(2) Demand deposits	+ 70.0

In the first step [entry (1)], investors sell 100 of securities, the buyers giving up 80 of demand deposits and 20 of currency, and the investors use the proceeds to acquire 100 of time deposits. Excess reserves of the banks are increased by 28 as a result of this transaction [20 of additional reserves resulting from the inflow of currency, plus 12 (15 percent of 80) of reserves released by the decline in demand deposits, minus 4 (4 percent of 100) of additional reserves needed to support the new time deposits]. With an average reserve requirement of 15 percent for demand deposits and a currency drain equal to 20 percent of any increase in the money supply, the banking system can expand credit [entry (2)] by 3.125 times any additional excess reserves.[12] Thus, secondary

[10]The article by Gramley and Chase (see footnote 6) deals with the effects of substitution between time deposits and securities on the interest rate on securities and on the money supply. The conclusions presented in that article are very similar to those derived here.

[11]The reader should understand that this illustration relates *only* to substitution between securities and time deposits. In the model we are considering there is also substitution between securities and money as reflected in the demand-for-money function [equation (9)].

[12]The standard "textbook" credit expansion multiplier is $1/[k(1-c)+c]$, where k is the reserve requirement for demand deposits and c is the currency drain as a proportion of the increase in the money supply. When $k = .15$ and $c = .20$, the multiplier is 3.125.

credit expansion amounts to 87.5 (3.125 times 28), of which the public takes 80 percent, or 70, in demand deposits, and 20 percent, or 17.5, in currency.

The result of this operation is to reduce the money supply by 12.5 — a drop of 10 in demand deposits and 2.5 in currency. And it is very important to note that the operation also reduces the total demand for loans and securities by 12.5: the public sells 100 of securities and the banking system acquires 87.5 of additional loans and investments. Thus, a decline in interest rates reduces not only the money supply but the demand for debt instruments as well. The decline in the demand for securities tends to check the fall in interest rates; this is the reason why the substitution between securities and time deposits reduces the absolute value of dr/dW as given by (11) above.

It is a simple matter to derive a general formula for the magnitude of the effect described above. If the change in time deposits is ΔT, the secondary contraction in money and bank credit is equal to the standard credit expansion multiplier times the amount of reserves released by the induced switch from money to time deposits, which is equal to $[k(1-c)+c-t]\Delta T$. Thus the secondary increase in the supply of money and bank credit is

$$\frac{k(1-c)+c-t}{k(1-c)+c}\Delta T$$

The initial shift of funds into time deposits changes the money supply and the public's demand for securities by $-\Delta T$. Thus, we have

$$\Delta M = \Delta S = \frac{k(1-c)+c-t}{k(1-c)+c}\Delta T - \Delta T$$

or   (14)

$$\Delta M = \Delta S = \frac{-t}{k(1-c)+c}\Delta T$$

In the above numerical example, $-t/[k(1-c)+c]$ is, of course, equal to $-.125$. Since ΔT is 100, we have

$$\Delta M = \Delta S = -12.5$$

Since $k(1-c)+c=m$, equation (14) can also be written

$$\Delta M = \Delta S = -\frac{t}{m}\Delta T \qquad (15)$$

Note that the coefficient of ΔT in (15) is precisely the same as the coefficient of $\delta T/\delta r$ in (13).

Discount-Rate Policy

Thus far, we have treated the Federal Reserve discount rate as a constant. However, the discount rate can be adjusted to changes in market rate or other variables in various ways, and the manner in which discount-rate policy is conducted will influence the effectiveness of monetary policy. Let us suppose that the discount rate is adjusted to market rate; the relation can be taken into account by introducing an additional equation

$$i = f(r) \tag{16}$$

This equation describes the behavior of the Federal Reserve in adjusting the discount rate to the market rate; the function f or its derivatives or other properties can presumably be chosen at will by the Federal Reserve. When the equation is introduced, the model becomes

$$W - F(r, i) = mM + tT \tag{8}$$
$$M = L(r, \bar{p}, \overline{Y}, \overline{K}) \tag{9}$$
$$T = T(r, \bar{p}, \overline{Y}, \overline{K}) \tag{10}$$
$$i = f(r) \tag{16}$$

Differentiating with respect to W and solving for dr/dW and dM/dW, we obtain

$$\frac{dr}{dW} = \frac{1}{m\dfrac{\delta L}{\delta r} + t\dfrac{\delta T}{\delta r} + \dfrac{\delta F}{\delta r} + \dfrac{\delta F}{\delta i}\dfrac{df}{dr}} \tag{17}$$

and

$$\frac{dM}{dW} = \frac{\dfrac{\delta L}{\delta r}}{m\dfrac{\delta L}{\delta r} + t\dfrac{\delta T}{\delta r} + \dfrac{\delta F}{\delta r} + \dfrac{\delta F}{\delta i}\dfrac{df}{dr}} \tag{18}$$

The money supply function for this model is

$$M = \frac{1}{m}\left[W - F(r, f(r)) - tT(r, \bar{p}, \overline{Y}, \overline{K})\right]$$

The response of the money supply to changes in the market rate of interest is obtained by differentiating this equation with respect to r:

$$\frac{dM}{dr} = -\frac{1}{m}\left(\frac{\delta F}{\delta r} + \frac{\delta F}{\delta i}\frac{df}{dr}\right) - \frac{t}{m}\frac{\delta T}{\delta r} \qquad (19)$$

It is possible, at least in principle, to choose a value of df/dr so as to satisfy the condition

$$\frac{\delta F}{\delta r} + \frac{\delta F}{\delta i}\frac{df}{dr} = 0$$

thereby eliminating the response of free reserves to the market rate of interest which reduces dM/dW [equation (18)] and the absolute value of dr/dW [equation (17)] and increases dM/dr [equation (19)]. Such a discount rate policy would be one in which

$$\frac{df}{dr} = -\frac{\dfrac{\delta F}{\delta r}}{\dfrac{\delta F}{\delta i}}$$

If $\delta F/\delta r$ and $\delta F/\delta i$ are known constants, it is a simple matter to formulate such a discount-rate policy. Suppose, for example, that $\delta F/\delta r = -2$ and $\delta F/\delta i = 4$. Then we would have $df/dr = .5$. That is, if the discount rate were changed consistently by one-half of a percentage point for every percentage point change in the market rate on securities, the interest response of free reserves would be eliminated. If it should happen that $\delta F/\delta i = -\delta F/\delta r$, the appropriate policy would be to change the discount rate by an amount equal to the change in the market rate.[13]

Since interest-induced changes in free reserves are primarily a result of changes in member-bank borrowing, as a practical matter the optimal way to conduct discount-rate policy would probably be to set the discount rate sufficiently above the market rate to make borrowing clearly unprofitable and then to maintain a constant differential between the two by adjusting the discount rate each week in response to changes in the market rate on new

[13]There is some evidence that $\delta F/\delta i$ may be approximately equal to $-\delta F/\delta r$. For example, Teigen, "Demand and Supply Functions for Money in the United States: Some Structural Estimates," *Econometrica*, Vol. 32, October 1964, found this to be the case for the postwar period, 1946–1959, but not for the prewar period, 1924–1941.

issues of Treasury bills.[14] Such a policy would eliminate borrowing entirely except in cases of emergency and should eliminate the
response of free reserves to the market interest rate regardless of
the "normal" values of $\delta F/\delta r$ and $\delta F/\delta i$. This is a policy that I have
recommended on several occasions, and I believe its adoption
would lead to a modest strengthening of monetary policy.[15]

Reserve Requirements
for Time Deposits

It is apparent from equations (11), (12), and (13) [or, alternatively,
(17), (18), and (19)] that if the objective is to set the reserve requirement for time deposits so as to eliminate the effects of interest-
induced substitution between securities and time deposits, the
reserve requirement should be set equal to zero. Thus, if $t = 0$, the
term $t(\delta T/\delta r)$ in equations (11) and (12) [or equations (17) and
(18)] is reduced to zero, as is the term $-(t/m)(\delta T/\delta r)$ in equation
(14) [or equation (19)].

The reason a policy of imposing zero reserve requirements on
time deposits will eliminate the effects on the money supply and
the interest rate of interest-induced substitutions between securities and time deposits is that in this case the banks will be able to
carry out a secondary expansion of loans and investments and the
money supply. This will precisely offset the effect on the demand
for securities of the initial security sales by investors shifting into
time deposits, and will restore the money supply to its initial level.
In the numerical illustration presented above, if reserve require-

---

[14]A policy approximating this was followed in Canada from November 1956
until June 1962, during which period the Bank of Canada followed the practice of
maintaining the Bank Rate—the minimum rate at which the Bank makes advances
to the chartered banks—at 1/4 of 1 percent above the average rate on three-month
treasury bills at the preceding weekly bill tender. As far as I can discover, this
policy was abandoned in Canada not because it did not work well but because the
Bank of Canada desired to raise the discount rate sharply at the time of the 1962
balance-of-payments crisis as a signal of the intention of the Canadian government
to take drastic action if necessary to deal with the crisis. The Canadian technique is
similar to the one I am proposing except that I would set the differential between
the discount and bill rates at 1 percent or more in order to eliminate borrowing
entirely except as a safety valve for individual banks in dealing with severe liquidity
problems.

[15]See W. L. Smith, "The Discount Rate as a Credit-Control Weapon," *Journal of
Political Economy*, Vol. 66, April 1958, pp. 171–177; and "The Instruments of General Monetary Control," *National Banking Review, I,* September 1963, pp. 47–76.

ments for time deposits were zero, excess reserves would increase by 32 rather than 28, and the banks would be able to expand loans, investments, and the money supply by 100 (32 × 3.125), thereby exactly offsetting the effect of the initial sale of 100 of securities by the nonbank investors who shifted funds into time deposits.

SUBSTITUTION BETWEEN MONEY AND TIME DEPOSITS

Much of the discussion of the impact of nonbank financial intermediaries has related to possible direct substitution between money and time-deposit-like claims. Let us now try to isolate this effect. The model we shall employ is as follows:

$$W - F(\dot{r}, i) = mM + tT \tag{8}$$
$$M = L(r, p, \overline{Y}, \overline{K}) \tag{20}$$
$$T = T(p, \overline{Y}, \overline{K}) \tag{21}$$
$$p = G(r) \tag{22}$$

In order to isolate the substitution between money and time deposits, we are here assuming that the demand for time deposits is dependent on the interest rate on time deposits but not on the interest rate on securities. We have also made the time deposit rate an endogenous variable by introducing a fourth equation [equation (22)] which reflects adjustment of the time deposit rate to the rate on securities. Even though investors do not shift funds between securities and time deposits in response to changes in relative rates of return, it is assumed that banks will at least partially adjust the rate paid on time deposits to changes in the interest rate on securities, because an increase in this rate will increase their incentive to attract funds in the form of time deposits for the purpose of investing in securities.

Effect of Open-Market Operations on r and M

Equations (8), (20), (21), and (22) contain four endogenous variables: r, p, M, and T. Differentiating with respect to W and solving for dr/dW and dM/dW, we obtain

$$\frac{dr}{dW} = \frac{1}{m\frac{\delta L}{\delta r} + m\frac{dG}{dr}\frac{\delta L}{\delta p} + t\frac{dG}{dr}\frac{\delta T}{\delta p} + \frac{\delta F}{\delta r}} \tag{23}$$

and

$$\frac{dM}{dW} = \frac{\frac{\delta L}{\delta r} + \frac{dG}{dr}\frac{\delta L}{\delta p}}{m\frac{\delta L}{\delta r} + m\frac{dG}{dr}\frac{\delta L}{\delta p} + t\frac{dG}{dr}\frac{\delta T}{\delta p} + \frac{\delta F}{\delta r}} \tag{24}$$

Since in this model, changes in the interest rate on time deposits are assumed to induce only direct substitution between money and time deposits, we may suppose that $\delta L/\delta p = -\delta T/\delta p$. Substituting this relationship into (23) and (24), we obtain

$$\frac{dr}{dW} = \frac{1}{m\frac{\delta L}{\delta r} + (m - t)\frac{dG}{dr}\frac{\delta L}{\delta p} + \frac{\delta F}{\delta r}} \tag{25}$$

and

$$\frac{dM}{dW} = \frac{\frac{\delta L}{\delta r} + \frac{dG}{dr}\frac{\delta L}{\delta p}}{m\frac{\delta L}{\delta r} + (m - t)\frac{dG}{dr}\frac{\delta L}{\delta p} + \frac{\delta F}{\delta r}} \tag{26}$$

In view of the fact that $\delta L/\delta p < 0$, $\delta L/\delta r < 0$, $dG/dr > 0$, and $\delta F/\delta r < 0$, it is clear that, if $t < m$, $dr/dW < 0$ and $dM/dW > 0$. If this condition is satisfied, an increase in the absolute value of $\delta L/\delta p$ $(=-\delta T/\delta p)$ will increase dM/dW and reduce the absolute value of dr/dW.[16]

The Money-Supply Function

In the case in which there is substitution between money and time deposits, the money-supply function can be obtained by substituting equations (21) and (22) into equation (8) and solving for M. This gives us

$$M = \frac{1}{m} [W - F(r, i) - tT(G(r), \bar{Y}, \bar{K})]$$

[16]The effect of an increase in $\delta L/\delta p$ on dr/dW is readily apparent from an examination of (25); the effect on dM/dW can easily be determined by differentiating (26) with respect to $\delta L/\delta p$.

The response of the money supply to the rate of interest on securities is obtained by differentiating with respect to r, giving

$$\frac{dM}{dr} = -\frac{1}{m}\frac{\delta F}{\delta r} - \frac{t}{m}\frac{dG}{dr}\frac{\delta T}{\delta p} \tag{27}$$

Since $\delta F/\delta r < 0$, $\delta T/\delta p > 0$, and $dG/dr > 0$, the first term of (27) is positive and the second term is negative. Hence the sign of dM/dr is uncertain in this case.

Interest-induced substitution between money and time deposits — the tendency of investors to shift funds from time deposits to money as the interest rate on time deposits declines — thus has three effects:

1. It reduces the absolute value of dr/dW, the power of open-market operations to change the interest rate on securities [equation (25)];
2. It increases dM/dW, the power of open-market operations to change the money supply [equation (26)]; and
3. It introduces a negative component into dM/dr, the interest-slope of the money supply function [equation (27)].

A numerical example of the substitution effect between money and time deposits may help to clarify these relationships.[17] Suppose, as in our earlier example, that reserve requirements are 15 percent for demand deposits and 4 percent for time deposits and that the cash drain is 20 percent of the money supply. Let us assume that as a result of a decline in the interest rate on time deposits, investors shift 100 of funds from time deposits to money. The results will be as follows:

Table 3

COMMERCIAL BANKS

(1) Currency	−20.0	(1) Time deposits	−100.0
(2) Loans and investments	−87.5	(1) Demand deposits	+80.0
(2) Currency	+17.5	(2) Demand deposits	−70.0

[17] In the model we are now considering there is also substitution between money and securities. This is not considered in the numerical example which relates only to substitution between money and time deposits.

In the first step [entry (1)], investors withdraw 100 from time accounts, taking 20 in currency and adding 80 to demand deposits. This reduces excess reserves by 28 [reduction of 20 due to cash outflow from banks to public, plus reduction of 12 (15 percent of 80) due to the tying up of additional reserves to support demand deposits, minus increase of 4 (4 percent of 100) due to release of reserves from support of time deposits]. Applying the "textbook" credit expansion multiplier of 3.125 to the reduction of 28 in excess reserves [entry (2)], a reduction of 87.5 in bank holdings of loans and securities is found to be necessary. This causes a secondary contraction of the money supply of 87.5, of which 80 percent, or 70, represents a reduction in demand deposits and 20 percent, or 17.5, represents an inflow of currency to the banks.

The result of the entire adjustment is to increase the money supply by 12.5 while reducing the demand for securities (supply of credit) by 87.5. That is, a shift of funds from time deposits to money, with the total reserve base held constant, will bring an increase in the stock of money (smaller than the amount of funds shifted). However, since money has higher reserve requirements than time deposits, the total amount of money plus time deposits that the given supply of reserves can support is reduced, and this produces a corresponding reduction in the total amount of credit supplied by the banks. The resulting decline in the total demand for securities tends to check the fall in the market rate of interest — that is, to reduce the absolute value of dr/dW.

General formulae for the effects of a shift from time deposits to money can be derived. If this shift into money is ΔL, the increase in money supply (ΔM) is equal to the initial shift of funds minus the secondary contraction of money and credit induced by the reduction in excess reserves. Thus,

$$\Delta M = \Delta L - \frac{m-t}{m}\,\Delta L = \frac{t}{m}\,\Delta L$$

or, since $\Delta L = -\Delta T$ (the change in time deposits),

$$\Delta M = -\frac{t}{m}\,\Delta T$$

Note that the coefficient of ΔT in (28) is the same as the coefficient of $(dG/dr)(\delta T/\delta p)$ in (27). In the above example, $t = .04$, $m = .32$, and $\Delta T = -100(\Delta L = 100)$, so that $\Delta M = 12.5$. The effect on the supply of credit (demand for securities) is equal to the contraction of bank credit—that is,

$$\Delta S = -\frac{m-t}{m}\,\Delta L$$

In the above example, this works out to −87.5.

Reserve Requirements for Time Deposits

In order to focus our attention on the effect of substitution between money and time deposits, let us eliminate the interest-sensitivity of free reserves by assuming that $\delta F/\delta r = 0$ in equations (25), (26), and (27). It is useful to consider the two cases in which the reserve requirement for time deposits is (a) equal to the reserve requirement for money ($t = m$), and (b) completely nonexistent ($t = 0$).[18] For these two cases, the expressions for dr/dW, dM/dW, and dM/dr are as shown in the following table:

Table 4

	$t = m$	$t = 0$
$\dfrac{dr}{dW}$	$\dfrac{1}{m\dfrac{\delta L}{\delta r}}$	$\dfrac{1}{m\left(\dfrac{\delta L}{\delta r}+\dfrac{dG}{dr}\dfrac{\delta L}{\delta p}\right)}$
$\dfrac{dM}{dW}$	$\dfrac{1}{m}+\dfrac{\dfrac{dG}{dr}\dfrac{\delta L}{\delta p}}{m\dfrac{\delta L}{\delta r}}$	$\dfrac{1}{m}$
$\dfrac{dM}{dr}$	$-\dfrac{dG}{dr}\dfrac{\delta T}{\delta p}$	0

If the reserve requirement for time deposits is the same as that for money ($t = m$), the influence of the substitution effect on the

[18]Throughout this paper, m, the reserve requirement applicable to money, is assumed to be given. Since $m = k(1-c)+c$, the value of m depends on the reserve requirement applicable to demand deposits, k, and public's propensity to hold currency in relation to demand deposits, c. For a discussion of various factors to be taken into account in deciding the appropriate value of k, see W. L. Smith, "Reserve Requirements in the American Monetary System," in *Monetary Management*, Englewood Cliffs, N.J.: Prentice-Hall, Inc., 1963, pp. 175–315.

rate of interest on securities is eliminated entirely. The reason for this is that if the two reserve requirements are equal, the amount of credit the banks can extend through acquisition of loans and securities is not affected by transfers of funds between money and time deposits. On the other hand, if the reserve requirement for time deposits is eliminated entirely $(t = 0)$, the substitution effect does not influence the money supply, the standard textbook theory of credit expansion $(dM/dW = 1/m)$ holds, and the money-supply function is completely insensitive to the interest rate on securities $(dM/dr = 0)$. But if the two reserve requirements are equal $(t = m)$, the power of open-market operations to change the money supply is even greater than under the standard text-

book theory $\left(\dfrac{dM}{dW} = \dfrac{1}{m} + \dfrac{dG}{dr} \dfrac{\delta L}{\delta p} \middle/ m \dfrac{\delta L}{\delta r} \right)$, and the money supply

function actually has a negative interest-slope $[(dM/dr) = -(dG/dr)(\delta T/\delta p)]$. Thus, if the reserve requirement for time deposits can be fixed between zero and the reserve requirement for money, the power of open-market operations to affect both the rate of interest on securities and the supply of money will be maximized by setting it at the latter level—that is, by setting $t = m$.[19]

[19]The model employed in this section is essentially the same as the one that underlies the analysis presented in my earlier paper, "Financial Intermediaries and Monetary Controls," *Quarterly Journal of Economics*, 73, November 1959, pp. 533–553, except that no allowance for the response of free reserves to the interest rate was made in that paper. It was shown in the earlier paper that if substitution between money and time deposits is not present, the orthodox theory of bank credit creation holds in the short run, although given time for interest rates to affect income and thereby saving, time deposit expansion may become involved in the credit expansion process. This is true in the present model: if $(dG/dr)(\delta L/\delta p) = 0$ (and $\delta F/\delta r = 0$), money creation is governed by the classical formula, $dM/dW = 1/m$, according to equation (15). However, in the longer run, the links connecting the financial and real sectors would have to be taken into account and the interest rate would affect income and the demand for time deposits, thereby making the process more complex. It was then pointed out in the earlier paper that the substitution effect, if present, would reduce the power of open-market operations to control the demand of financial institutions for loans and securities. This is analogous to the result derived in this paper [equation (25)] that the substitution effect reduces the power of open-market operations to influence the interest rate on securities. The earlier paper also showed that if interest-induced substitutions involving money and time-deposit-type claims should significantly weaken monetary policy, these effects could be neutralized by equalizing reserve requirements. This is essentially the same as the conclusion presented above that the substitution effect can be neutralized by setting $t = m$.

BOTH SUBSTITUTION EFFECTS PRESENT

We shall now consider a model that contains both substitution between time deposits and securities and substitution between money and time deposits.[20] At the same time, we shall allow for adjustment of the discount rate to the interest rate on securities. The model is as follows:

$$W - F(r, i) = mM + tT \tag{8}$$
$$i = f(r) \tag{16}$$
$$M = L(r, p, \overline{Y}, \overline{K}) \tag{20}$$
$$p = G(r) \tag{22}$$
$$T = T(r, p, \overline{Y}, \overline{K}) \tag{29}$$

It differs from our previous models because we now assume that the demand for time deposits depends on both the interest rate on time deposits and the interest rate on securities, and we treat both interest rates as variables. Differentiating with respect to W and solving for dr/dW and dM/dW, we obtain

$$\frac{dr}{dW} = \frac{1}{m\left(\dfrac{\delta L}{\delta r} + \dfrac{dG}{dr}\dfrac{\delta L}{\delta p}\right) + t\left(\dfrac{\delta T}{\delta r} + \dfrac{dG}{dr}\dfrac{\delta T}{\delta p}\right) + \dfrac{\delta F}{\delta r} + \dfrac{\delta F}{\delta i}\dfrac{df}{dr}} \tag{30}$$

and

$$\frac{dM}{dW} = \frac{\dfrac{\delta L}{\delta r} + \dfrac{dG}{dr}\dfrac{\delta L}{\delta p}}{m\left(\dfrac{\delta L}{\delta r} + \dfrac{dG}{dr}\dfrac{\delta L}{\delta p}\right) + t\left(\dfrac{\delta T}{\delta r} + \dfrac{dG}{dr}\dfrac{\delta T}{\delta p}\right) + \dfrac{\delta F}{\delta r} + \dfrac{\delta F}{\delta i}\dfrac{df}{dr}} \tag{31}$$

In the context of the present model, any shift of funds into time deposits as a result of a rise in the interest rate on time deposits must come either from money or from securities. If it is assumed that a given rise in the interest rate on time deposits will induce the shifting of the same amount of funds from securities to time deposits as will be induced by an equal decline in the interest rate on securities, we can write

[20]It is not difficult to extend the model to include time-deposit-like claims in institutions (such as savings and loan associations and mutual savings banks) which hold their reserves in the form of demand deposits in commercial banks. However, the added complexity hardly seemed worthwhile for purposes of this paper.

$$\frac{\delta T}{\delta p} = -\frac{\delta L}{\delta p} - \frac{\delta T}{\delta r} \tag{32}$$

In the case of a rise in the interest rate on time deposits, the term on the left measures the total volume of funds attracted into time deposits. The first term on the right measures the portion of these funds derived from a shift out of money balances, while the second term on the right measures the portion derived from a shift out of securities.

Making use of (32), it is possible to write (30) and (31) in the following form:

$$\frac{dr}{dW} = \frac{1}{m\dfrac{\delta L}{\delta r} + (m-t)\dfrac{dG}{dr}\dfrac{\delta L}{\delta p} + t\left(1 - \dfrac{dG}{dr}\right)\dfrac{\delta T}{\delta r} + \dfrac{\delta F}{\delta r} + \dfrac{\delta F}{\delta i}\dfrac{df}{dr}} \tag{33}$$

and

$$\frac{dM}{dW} = \frac{\dfrac{\delta L}{\delta r} + \dfrac{dG}{dr}\dfrac{\delta L}{\delta p}}{m\dfrac{\delta L}{\delta r} + (m-t)\dfrac{dG}{dr}\dfrac{\delta L}{\delta p} + t\left(1 - \dfrac{dG}{dr}\right)\dfrac{\delta T}{\delta r} + \dfrac{\delta F}{\delta r} + \dfrac{\delta F}{\delta i}\dfrac{df}{dr}} \tag{34}$$

The terms in the denominator of (33) and (34) may be identified with the effects we have been discussing in the following way:

Table 5

EFFECT	REPRESENTED IN (33) AND (34) BY:
Substitution between time deposits and securities	$t\left(1 - \dfrac{dG}{dr}\right)\dfrac{\delta T}{\delta r}$
Substitution between money and time deposits	$(m-t)\dfrac{dG}{dr}\dfrac{\delta L}{\delta p}$
Interest-induced response of free reserves	$\dfrac{\delta F}{\delta r} + \dfrac{\delta F}{\delta i}\dfrac{df}{dr}$

The factors determining the relative importance of the two substitution effects can be summarized as follows:

1. If interest rates on time deposits are quite flexible (dG/dr is close to unity), substitution between money and time deposits will be relatively important while substitution between securities and time deposits will be relatively unimportant (because there will be little *relative* change in interest rates on securities and time deposits). On the other hand, if interest rates on time deposits are quite inflexible (dG/dr is close to zero), substitution between money and time deposits will be relatively unimportant, while substitution between securities and time deposits will be relatively important.
2. Substitution between money and time deposits will be more important the greater in absolute value is $\delta L/\delta p$.
3. Substitution between securities and time deposits will be more important the greater in absolute value is $\delta T/\delta r$.

The Money-Supply Function

The money-supply function for this model can be obtained by substituting (16), (22), and (29), into (8) and solving for M. This yields

$$M = \frac{1}{m} [W - F(r, f(r)) - tT(r, G(r), \overline{Y}, \overline{K})] \tag{35}$$

Differentiating with respect to r, we obtain

$$\frac{dM}{dr} = -\frac{1}{m}\left(\frac{\delta F}{\delta r} + \frac{\delta F}{\delta i}\frac{df}{dr}\right) - \frac{t}{m}\left(\frac{\delta T}{\delta r} + \frac{dG}{dr}\frac{\delta T}{\delta p}\right)$$

Using the condition, $\delta T/\delta p = -\delta L/\delta p - \delta T/\delta r$ [(equation (32)], this becomes

$$\frac{dM}{dr} = -\frac{1}{m}\left(\frac{\delta F}{\delta r} + \frac{\delta F}{\delta i}\frac{df}{dr}\right) - \frac{t}{m}\left(1 - \frac{dG}{dr}\right)\frac{\delta T}{\delta r} + \frac{t}{m}\frac{dG}{dr}\frac{\delta L}{\delta p} \tag{36}$$

The term $-t/m\ (1 - dG/dr)\ \delta T/\delta r$ is positive and represents the effect of substitution between time deposits and securities which increases the responsiveness of the money supply to the interest rate. The term $(t/m)(dG/dr)(\delta L/\delta p)$ is negative and reflects the effect of substitution between money and time deposits which reduces the responsiveness of the money supply to the interest rate. Since the first two terms of (36) are positive and the last term is negative, the sign of dM/dr is uncertain.

Reserve Requirements
for Time Deposits

In order to analyze the effects of the reserve requirement for time deposits on dr/dW, let us replace $\delta L/\delta p$ and $\delta T/\delta r$ with their respective absolute values, $\left|\dfrac{\delta L}{\delta p}\right|$ and $\left|\dfrac{\delta T}{\delta r}\right|$, in the middle two terms of the denominator of (33) and write

$$V = (m - t)\frac{dG}{dr}\left|\frac{\delta L}{\delta p}\right| + t\left(1 - \frac{dG}{dr}\right)\left|\frac{\delta T}{\delta r}\right| \tag{37}$$

where $1 > dG/dr > 0$, so that both effects are present. Let us suppose it is feasible to vary the reserve requirement for time deposits between zero and the given reserve requirement for money (that is, $0 \leq t \leq m$). We can write (37) as

$$V = m\frac{dG}{dr}\left|\frac{\delta L}{\delta p}\right| - t\left[\frac{dG}{dr}\left|\frac{\delta L}{\delta p}\right| - \left(1 - \frac{dG}{dr}\right)\left|\frac{\delta T}{\delta r}\right|\right]$$

This function can be plotted as follows:

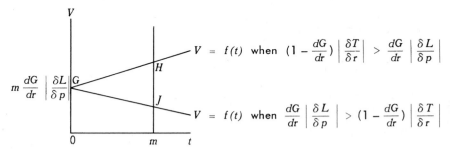

Suppose the object is to select the value of t so as to minimize V, thereby maximizing the absolute value of dr/dW. If $\left(1 - \dfrac{dG}{dr}\right)\left|\dfrac{\delta T}{\delta r}\right| > \dfrac{dG}{dr}\left|\dfrac{\delta L}{\delta p}\right|$ (that is, when substitution between time deposits and securities is stronger than substitution between money and time deposits), the function $V = f(t)$ will be an upward-sloping line such as GH, and the minimum will be at point G where $t = 0$. On the other hand, if $\frac{dG}{dr}\left|\frac{\delta L}{\delta p}\right| > \left(1 - \frac{dG}{dr}\right)\left|\frac{\delta T}{\delta r}\right|$ (that is, substitution between money and time deposits is stronger than substitution between time deposits and securities), the function $V = f(t)$ will be a downward-sloping line such as GJ and the minimum will be at point J where $t = m$.

It is not easy to tell which of two substitution effects is dominant. Prior to the introduction of the negotiable time certificate of deposit in 1961, most time deposits were held by the household sector. Under such conditions, it seems unlikely that systematic interest-induced substitution either between money and time deposits or between time deposits and securities was very important. However, the rise of the CD attracted a more sophisticated class of investors—especially nonfinancial corporations—into the market for time deposits. This probably increased the importance of both substitution effects, although I would judge substitution between time deposits and securities to be more important than substitution between money and time deposits in this new setting—that is, I suspect that $\delta T/\delta r$ is greater in absolute value than $\delta L/\delta p$. At the same time, the tendency for interest rates on time deposits to adjust to interest rates on securities has probably increased, although judgments concerning this matter are complicated by the existence of—and increases in—the Regulation Q ceilings on interest rates on time deposits. If this tendency has strengthened, however, it means dG/dr has increased, thereby reducing the weight attaching to substitution between time deposits and securities ($\delta T/\delta r$), and increasing the weight attaching to substitution between money and time deposits ($\delta L/\delta p$) in the denominator of (33). The overall result is difficult to evaluate, but in my own judgment, substitution between time deposits and securities is probably the dominant effect in the present setting.

The Effects
of Interest-Rate Ceilings

Whether the existence of effective ceilings on interest rates on time deposits under Regulation Q will increase or decrease the effectiveness of monetary policy (as measured by dr/dW) depends on the relative strength of the two substitution effects we have been considering. If the ceiling is effective—that is, if the actual rate is equal to the ceiling—the effect is to make dG/dr equal to zero for upward movements of interest rates. Whether this will strengthen or weaken monetary policy depends upon its effect on the value of V [equation (37)]. If $dG/dr = 0$, (37) becomes

$$V = t\left|\frac{\delta T}{\delta r}\right|$$

Monetary policy (as measured by dr/dW) will be stronger with the ceilings than without them if

$$t\left|\frac{\delta T}{\delta r}\right| < (m - t)\frac{dG}{dr}\left|\frac{\delta L}{\delta p}\right| + t\left(1 - \frac{dG}{dr}\right)\left|\frac{\delta T}{\delta r}\right|$$

which reduces to

$$\left|\frac{\delta T}{\delta r}\right| < \frac{m - t}{t}\left|\frac{\delta L}{\delta p}\right|$$

If, as in our earlier example, $t = .04$, while $k = .15$, and $c = .20$, so that $m[= k(1 - c) + c] = .32$, the condition becomes

$$\left|\frac{\delta T}{\delta r}\right| < 7\left|\frac{\delta L}{\delta p}\right|$$

That is, unless the responsiveness of the demand for time deposits to the interest rate on securities is more than seven times as great as the responsiveness of the demand for money to the interest rate on time deposits, monetary policy will be strengthened by the existence of the ceilings. Of course, the effect of the ceilings is not symmetrical—they may help to make restrictive monetary policy effective, but they will not affect the potency of expansionary policy one way or the other.[21]

[21]The effects of *changes* in the Regulation Q ceilings—which have been used as a discretionary weapon of monetary policy on occasion in recent years—cannot be satisfactorily handled within the confines of a static equilibrium model of the type employed in this paper, because the changes in the ceilings will only be effective if the ceiling is initially such as to prevent the attainment of equilibrium and because an essential objective of changes in the ceilings has commonly been to produce effects on the *structure* of interest rates.

TIME DEPOSITS
AND FREE RESERVES
IN THE KEYNESIAN MODEL

It is possible with little difficulty to fit the analysis developed above into the overall framework of Keynesian—or post-Keynesian—monetary theory.

The LM Curve

The responsiveness of free reserves to the market rate of interest and the discount rate, as well as substitution between time deposits and securities and between money and time deposits, can readily be incorporated into the LM curve, which has come to be a standard analytical construct in post-Keynesian macroeconomic theory.[22] For the model discussed in the previous section, which incorporates all three of these effects, the LM curve can be obtained by substituting equation (22) into the demand for money equation (20) and setting the latter equal to the supply of money equation (35). Treating Y (but not K) as a variable, we have [23]

$$L\ (r,\ G\ (r),\ Y,\ \bar{K}) = \frac{1}{m}\ [W - F\ (r, f\ (r)) - tT\ (r,\ G(r),\ Y,\ \bar{K})] \quad \text{(38)}$$

This is the equation of the LM curve. It contains only two variables, Y and r; and its slope, dr/dY, can be obtained by differentiating with respect to Y, treating r as a variable. This differentiation produces the following equation:

$$\frac{dr}{dY} = \frac{-m\dfrac{\delta L}{\delta Y} - t\dfrac{\delta T}{\delta Y}}{m\dfrac{\delta L}{\delta r} + m\dfrac{dG}{dr}\dfrac{\delta L}{\delta p} + t\dfrac{dG}{dr}\dfrac{\delta T}{\delta p} + t\dfrac{\delta T}{\delta r} + \dfrac{\delta F}{\delta r} + \dfrac{\delta F}{\delta i}\dfrac{df}{dr}}$$

[22]See J. R. Hicks, "Mr. Keynes and the 'Classics': A Suggested Interpretation," *Econometrica,* Vol. 5, April 1937, pp. 147–159, reprinted in W. Fellner and B. F. Haley (Eds.), *Readings in the Theory of Income Distribution,* Philadelphia: The Blakiston Co., 1951, pp. 461–476; and A. H. Hansen, *Monetary Theory and Fiscal Policy,* New York: McGraw-Hill, 1949, Chap. 5.

[23]It is a defect in the analysis that K is regarded as a constant; however, this defect is related to the shortcoming of all static Keynesian-type models that capital accumulation is neglected.

Assuming, as we did earlier [equation (32)], that $\delta T/\delta p = (-\delta L/\delta p) - (\delta T/\delta r)$, this reduces to

$$\frac{dr}{dY} = \frac{-m\dfrac{\delta L}{\delta Y} - t\dfrac{\delta T}{\delta Y}}{m\dfrac{\delta L}{\delta r} + (m-t)\dfrac{dG}{dr}\dfrac{\delta L}{\delta p} + t\left(1 - \dfrac{dG}{dr}\right)\dfrac{\delta T}{\delta r} + \dfrac{\delta F}{\delta r} + \dfrac{\delta F}{\delta i}\dfrac{df}{dr}} \quad (39)$$

Since $\delta L/\delta Y$ and $\delta T/\delta Y$ are both positive, the *LM* curve is clearly upward sloping ($dr/dY > 0$), all of the terms in both the numerator and denominator of (39) being negative. The denominator of (39) is exactly the same as the denominator of the expressions for dr/dW and dM/dW [equations (33) and (34)]. Consequently, the same policies with respect to the discount rate and reserve requirements for time deposits that would maximize dM/dW and the absolute value of dr/dW would also maximize the slope of the *LM* curve, dr/dY, as given by (39).

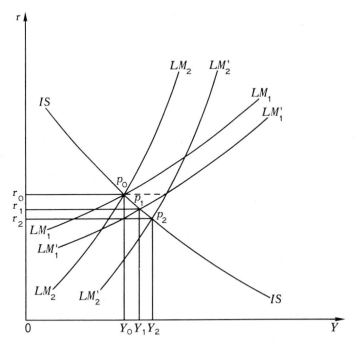

FIGURE 1

It can be seen from the *IS-LM* curve diagram in Figure 1 that an increase in the slope of the *LM* curve that is associated with an increase in dr/dW [equation (33)] will mean an increase in the effectiveness of monetary policy. The initial equilibrium is at P_o ($Y=Y_o$, $r=r_o$), where the *IS* and *LM* curves intersect. Two alternative *LM* curves are shown—LM_1 and LM_2—which intersect the *IS* curve at P_o. LM_2 has a steeper slope (a greater value of dr/dY) than LM_1. Open-market purchases by the Federal Reserve—an increase in W in the model—would shift the *LM* curve to the right. If we assume that the same amount of open-market purchases would shift each of the two alternative *LM* curves horizontally by the same amount,[24] we find that the steeper *LM* curve (LM_2) will produce a greater fall in the interest rate and a greater increase in income than will the less steep *LM* curve.[25]

Are Banks Different from Intermediaries?

The above analysis shows that the operations of nonbank financial intermediaries can be fitted into the standard post-Keynesian framework of monetary theory with relatively little difficulty. With respect to the controversy about whether banks and nonbank intermediaries are basically different in their operations and their role

[24]Differentiating equation (38) with respect to W, treating Y as a variable and r as a constant, we obtain

$$\frac{dY}{dW} = \frac{1}{m\frac{\delta L}{\delta Y} + t\frac{\delta T}{\delta Y}} > 0$$

If a steepening of the slope of the *LM* curve is a result solely of changes that produce an increase in dr/dW [equation (33)], it will be reflected entirely in a reduction of the denominator of (39). If the numerator of (39) remains unchanged, it is apparent from the expression above that every point on the new *LM* curve will be shifted to the right by open-market operations to the same degree as would the point corresponding to the same interest rate on the original *LM* curve.

[25]The argument presented in Figure 1 is developed analytically in the first section of the Appendix. It is further shown there that the argument holds only in the "normal" case in which the *IS* curve has a negative slope. The system will be stable with a positively sloping *IS* curve provided the slope of the *IS* curve is less than the slope of the *LM* curve. However, in such a case, the more responsive the money supply is to the interest rate (that is, the smaller the slope of the *LM* curve), the greater will be the effect of open-market operations on income.

in the economy, it is interesting to note that the analysis can be carried through in a slightly different way, focusing on time deposits (that is, intermediary claims) rather than on money. Substituting equation (22) into equation (20) and equations (20) and (16) into equation (8), we obtain (treating Y as a variable)

$$W - F(r, f(r)) = mL(r, G(r), Y, \overline{K}) + tT$$

or, solving for T,

$$T = \frac{1}{t} [W - F(r, f(r)) - mL(r, G(r), Y, \overline{K})] \qquad . \qquad (40)$$

This can be viewed as a supply function for time deposits. Substituting equation (22) into the demand equation for time deposits [equation (29)] and equating the demand for and supply of time deposits, we obtain

$$T(r, G(r), Y, \overline{K}) = \frac{1}{t}[W - F(r, f(r)) - mL(r, G(r), Y, \overline{K})]$$

This is an alternative formulation of the LM curve [equation (38) above]. That it is precisely the same equation can be easily seen by a simple rearrangement of terms. Actually, equation (8) is a joint supply equation for demand and time deposits, and it can be converted into an explicit supply equation for either by appropriate substitution. In the context and at the level of abstraction employed in this paper, money and time deposits play entirely symmetrical roles.

Automatic versus Discretionary Monetary Policy

It is not always recognized that the economy contains automatic monetary stabilizers as well as automatic fiscal stabilizers. For example, if income falls in recession, the demand for money will fall and this will lead to a decline in interest rates which will help to check the decline in income and employment.

The working of the automatic monetary stabilizers is depicted in Figure 2. The initial equilibrium is at P_o ($r = r_o$, $Y = Y_o$), where the curve IS intersects the curves LM_1 and LM_2. Suppose that an autonomous decline in private demand for goods and services

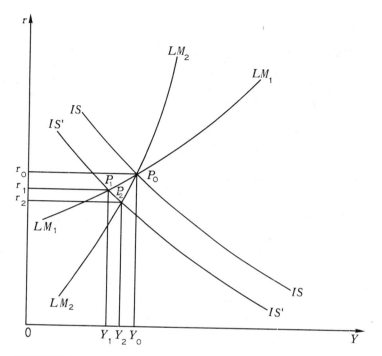

FIGURE 2

causes the *IS* curve to fall to *IS'*.[26] If the *LM* curve has a relatively small slope (that is, dr/dY is small) as in the case of LM_1, the equilibrium point will shift to P_1 ($r=r_1$, $Y=Y_1$). On the other hand, if

[26]The results presented in Figure 2 are for the case in which fluctuations originate in the real sector (that is, from autonomous changes in demand for goods and services which produce shifts in the *IS* curve) and in which the *IS* curve has a negative slope. It is shown in the second part of the Appendix that if fluctuations originate in the monetary sector (that is, from autonomous changes in the demand for money which produce shifts in the *LM* curve) and if the *IS* curve is negatively sloped, the automatic monetary stabilizers will be more effective the more responsive are the demand for and supply of money to the interest rate (that is, the smaller is the slope of the *LM* curve). On the other hand, if the slope of the *IS* curve is positive (but less than the slope of the *LM* curve so that the system is stable), a steeply sloped *LM* curve increases the strength of the automatic monetary stabilizers in defending against fluctuations originating in either the real or the monetary sector.

the *LM* curve is steeper, as in the case of LM_2, the equilibrium point will shift to P_2 $(r = r_2, \dot{Y} = Y_2)$. Note that the decline in income is smaller and the decline in interest is greater when the *LM* curve has a steep slope than when it has a flat slope (that is, $Y_2 > Y_1$, and $r_2 < r_1$). In other words, the automatic stabilizing properties of the monetary system are greater the greater is the slope of the *LM* curve. Thus, the previously discussed structural reforms of reserve requirements and discount rate policy which strengthen discretionary monetary policy by increasing dr/dW also serve to steepen the *LM* curve and strengthen the automatic stabilizer properties of the monetary system.

It is interesting to note that the three effects discussed in this paper — (a) interest-induced substitution between money and time deposits, (b) interest-induced substitution between time deposits and securities, and (c) interest-induced adjustments of free reserves — operate as automatic monetary *destabilizers*. That is, they serve to cancel out a portion of the automatic stabilizing effects of the monetary system, thereby presumably contributing to overall economic instability. Eliminating — or at least minimizing — them by appropriate changes in reserve requirements applicable to time deposits and in the conduct of discount-rate policy would therefore presumably be doubly desirable, since it would strengthen both automatic and discretionary monetary policy.

APPENDIX

Relation between Interest-Rate Responses and Income Responses

A static model of the whole economy incorporating the analysis of the financial sector discussed in this paper is necessary to derive formally some of the conclusions that are presented. Such a model is the following:

$$Y = E(Y, b) + A \tag{i}$$
$$M = L(s, p, Y, \overline{K}) + B \tag{ii}$$
$$T = T(s, p, Y, \overline{K}) \tag{iii}$$
$$W - F(s, i) = mM + tT \tag{iv}$$
$$p = G(s) \tag{v}$$

$$i = f(s) \tag{vi}$$
$$b - \bar{r} = a(s - \bar{r}) \tag{vii}$$

The first equation is the condition for equilibrium in the market for goods and services. It indicates that GNP (Y) is the sum of induced expenditures $E(Y, b)$, which are determined by GNP (Y), the long-term interest rate (b), and autonomous expenditures (A). Otherwise the model is the same as the complete model of the financial sector given in the body of this paper, except that two interest rates on securities are included and a shift parameter (B) is introduced into the demand for money. It is assumed that investment expenditures are affected by the long-term rate (b), but the rate that is relevant to the financial sector is the short-term rate (s). The two rates are connected by a very simple interest-rate structure equation [equation (vii)] which simply shows the difference between the long-term rate and the financial community's idea of the "normal" level of interest rates $(\bar{r})$ changing by some fraction (a) of the change in the difference between the short-term rate and the "normal" level of rates. This equation might be interpreted as embodying a simple version of the expectations hypothesis with respect to the term-structure of interest rates, since it will result in the short-term rate sweeping over a wider range than the long-term rate, lying above it when rates are high and below it when rates are low.

This model contains seven equations and seven endogenous variables $(Y, M, T, b, s, p,$ and $i)$. Equation (vi), of course, reflects Federal Reserve behavior in adjusting the discount rate to the short-term market rate. To find the effect of open-market operations on income, we differentiate with respect to W and solve for dY/dW. If we make the assumption that $\delta T/\delta p = -(\delta L/\delta p + \delta T/\delta s)$ as we did in the body of this paper, the differentiation yields the following expression:

$$\frac{dY}{dW} = \frac{a\dfrac{\delta E}{\delta b}}{\left(1 - \dfrac{\delta E}{\delta Y}\right)Z + a\dfrac{\delta E}{\delta b}\left(m\dfrac{\delta L}{\delta Y} + t\dfrac{\delta T}{\delta Y}\right)} \tag{viii}$$

where

$$Z = m\frac{\delta L}{\delta s} + (m - t)\frac{dG}{ds}\frac{\delta L}{\delta p} + t\left(1 - \frac{dG}{ds}\right)\frac{\delta T}{\delta s} + \frac{\delta F}{\delta s} + \frac{\delta F}{\delta i}\frac{df}{ds} \tag{ix}$$

We may assume, on the basis of *a priori* reasoning supported in most instances by a substantial amount of empirical evidence, that $\delta L/\delta s < 0$, $\delta L/\delta p < 0$, $0 < dG/ds < 1$, $\delta T/\delta s < 0$, $0 < df/ds \leqq 1$, $\delta F/\delta s < 0$, $\delta F/\delta i > 0$, $\delta E/\delta b < 0$, $0 < a < 1$, $\delta L/\delta Y > 0$, and $\delta T/\delta Y > 0$.

We shall take the stability condition to be[27]

$$\left(1 - \frac{\delta E}{\delta Y}\right)Z + a\frac{\delta E}{\delta b}\left(m\frac{\delta L}{\delta Y} + t\frac{\delta T}{\delta Y}\right) < 0 \qquad \text{(x)}$$

The equation of the *IS* curve as a function relating income (Y) to the short-term interest rate (s) can be obtained by solving equation (vii) for b and substituting this value in equation (i). The equation of the *LM* curve as a function relating Y to s can be obtained by substituting equations (ii), (iii), (v), and (vi) into (iv). When the equations for the *IS* and *LM* curves are differentiated with respect to Y treating s as a variable, the following equations are obtained:

$$\frac{ds}{dY} = \frac{1 - \dfrac{\delta E}{\delta Y}}{a\dfrac{\delta E}{\delta b}} \qquad \text{slope of } IS \text{ curve}$$

and

$$\frac{ds}{dY} = \frac{-m\dfrac{\delta L}{\delta Y} - t\dfrac{\delta T}{\delta Y}}{Z} \qquad \text{slope of } LM \text{ curve}$$

The stability condition (x) can be rewritten as

[27]Strictly speaking, it is possible to derive the stability conditions for the model represented by equations (i) through (vii) only by introducing specific time lags into the equations and analyzing the properties of the resulting dynamic model. For example, by lagging income in equation (i) and taking the first terms of a Taylor expansion around the equilibrium point, it is possible to derive the stability condition (x). Actually, however, this is only one of several possible stability conditions that can be derived in this way, depending on the precise nature of the lags introduced. Since many alternative sets of lags seem reasonable and since no feasible set is likely to correspond at all closely to reality, a more commonsense approach seems preferable. Since open-market purchases (an increase in W) must lower the interest rate initially, thereby stimulating investment and setting off a rise in income, it seems reasonable to suppose that the new equilibrium income corresponding to the increased value of W must be higher than the original level if the system is to be stable. Thus, stability would appear to require that dY/dW be positive. This means that the denominator of (viii) must be negative, and this is the condition given by (x).

$$\frac{1 - \dfrac{\delta E}{\delta Y}}{a\dfrac{\delta E}{\delta b}} < \frac{-m\dfrac{\delta L}{\delta Y} - t\dfrac{\delta T}{\delta Y}}{Z}$$

or

slope of IS curve $<$ slope of LM curve.

The slope of the LM curve is unambiguously positive. There are two possible cases with respect to the IS curve:

1. The IS curve has a negative slope. This case will occur if $0 < \delta E/\delta Y < 1$, so that both of the terms in the denominator of (viii) are negative.

2. The IS curve has a positive slope but is less steep than that of the LM curve. This case will arise if

$$1 < \frac{\delta E}{\delta Y} < 1 + \frac{a\dfrac{\delta E}{\delta b}\left(m\dfrac{\delta L}{\delta Y} + t\dfrac{\delta T}{\delta Y}\right)}{Z}, \text{ so that the first term}$$

$\left[\left(1 - \dfrac{\delta E}{\delta Y}\right)Z\right]$ in the denominator of (viii) is positive but smaller in magnitude than the second term.

Differentiation of equations (ii) through (vi) with respect to W, treating Y as a constant, and solving for ds/dW yields

$$\frac{ds}{dW} = \frac{1}{Z} \qquad\qquad \text{(xi)}$$

This expression measures the response of the interest rate on short-term securities to open-market operations, taking account of reactions in the financial sector only (that is, disregarding the links and feedbacks connecting the financial and real sectors). Equation (xi) is the same as equation (39), with s substituted for r to take account of the distinction being made in this appendix between short-term and long-term interest rates. When equation (xi) is substituted into equation (viii), the result is

$$\frac{dY}{dW} = \frac{a\dfrac{\delta E}{\delta b}}{\left(1 - \dfrac{\delta E}{\delta Y}\right)\dfrac{1}{\dfrac{ds}{dW}} + a\dfrac{\delta E}{\delta b}\left(m\dfrac{\delta L}{\delta Y} + t\dfrac{\delta T}{\delta Y}\right)} \qquad \text{(xii)}$$

It is apparent from (xii) that if the IS curve has a negative slope $(0 < \delta E/\delta Y < 1)$, an increase in the absolute value of ds/dW

will be associated with an increase in dY/dW. This is the situation depicted in Figure 1. However, if the IS curve has a positive slope but is less steep than the LM curve so that the system is stable, the first term in the denominator of (xii) will be positive but of smaller size than the (negative) second term. In this case, an increase in the absolute value of ds/dW will be associated with a decrease in dY/dW.

Effects on Income
of Autonomous Changes
in Private Demand

CHANGES IN DEMAND FOR GOODS AND SERVICES.   Differentiating equations (i) through (vii) with respect to A (the autonomous component in the demand for goods and services) and solving for dY/dA, we obtain

$$\frac{dY}{dA} = \frac{Z}{\left(1 - \frac{\delta E}{\delta Y}\right)Z + a\frac{\delta E}{\delta b}\left(m\frac{\delta L}{\delta Y} + t\frac{\delta T}{\delta Y}\right)} \qquad \text{(xiii)}$$

As indicated above, stability of the system requires that the denominator of (xiii) be negative. Dividing numerator and denominator by Z, we obtain

$$\frac{dY}{dA} = \frac{1}{1 - \frac{\delta E}{\delta Y} + \frac{a}{Z}\frac{\delta E}{\delta b}\left(m\frac{\delta L}{\delta Y} + t\frac{\delta T}{\delta Y}\right)} \qquad \text{(xiv)}$$

If $\delta E/\delta Y < 1$, both of the terms in the denominator of (xiii) will be negative, and both of the terms in the denominator of (xiv) will be positive. This is the case of the downward sloping IS curve. In this situation a decrease in the absolute value of Z, which will increase dr/dW [by equation (39)] and increase the slope of the LM curve [by equation (45)] must decrease dY/dA, which indicates a strengthening of the automatic monetary defenses against fluctuations originating in the real sector of the economy.

On the other hand, if $\delta E/\delta Y > 1$, the first term in the denominator of (xiii) will be positive, and the first term in the denominator of (xiv) will be negative. This is the case of the positively sloped IS curve. Stability in this case requires that the second term in the denominator of (xiii) exceed the first term in absolute value so that the entire denominator is negative. Likewise, the second term in the denominator of (xiv) must exceed the first in absolute value so that the entire denominator is positive. In this case, a decrease in the absolute value of Z will increase the size of the dominant second term in the denominator of (xiv), thereby decreasing dY/dA and representing an increase in the strength of the automatic monetary defenses against fluctuations originating in the real sector.

CHANGES IN DEMAND FOR MONEY. Differentiating equations (i) through (vii) with respect to B (the autonomous component in the demand for money) and solving for dY/dB, we obtain

$$\frac{dY}{dB} = \frac{-\,ma\dfrac{\delta E}{\delta b}}{\left(1 - \dfrac{\delta E}{\delta Y}\right)Z + a\dfrac{\delta E}{\delta b}\left(m\dfrac{\delta L}{\delta Y} + t\dfrac{\delta T}{\delta Y}\right)} \qquad \text{(xv)}$$

Stability requires that the denominator of (xv) be negative; the numerator is unambiguously positive. Hence dY/dB must be negative. If $\delta E/\delta Y < 1$ so that the IS curve has a negative slope, a decrease in the absolute value of Z (which will increase dr/dW and also the slope of the LM curve) must increase dY/dB, thereby representing a weakening of the automatic defenses against fluctuations originating in the demand for money. On the other hand, if $\delta E/\delta Y > 1$ so that the first term in the denominator of (xv) is negative but the second term exceeds the first so that the system is stable, a decrease in the absolute value of Z will increase the denominator of (xv) and decrease the size of dY/dB, thus representing a strengthening of the automatic defenses against fluctuations originating in the demand for money.

SUMMARY. The results derived above are summarized in the following table:

Table 6

Slope of IS curve	Direction of effect of an increase in absolute value of Z on:	
	$\dfrac{dY}{dA}$	$\dfrac{dY}{dB}$
Negative	Decrease	Increase
Positive but less than slope of LM curve	Decrease	Decrease

Commentary [1]

G. L. Bach

Professor Smith's paper on "Time Deposits, Free Reserves, and Monetary Policy" is a careful, thorough analysis. It is an exercise — and a taxing one — in monetary mechanics, involving especially the interrelationships between the reserve base, demand deposits, time deposits, and interest rates on securities. Like most thorough exercises, it demands care on the part of the reader lest he forget precisely what assumptions are being made when, and give more generality to the conclusions than they may deserve.

In my opinion, Smith's statement of monetary mechanics is sound. Instead of searching for minor faults, I propose instead merely to append a list of observations that his interesting analysis has brought to my mind. Partly these observations raise some questions about the assumptions made; more generally, they raise issues as to the meaningfulness and usefulness of some of his conclusions in the real world about us; and they supplement some of Smith's policy observations.

Professor Smith's most interesting conclusions deal with reserve requirements for time deposits. He demonstrates elegantly that if demand and time deposits are close substitutes, identical reserve requirements against them will minimize the disruptive effects of shifts by the public between demand and time deposits on the impact of monetary policy; however, if time deposits and securities are close substitutes, identical reserve requirements (zero on time deposits) will minimize the disruption introduced by the public's shifting between these forms of quasi-monies. This is hardly a startling conclusion. But more interestingly, Smith goes on to imply (though he avoids the specific statement) that optimal reserve policy would *in fact* mean zero (or very low) reserve requirements against time deposits. This would eliminate (or substantially reduce) both the slippage and the uncertainty in the

---

[1] This comment was prepared on the basis of a preliminary draft of Professor Smith's paper.

impact of monetary policy which arises from shifts in asset holdings by the public among demand deposits, time deposits, and securities.

It is important to recognize that this interesting conclusion derives from an empirical proposition that *in fact* there is limited substitution between demand and time deposits in response to changing interest rate differentials, while the substitution between time deposits and securities is strong. Smith indicates that this is merely his qualitative impression from the evidence he knows, and he may well be right. But it would be dangerous to accept his conclusion on optimal policy without a hard look at the empirical evidence on which it rests. If in fact the elasticity of substitution with reference to interest rate changes should turn out to be the reverse of the one he considers, Smith's suggested policy would weaken both automatic and discretionary monetary policy, and the arguments he presents at the end of his paper would have to be reversed.

The section of Smith's paper in which he examines the effects of interest rate changes on the supply of money, once we recognize banks' interest elasticity of demand for free reserves and likely public shifts between time and demand deposit holdings, should be read with care. It may appear from the mechanics that the money supply responds *positively* to changes in the interest rate — that is, a rise (or fall) in the interest rate on securities would induce a rise (or fall) in the money stock.

This result would, of course, be extraordinary, for normally when the Federal Reserve buys securities in the open market, providing more reserves and driving prices up and interest rates down, the money stock is *increased,* not decreased. If one begins merely with a lower interest rate, rather than by recognizing the policy action which lowers the rate, one may be misled as to the direction of effect. Smith's new model tells us that introduction of these additional factors will *reduce the increase* in the money stock induced by Federal Reserve open-market operations which bid down the interest rate on securities — not, of course, that they will produce an absolute decrease in the money stock, as might appear from the numerical examples in the paper.

In a brief section, Smith asks: "Are banks different from other intermediaries?" and concludes that there really is not much difference. He points out that one can fit nonbank intermediaries into either a standard monetary or neo-Keynesian analysis with little difficulty. We could readily focus on demand and supply functions for time deposits instead of for demand deposits. In fact, the standard supply equations, once we take into account both demand and time deposits as is done in the more sophisticated versions, are in fact joint supply equations for demand and time deposits. As Smith points out, in this context money and time deposits play symmetrical roles.

I am sure Smith is right on his mechanics, but this kind of example leaves me uncomfortable. If indeed we are to view time and demand deposits symmetrically, and commercial banks and nonbank financial institutions equally symmetrically, one begins to wonder why there is any difference at all in reserve requirements between the different types of deposits generated by the different types of institutions. Why should there be reserve requirements against demand deposits? I am old-fashioned enough to think that money (currency and demand deposits) does indeed matter for economic analysis, and that money is indeed significantly different from quasi-monies for a fundamental reason. Money is what people buy things with in the marketplace, even though quasi-monies fulfill many of the other nontransactions functions of money. There is indeed a lot of similarity between money and quasi-monies, and a lot of shiftability between them. But in the end, it is money that people spend for goods and services, and it is the production of goods and services in which we are especially interested in many of our fundamental macro-economic analyses. Even with the "new look," it is hard to avoid the old conclusion that the supply of money is, and should be, under the control of the governmental monetary authorities; and certainly there is far from perfect substitutability between demand and time deposits. One may wonder whether concern with the logical niceties of monetary mechanics may not sometimes get in the way of our remembering what really matters for the central, real-world economic issues we face.

In an excellent little section on optimal discount-rate policy, Smith points out that tying the discount rate to the Treasury bill rate, with the former perhaps a half point higher than the latter, would substantially eliminate the effect of bankers' interest elasticity of demand for free reserves, and thereby increase the potency of monetary policy and decrease the uncertainty as to its impact. Such a policy would eliminate banks' borrowing entirely except in cases of emergency and would substantially eliminate the response of free reserves to market interest rate changes. I think he is quite right. But it may be worth remembering that one does not need this particular elaborate demonstration of monetary mechanics to arrive at this conclusion, even though the mechanics are correct.

The paper is essentially an exercise in comparative statics, as Smith points out in the outset. For most of what it does, this approach is satisfactory. But at some points, one must be careful not to take conclusions derived from such a model and generalize them to a world in which dynamic reactions are important. As Smith notes, the interactions between the monetary and the real sectors may take more time than the adjustments with which he is concerned, but they do exist.

In particular, the discussion of the built-in (automatic) stabilizing effects of the demand for money are correct in the comparative statics sense in which Smith presents them. But in a world of dynamic interactions, a decline in money and real incomes for the economy, associated, for example, with a collapse of expectations and capital values, may well *increase* the demand for money rather than decrease it as would be predicted by the standard comparative statics (which rest on falling transactions demand for money with falling income). In other words, shifts in the demand for money exogenous to the Smith model may dominate this mechanism in a dynamic real world. Thus, it is not clear that in the real world the "automatic monetary stabilizers" will always work in the right direction; in severe collapses especially, these mechanisms are likely to act as automatic monetary *destabilizers* over critical periods. Smith's parallel with the automatic fiscal stabilizing effect of the federal tax system is important, but it may also be misleading.

Chapter 4

Introduction

I n the preceding paper by Professor Smith, the primary emphasis is on the importance of interest rates in equilibrating the money and capital markets. In Professor Smithies' paper in Chapter 5 the central focus is on the problem of the appropriate combination of monetary and fiscal policy needed to achieve economic stabilization and growth. In the intervening paper, Professor Albert G. Hart, like Smithies, considers primarily the impact of monetary policy upon the goods-and-services sector rather than on financial markets. On the other hand, like Smith, Hart limits himself to the monetary side. This is particularly appropriate at this time (the Fall of 1966), since the burden of stabilization policy for the last year

119

has been thrown almost exclusively upon the monetary authorities.

Hart's paper is frankly exploratory, with no pretense of offering definitive findings. The evidence he produces suggests that in the critical area of decisions about investing in business plant and equipment or in housing, the customary linkages of monetary policy to the goods-and-services sphere via changes in the amount, availability, or price of money or of bank loans are in doubt. *Expenditures* in this forward-looking area lag behind *decisions to spend.* Hart presents data suggesting that investment-spending decisions change earlier than the price of money, the money supply, or the volume of loans, and he recommends a research agenda organized around the possibility that *expectations* affecting investment decisions may be affected by monetary policy through variations in free reserves.

CONNECTING LINKS BETWEEN MONETARY POLICY AND FIXED INVESTMENT

Albert G. Hart

The growing economy of the United States has always shown intermittent tendencies to drift off its course—veering either toward inflation or toward depression. Course-correction adjustments can in principle be made through any one of a number of fiscal and monetary instruments. But in practice, since monetary policy recovered its freedom of action early in 1951, most short-term adjustments have been made through policies toward money and credit. Hence the post-1951 period both emphasizes the importance of monetary policy and offers a field of observation as to how it works.

All of the elements of aggregate demand for gross national product (including consumption and even the expenditures of government bodies) may be influenced by monetary policy. But it is generally agreed that the sharpest impact of monetary policy upon the goods-and-services economy should be found in the sector of private fixed investment. The present paper reports upon a search for traces in the post-1951 record of the impact of monetary policy in this sector—broken down into a moderate number of subsectors. This report is exploratory rather than definitive, but I think it gives reason for skepticism about widely held views and for much more intensive examination of *ex ante* data bearing upon investment decisions.

There has been much discussion among monetary economists about the way to view the linkage between the variables directly controlled by monetary policy and the course of events in the goods-and-services economy. One school of monetary monists holds that changes in the supply of money show such simple and clearcut relations to changes in the flow of expenditures on GNP that it is unnecessary to explore "connecting links." Another school holds that interest rates so far dominate the field of fixed investment (and by implication, activity in general) that we need only trace monetary influences on interest rates and our problems are solved. Quite a different view is taken by the "credit-availability" school, which stresses changes on the asset side of the bank balance sheet together with similar processes in other lending institutions—with special attention given to types of credit, such as goods-and-services operations that have especially wide amplitude of fluctuations. Those who complain that monetary policy has been trying to reduce fluctuations in the economy as a whole by imposing especially sharp fluctuations upon construction are an interesting wing of this school.

The view toward which I am pushed by the evidence sketched in this paper may be described as a variant of the credit-availability interpretation. However, I diverge from all the schools mentioned above at one important point. All analysts agree that the problem is to trace monetary influences upon investment decisions taken by firms and households, but virtually all the published literature takes it for granted that these decisions can be measured by tracing the path through time of capital expenditures. I would argue that such use of *ex post* data risks a major distortion of the crucial aspect of timing of decisions. The data for the postwar period include important series of *ex ante* figures which purport to tell us about commitments to processes which will generate expenditures for ensuing months or years. In particular, I use in this paper the series which measure orders placed for machinery and equipment, appropriations for corporate capital expenditures, and starts of residential construction. The timing of changes in the rates of flow of such commitments casts serious doubt as to whether the conventional connecting links move early enough to be considered as causes of changes in the flow-of-investment decisions—a point which has not received the attention it deserves in the literature because the "gestation lag" between decisions and expenditures is long enough so that when expenditures are taken directly as the object of explanation, they can plausibly be pictured as coming in appropriate time-sequence with the conventional link-variables.[1]

[1]To avoid claiming too much, I must enter here a proviso about the timing of "decisions to invest." Numerical expressions about investment (including those in this paper) are likely to be used in ways that imply that investment decision is an *event*, whereas it is more properly to be seen as a *process* extending over considerable time.

Consider the important example of the acquisition of new machinery. The firm that wants this machinery will have been studying its engineering, cost, and marketing aspects for months or even years before an order is placed; very likely it has carried on negotiations with several alternative suppliers. The fact that the firm has placed an order on a stated date for a stated dollar value of machinery —the sort of fact which enters *ex ante* statistics that we use to register "decision"—indicates that the decision process has passed a crucial stage. Henceforth all possible suppliers but one have been eliminated; so have almost all of the possible alternative designs for the machinery. Cancellation or major modification of the machinery has been made subject to a substantial financial penalty. Authority over the investment project in question has been delegated by the firm's top policymakers to operating managers.

Yet to place the order does not put an end to all elements of flexibility in the decision. Secondary modifications of design remain possible. Furthermore, it may be possible without penalty to add or subtract a few units of machinery before the order is filled. The contemplated delivery date may be set back if the supplier has difficulty with his other work, and/or if the buyer finds his needs less urgent (or his financing more difficult) than he had expected.

In interpreting statistics which purport to register "decisions," moreover, we have to remember that important dimensions of the provisional decision upon which buyer and supplier have agreed are not explicitly represented in these statistics. The timetables of work by the supplier, deliveries and installation, and

INDICATORS OF MONETARY-POLICY PRESSURE

To open the discussion, it is essential to adopt a measure of the pressure being applied by the monetary authorities to correct the course of the economy. I propose to use what I call the *F-ratio*, which is a percentage with free reserves of member banks as numerator and their required reserves as denominator. In quarter-to-quarter comparisons, movements of this ratio are dominated by changes in free reserves. However, the inclusion of required reserves as a denominator corrects important defects which students of monetary economics find in the free reserve series taken alone. In particular, the denominator provides a built-in correction for the effects of the long-term down-drift in the level of required reserve-percentages, as well as for changes in the proportions of deposits subject to different reserve requirements (in particular between demand and time deposits), and for growth in the general scale of economic operations (which in monetary terms doubled during the period of observation). The numerator sums up the impact of Federal Reserve open-market operations, changes in reserve requirements, international gold flows, gold production, and internal paper-currency flows. A curve for the *F*-ratio is included in each of the figures which illustrate the argument of this paper.

It will be obvious that there are other series which might be advocated as measures of the pressure of monetary policy. In particular, one might use a curve of discount rates; or one might use a curve of open-market interest rates. But for the problems

payments by the buyer are presumably set at least provisionally at the time the order is placed; but I am aware of no compilation which tries to give a time-series taking account of these dimensions. Orders data, therefore, fall a good deal short of being data on future expenditures to which we can assign dates, though useful. Strictly, orders and the like should be regarded as gross additions to the backlog of investment commitments.

With all their defects, however, *ex ante* data such as orders are likely to be revealing as to the timing of influences on investment decisions. Certainly their timing is much more significant in this respect than is the timing of expenditures—which in good part measure a financial cleanup on installations that may have been decided upon several years in the past, and on which the actual productive operations of fabrication and installation run a good deal ahead of final settlements.

under analysis here, neither of these two curves would serve, as will be shown in the course of the argument. The discount rate may at times be "out of touch with the market"; and by the test of apparent effects on investment decisions, it seems to have too indefinite a shape to show much. Representative market rates (of which I use the rate on finance-company paper to typify short rates, and the Moody average for Aaa corporate bonds to typify long rates) have a much more clear-cut shape, but on the whole seem to change too late to explain investment-decision developments.

The relation of monetary policy to the events which show whether the economy is getting off course may be seen from Figure 1. The F-ratio curve appears near the bottom of the chart. To provide a base-line for analysis, I have intertwined with the F-ratio curve a more slow-moving "accustomed-situation curve." This curve (to which there are counterparts on all the other series graphed for this paper) is a weighted average of the F-ratio at recent dates, with heavier weights for the most recent than for somewhat-less-recent observations.[2] I assume that the banks will

[2]In calculating all the "accustomed-situation" indexes of this paper, I have used a uniform system of declining weights. To set up the index for quarter (t), I have calculated moving four-quarter averages for previous periods, and combined them with the following weights:

QUARTERS COVERED BY FOUR-QUARTER AVERAGES	WEIGHTS FOR AVERAGES
(t-4) to (t-1)	0.4154
(t-8) to (t-5)	0.2769
(t-12) to (t-9)	0.1846
(t-16) to (t-13)	0.1231
	1.0000

It will be seen that the weights decline by one-third each year (a rate of decay which has become a favorite in "learning-theory" models applied to the effect of experience on people's views of a "normal" situation). It might be better to let the weights decline by a little bit each quarter rather than jump them downward every four quarters. But this complication would not much affect the outcome; and reports in the business press suggest that it is typical to give special emphasis to twelve-month periods in looking at recent experience.

It will be seen that this "accustomed level" device is an adaptation of the concept popularized by Milton Friedman in his discussions of "permanent income." But it will be noted that most of the indexes to which I give this treatment in the present paper measure *rates of change* of the variables under analysis. I adopt the expression "accustomed" rather than "permanent" in recognition of the semantic awkwardness of tagging as "permanent" (for example) a 4 percent-per-quarter rate of rise of prices on the stock market or of capital appropriations.

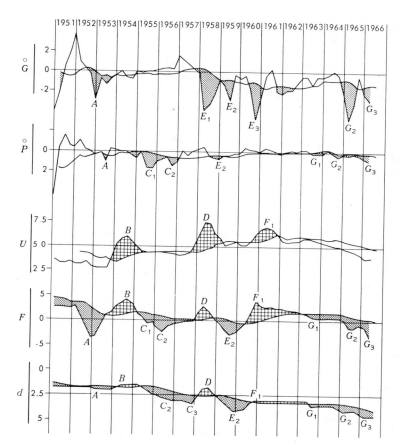

FIGURE 1. Free-Reserve Ratio and Discount Rate in Relation to Signals of Need for Expansion or Contraction, Quarterly Figures, 1951–1966.

Variables Graphed

G: Monetary gold stock, quarter-to-quarter % change.[1]

P: Wholesale prices (excluding farm products and foods), quarter-to-quarter % change, inverted.[2]

U: Unemployment, percent of civilian labor force, quartererly average.[2]

F: Ratio of free to required reserves, all member banks, quarterly average.[1]

D: Discount rate, Federal Reserve Bank of New York, quarterly average, inverted.[1]

Number following explanation of variables graphed refers to the source of information from which the graphs were developed: (1) Various *Federal Reserve Bulletins*; Board of Governors of the Federal Reserve System; (2) Bureau of Labor Statistics, U.S. Department of Labor; (3) U.S. Housing and Home Finance Agency; (4) Office of Business Economics, U.S. Department of Commerce.

feel under pressure to restrict credit when the F-ratio is below the accustomed level, and feel free to expand when the F-ratio is above the accustomed level. As a graphical convention to bring out the contrast between these situations, I have adopted a dotted shading of the area between the actual and accustomed-level curves during periods when the F-ratio is below the accustomed level, and cross-hatching where the F-ratio is above the accustomed level.

The upper curves of Figure 1 record the signals by which the Federal Reserve authorities may be presumed to judge whether the economy needs a course-correction. The top curve represents the balance-of-payments situation, as measured by quarter-to-quarter percentage changes in the monetary gold stock ($\mathring{G}$-curve). The second represents the movement of the price level, as measured by quarter-to-quarter percentage changes in the index of wholesale prices excluding farm products and foods ($\mathring{P}$-curve). This $\mathring{P}$-curve is graphed upside down. The third (U-curve) shows the seasonally adjusted ratio of unemployment to civilian labor force.[3] In viewing these signals, a certain asymmetry should be noted. While a high level of unemployment suggests the need for expansive pressure, a low level suggests not that contraction is needed but merely that it is permissible. Reciprocally, a rapid loss of gold or a rapid rise of prices suggests the need for contraction, while stability of gold stocks or prices suggests not that expansion is needed but merely that it is permissible. In line with this view, I have shaded only the below-accustomed-level segments of the G-curve and $\mathring{P}$-curve, and only the above-accustomed segments of the U-curve.

It will be seen that each of the major episodes where the F-ratio lies above or below the "accustomed" level is readily matched with a relevant signal. The three expansion-episodes tagged on the F-curve by letters B, D and F are highly comparable in timing and intensity with the three high-unemployment episodes tagged on the U-curve by the same letters. Contraction-episode A on the F-curve has its warrant in the gold-loss episode tagged A on the G-curve; and contraction-episode C on the F-curve (including its double bottom) has a counterpart in the price-inflation episode tagged with the same letter on the $\mathring{P}$-curve. The contraction-

[3]Note that quarter-to-quarter changes in G and P are graphed at between-quarter dates; while levels of U, the F-ratio and the discount rate are graphed at mid-quarter dates.

episodes tagged with letters E and G are more complex. They may be interpreted as meaning that contraction-signals from the $\overset{\circ}{G}$-curve or $\overset{\circ}{P}$-curve tend to be dominated by simultaneous strong expansion-signals from the U-curve; but once unemployment gets below some such level as 5 percent, contraction-signals will be obeyed.

The bottom curve of the figure (d-curve) traces the discount rate of the Federal Reserve Bank of New York—in quarterly-average levels. On the whole, its deviations from "accustomed level" match those of the F-curve. But the various episodes come later on the d-curve, and do not reflect the *intensity* we can observe on the F-curve. I infer that for present purposes, the d-curve is essentially a less effective version of the same information carried by the F-curve.

THE CONVENTIONAL MONETARY LINKS

Comparison of the course of the F-ratio with that of the variables conventionally viewed as connecting links between monetary policy and the goods-and-services economy may be undertaken with the aid of Figure 2. It shows much of the pattern of relationships that would be expected from the folklore of the monetary economists—but with one or two interesting differences.

The curve for the F-ratio, transferred from Figure 1, lies at the top of the figure. Below it come two curves for short-term and long-term interest rates. The former are represented by the rate on new 3–6 month finance-company paper privately placed; the latter by Moody's series of yields on long-term grade Aaa corporate bonds. (Both series are averages of daily figures, like the data underlying the F-ratio, reduced here to quarterly averages.) As with the curves of Figure 1, each of these has a curve intertwined for the "accustomed level," with areas between the curves shaded on the same system as on Figure 1; the interest curves are of course graphed with an inverse scale so as to make low rates correspond to large free reserves. Each of the easy-money phases tagged with the letters B, D and F, and each of the tight-money phases tagged with the letters A, C, and E can be readily seen on the R-curve for short-term rates. The points of maximum expansive and contractive pressure (crests and troughs of the curves) and the points where rates pass through the accustomed level

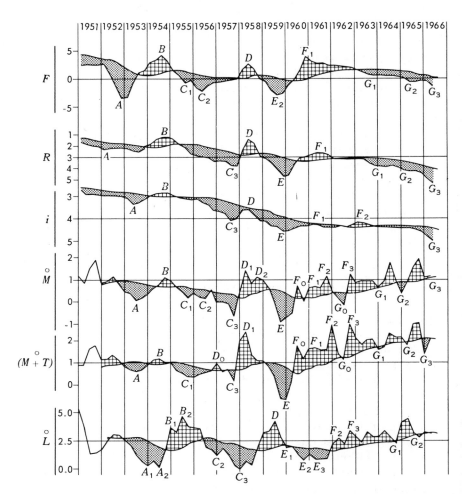

FIGURE 2. Free-Reserve Ratio in Relation to Monetary-Link Variables, Quarterly Figures, 1951–1966.

Variables Graphed

F: Ratio of free to required reserves, all member banks, quarterly average.[1]

R: Interest rate on finance-company paper directly placed, quarterly average, inverted.[1]

i: Bond yield, corporate Aaa, Moody, quarterly average, inverted.[1]

M: Money stock, quarter-to-quarter % change.[1]

(M+T): Money stock plus commercial-bank time deposits, quarter-to-quarter % change.[1]

L: Commercial-bank total loans outstanding, quarter-to-quarter % change.[1]

128

come with or slightly later than corresponding points on the *F*-curve. Note however that the *R*-curve suggests more intense pressure toward contraction in 1963–1966 than in 1952–1953, while the *F*-curve suggests the contrary. The long-term interest rate (shown by the *i*-curve) has a somewhat similar shape. But because the long-term rate rarely fell appreciably during the 1951–1966 period, the calibrating device of the accustomed-level curve does not work as well as for the other series charted; the actual- and accustomed-level curves almost never cross, so that key points of the series are not well mapped. This is unfortunate, since in the conventional view it is the long-term rate rather than the short-term rate that links directly with investment decisions for fixed capital. I would comment, however, that in the period of observation, the long-term rate tends to move later than the fixed-investment decisions. My tentative interpretation is that the *execution* of investment decisions affects pressure upon the capital market, and that in the causal chain the long-term rate is an effect rather than a cause of these decisions.

The stock of money is represented by the next two curves. Following the logic of the "modern quantity theory" and the procedure of *Business Cycle Developments*, I show these variables in the form of percentage rates of change from quarter to quarter.[4] The *M*-curve registers changes in the stock of money in the everyday sense (currency plus demand deposits adjusted); the (*M+T*)-curve registers changes in what Milton Friedman prefers to treat as the money stock (including time deposits at commercial banks). Once more the phases tagged by the letters *A*, *B*, *C*, *D*, *E* and *F* are readily seen in these curves—but with differences such as the shorter duration and faint intensity of the expansion-episode "*B*" of 1954. Furthermore, both money-stock curves disagree with the *F*-curve and *R*-curve in that they indicate expansion rather than tightness for 1951–1952 and for most of the period 1963–1966. The sharp drop to approximately the "accustomed" rate of expansion on both money-stock curves in 1962, furthermore, has no counterpart on the *F*-curve or *R*-curve.

The final curve of Figure 2 (the *L*-curve) shows quarter-to-quarter percentage changes in total loans outstanding at com-

[4]The data are published in monthly form in *Business Cycle Developments*, U.S. Dept. of Commerce, Bureau of the Census, (series 85 and 98); my quarterly-change figures are simply sums of the *BCD* monthly-percentage-change figures (reduced from an annual to a monthly rate by dividing all *BCD* figures by 12).

mercial banks.[5] Again it has counterparts to the main fluctuations
shown by the F-curve—but with lags of a year or more. As will appear presently, the investment-decision variables seem to move
sooner than the L-curve. My tentative interpretation is that fluctuations in loans are completely untenable as causal explanations for
fluctuations in fixed investment.[6]

On the whole, this part of the record seems to bear out the
impressions of monetary economists as to the way the monetary
pressure indicated by the free-reserve situation transmits itself to
interest rates and to the volume of bank assets and liabilities. But
as the next part of the paper will show, the "link variables" do not
seem to have a convincing relation to the variables which measure
investment decisions; so that the impression that the course of
real investment is determined by monetary policy via the conventional links needs to be reexamined.

FREE RESERVES, MONETARY LINKS,
AND BUSINESS INVESTMENT DECISIONS

The next stage of this exploration is to compare the course of free
reserves and of the monetary-link variables with that of investment
decisions in the business sphere. This is done in Figure 3. I have
carried forward from Figure 2 the F-ratio curve and two monetary-
link variables: the short-term interest-rate curve (R-curve), and the
curve for the change in money stock in Friedman's sense ($M + T$-
curve), which is preferred to the M-curve because on the whole it
moves sooner in each fluctuation.

Broad data on investment decisions by business enterprises are
not as plentiful as would be desirable; contracts for non-residential

[5] I have not been able to adopt the corresponding *BCD* data (series 113)
because *BCD* figures are stated in absolute increments (billions of dollars at annual
rates) and the denominator which should be applied to calculate a percentage
change is unclear. Hence I have gone back to the Federal Reserve's seasonally
adjusted series for the month-end level of total loans outstanding at commercial
banks, combined month-end figures into quarterly averages, and calculated
percentage changes in these averages from quarter to quarter.

[6] Inventory investment, not treated in this paper, shows a pattern very like that
of bank loans, and *also* behaves much as if it reflected accelerator-effects of
changes in final sales. I am inclined to guess that, in the period of observation,
inventory investment was primarily an adjustment to sales, and that loan fluctuations were largely induced by inventory fluctuations.

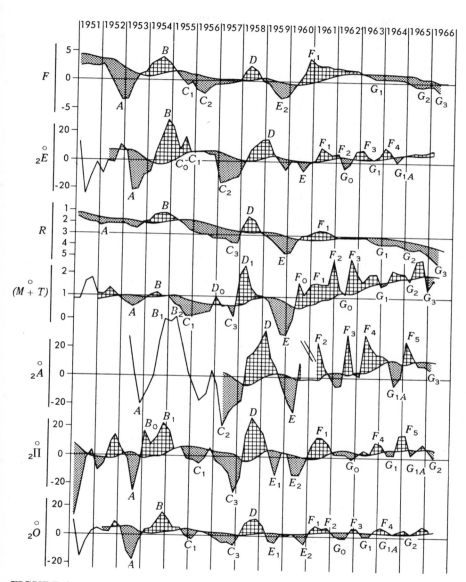

FIGURE 3

construction, in particular, have been reported with so many discontinuities that I have not been able to give them coherent form. But for the entire postwar period, we have a series for orders placed with "machinery and equipment industries," which may be taken to be commitments by enterprises for equipment (as distinct from plant). For symmetry with the monetary variables, I have expressed this series in quarter-to-quarter percentage changes. This implies that an unchanging monetary pressure (constant F-ratio, or constant rate of growth of money stock, or constant interest rate acording to one's hypothesis) would favor a constant growth-rate for equipment expenditures. Because there is a good deal of random noise in this and the other investment-decision series used in this paper, I have smoothed it to the minimum extent by combining pairs of adjacent quarter-to-quarter changes into two-quarter percentage changes (graphed at the center of the intervening quarter). Using a subscript to show that the rate of change is for two successive quarters, this is labeled as the $_2\mathring{E}$-curve. In the same figure, I present a similar $_2\mathring{A}$-curve, which shows from 1953 on the course of two-quarter percentage changes in capital appropriations of large manufacturing corporations (for equipment plus plant) as reported by NICB.

It will be evident at once that the $_2\mathring{E}$-curve shows a complete set of counterparts to the fluctuations of the F-curve tagged by the letters A, B, C, D, E, F; and with limitations imposed by the lack of pre-1953 data and by a discontinuity at the end of 1960, the same is true of the $_2\mathring{A}$-curve. (Differences at both ends of the period of observation will be examined in a moment.) It will be evident also that each of these fluctuations in the rate of growth comes somewhat later in time than the counterpart fluctuation in the F-curve. Furthermore, the $_2\mathring{E}$-curve and $_2\mathring{A}$-curve agree with the F-curve in showing a progressive diminution of amplitude—as if the massive disturbance of the Korean conflict had set up a strongly damped cycle.

If we compare the $_2\mathring{E}$-curve and $_2\mathring{A}$-curve with the interest-rate curve (R-curve) and with the ($M + T$)-curve, we can, of course, also establish counterpart-series of fluctuations. However, on several occasions the fluctuations in the investment-decision curves come a little earlier than their counterparts on the money-stock-change curve, and no later than their counterparts on the interest curve. Since the crystalization of an investment decision in an equipment order or capital appropriation requires previous negotiations and engineering studies, we would expect causal variables uniformly to move ahead of the investment decisions; so that on grounds of timing, the F-curve offers a more convincing "explanation" of the investment decisions than do the R-curve and $(M + T)$ curve. Furthermore, the R-curve shows maximum amplitude of fluctuation at the middle (expansion D and contraction E), while the $(M + T)$ curve shows increasing rather than decreasing deviations from the "accustomed" rate of expansion. Hence the general profile as well as the timing of fluctuations in these curves matches less well with the $_2\overset{\circ}{E}$-curve and $_2\overset{\circ}{A}$-curve than does the profile of the F-curve.

The two curves at the bottom of Figure 3 trace the course of two variables which would be expected to make strong contributions to investment decisions—profits and new orders. Both variables are measured (to give dimensional comparability with other variables and to smooth slightly their strong random bounce) in the form of two-quarter percentage changes. The $_2\Pi$-curve shows changes in profits after taxes of corporations (the Department of Commerce series carried in *Business Cycle Developments* as series number 16). The $_2\overset{\circ}{O}$-curve shows changes in new orders received by all manufacturing *excluding* the equipment-and-machinery orders represented by the $_2\overset{\circ}{E}$-curve. Here again we can find counterpart-fluctuations to those we found in the F-curve and in the $_2\overset{\circ}{E}$-curve; but a number of the fluctuations in profits and in orders come too late to be helpful as explanations of investment decisions—at least if we allow any time for the crystallization of decisions. It is not unlikely that the fluctuation of orders is in part a feedback of the investment decisions themselves.[7]

If we go outside the period 1953–1961 for which the matching

---

[7]My precaution of subtracting out the machinery-and-equipment orders may be insufficient, because orders include a good deal of duplication at different levels of industry. Insofar as machinery-and-equipment producers order from each other, this duplication will do us no harm; but insofar as they order (for instance) primary metals in response to orders received, the expansion of machinery-and-equipment orders may generate expansion of other orders with a rapidity which (in terms of my quarterly time-unit) approaches instantaneity.

The relation of the inflow of orders to the flow of capital appropriations seems clear from preliminary work at the level of two-digit industries, within which the feedback of appropriations into orders should in most cases be of second magnitude. But since orders (as distinct from appropriations) cannot be classified by the industrial classification of the buyer, the orders-orders relationship may be more slippery than the orders-appropriations relationship.

of counterpart fluctuations is strongest, there are several indications that these supplementary variables will be important in any thoroughgoing analysis. During the shakedown period of monetary policy in 1951–1952, immediately after the "accord" between Treasury and Federal Reserve which restored freedom of action to monetary policy after its "Babylonian captivity" at the hands of the Treasury, the conformation of the $_2\mathring{E}$ curve is remarkably like that of the $_2\mathring{\Pi}$-curve. The sharp deceleration of investment decisions in 1964, for which the monetary curves offer no warrant, also has a counterpart in profits. The generally level tendency of the rate of growth of investment decisions in 1961–1965 (despite increasing tightness as shown by the F-ratio and interest rate) may also be related to the sustained general rate of growth of profits and of orders; at this point, the sustained acceleration in growth of the money stock would seem to imply too much investment.

On the whole, if we had to adopt a monistic explanation of business fixed-investment decisions from one monetary variable, we would be forced to drop out the links and rest our case primarily upon the F-ratio. We are, of course, not obliged to assume that there is only one channel of monetary influence; and any reasonably conclusive explanation must clearly be eclectic enough to take account of profits and of orders. But the money-stock link, on the face of the record, would not seem to have explanatory force; and the interest-rate link has drawbacks. I would suggest that a direct link from the F-ratio to investment decisions can be rationalized in expectational terms. A firm which has a close investment decision to make has reason to inquire at its bank about financing prospects. If the free-reserve situation is clearly easy or clearly tight (as it was almost all the time from late 1952 through 1961), we must suppose that the banker will reply in the first case, "We think we will be able to provide interim financing if you need it, and think the market will be receptive if you want to sell securities;"—and in the second case, "Our reserve position will force us to restrict loans for awhile; and the market as a whole is so tight that security flotation may be harder than usual." While the large firms which dominate the fixed-investment situation may be dependent on bank financing only contingently, a tight-money report will be disturbing: it indicates a prospect that if the firm commits itself to investment beyond what its own cash flow will finance, a series of worrisome financial decisions may be necessary, whereas most managements would probably rather concentrate on technical, organizational, and marketing decisions. Furthermore, a tight-money report will suggest that the smaller firms, important as customers, may have to reduce their orders, and that such customers are likely to finance themselves to a greater extent on trade credit, increasing the supplier's needs for working capital. On this rationalization, the backing and filling of the rate of growth in investment decisions (within a rather narrow range) during 1962 – 1966 can be explained on the basis that when the free-reserve position shifts very little and thus is close to the "accustomed" situation, the bankers' view will not be clearcut, and decision factors which at other times are dominated by considerations of outside finance may take the leading role.

THE HOUSEHOLD-DECISION SPHERE

One of the major areas of fixed investment—housing—presents a very different decision mechanism from business plant and equipment. Although most new private housing units are put up on the initiative of builders, the ability of such builders to carry an unsold inventory, or to absorb losses by selling much below the contemplated price, is narrowly limited. Hence their decisions to accelerate construction must be *ratified* within a few weeks by an acceleration in household decisions to buy, or the acceleration will be reversed. Similarly, decisions by builders which decelerate the rate of construction will be reversed if households fail to decelerate their purchases.

This area, in which the more fundamental investment decision rests with the household rather than with business firms, is examined in Figure 4. To get as close as possible to a decision footing, I work with housing *starts* rather than with construction activity. Once more I match the dimensional character of the monetary variables by showing percentage rates of change, and smooth out much of the random variation by using two-quarter changes; the result is the $_2\mathring{H}$-curve near the top of the figure. Comparison with the F-curve carried forward from previous figures to the top of Figure 4 shows that again we can identify accelerations and decelerations of investment decisions that are counterparts to periods of easy and tight money; and as before, we find that the main features of the $_2\mathring{H}$-curve show slight lags in comparison to their counterparts tagged by A, B, C, D, E, F. Comparison with the other monetary-variable curves—the R-curve and $(M + T)$-curve, as in Figure 3—shows that in this case the timing of the main shifts in investment is so close to that of the F-ratio that at several points the $_2\mathring{H}$-curve leads the monetary variables. Furthermore, the

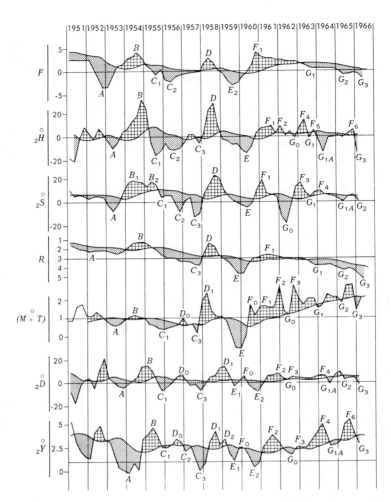

FIGURE 4. Monetary Variables and Two-Quarter Changes in Disposable Income, in Relation to Two-Quarter Changes in Housing Starts, Consumer Durables and Stock Prices, Quarterly Figures 1951–1966.

F: Ratio of free to required reserves, all member banks, quarterly average.[1]

$_2H$: Housing starts, non-farm, two-quarter % change.[3]

$_2S$: Stock prices (Standard and Poors, 500 stocks), two-quarter % change.[1]

R: Interest rate on finance-company paper directly placed, quarterly average, inverted.[1]

$(M + T)$: Stock of money including time deposits in commercial banks, quarter-to-quarter % change.[1]

$_2D$: Consumer durable goods, two-quarter % change.[4]

$_2Y$: Consumer disposable income, two-quarter % change.[4]

136

housing-starts curve, like the previous investment curves, agrees with the F-curve in showing a decreasing amplitude of fluctuation (damped cycle), in contradiction to the R-curve and $(M + T)$-curve. Still further, the $_2\mathring{H}$-curve (unlike the business-investment curves) agrees with the F-curve [but disagrees with the $(M + T)$-curve] in showing deceleration after early 1963. I would argue that the behavior of housing starts reinforces the argument sketched above in favor of a direct expectational link from free reserves to investment decisions (operating presumably through the spread of information from bankers) rather than of a causal sequence with money stocks or interest rates as intervening variables.

Another important area of the consumer domain where there is scope for more or less autonomous acceleration or deceleration of decisions is the purchase of consumer durables — though in this area we have no time series which represent decisions in advance of action. Two-quarter percentage changes in durable-goods purchases by consumers are traced in the $_2\mathring{D}$-curve near the bottom of the Figure 4. Here again it is possible to find counterparts to the tight- and easy-money periods tagged by A, B, C, D, E, F on the F-curve. But the lags are very great, and several features (notably the acceleration of durable-goods purchases in 1956 and briefly in 1960) have no counterparts in the F-curve and very doubtful counterparts in the $_2\mathring{H}$-curve. Durable-goods expenditures obviously stand at the frontier between consumption and investment operations, so it is interesting to compare the $_2\mathring{H}$-curve with a curve of the same dimensions which traces the course of two-quarter percentage changes in consumer disposable income — the $_2\mathring{Y}$-curve at the bottom of the Figure 4. Broadly speaking, the accelerations and decelerations of the $_2\mathring{D}$-curve (including the features of the curve in 1956 and 1960 just mentioned) match better with the movements of disposable income than with those of free reserves or other monetary variables. I would suggest, however, that careful examination will probably show a net positive partial relation of durable-goods to monetary variables after the effect of income is allowed for.

STOCK-MARKET BEHAVIOR

On the hypothesis that investment decisions are powerfully influenced by changes in expectations induced by information about tight or easy money, we should expect to find counterparts to the accelerations and decelerations of fixed-investment decisions in another area—namely the stock market. Since this is an area where any action initiated by the professionals must be ratified by people's decisions as managers of household affairs, I have included the evidence in Figure 4 as part of the household-decision area. However, it might reasonably be put with the business-decision variables, on the ground that the decisive voice on the stock market is probably that of the managers who make fixed-investment decisions, operating in their personal capacity on the stock-market. Equally well, it might be argued that since stock-market conditions have a great deal to do with the ability of firms to obtain external financing (particularly by issuing new stock or convertible debentures), the stock market should be viewed as a connecting link between monetary policy and the goods-and-services sphere.

The stock market is notoriously very eccentric; being hung on sky-hooks anyhow, it responds in part emotionally to economic and political events, and is very subject to bandwagon movements of market psychology. Yet when we transform stock-market prices (the Standard and Poor index of 500 shares) into the form of two-quarter percentage changes, we obtain the $_2\overset{\circ}{S}$-curve of Figure 4, which bears a remarkable similarity to the investment-decision curves and to the curves for monetary variables. The $_2\overset{\circ}{S}$-curve has clear counterparts to the tight-money and easy-money periods tagged by A, B, C, D, E, F; and it agrees with the F-curve and investment-decision curves in showing a damped-cycle pattern of decreasing amplitude.[8] Furthermore, like the $_2\overset{\circ}{H}$-curve, it shows deceleration in recent years, though starting rather later than the F-curve and $_2\overset{\circ}{H}$-curve.[9]

It is interesting to observe that besides showing the main features of the F-curve, the $_2\overset{\circ}{S}$-curve has several idiosyncratic features.

[8]The sharp decline of 1966, however, is not fully registered at the right-hand end of the curve, since the latest entry on the chart shows the percentage change from October–December 1965 to April–June 1966. The decline from January –March to July–September of 1966 will register as of the order of 20 percent.

[9]It might be supposed, because of the highly psychological character of the stock market, that our intrepretation would be extremely sensitive to the manner in which we calculated the "accustomed-level curve" intertwined with the curve of actual entries. But examination of Figure 4 suggests that if we substituted (for example) a horizontal straight line showing the average rate of change from 1951 through 1965 for the "accustomed-level" curves of F and $_2\overset{\circ}{S}$, the agreement would be almost exactly like the agreement we find in Figure 1.

The most conspicuous of these is the sharp deceleration (leading into a substantial absolute decline) in 1962; but the triple-bottom (C_1, C_2, C_3) in 1955–1956, the double-top (B_1, B_2) in 1954–1955, and the double-top (F_3, F_4) in 1963–1964 are also interesting. None of these features has any warrant in the F-curve or the other monetary curves. But each has counterparts in some of the minor movements of the $_2\overset{\circ}{H}$-curve and (if we look back at Figure 3) of the $_2\overset{\circ}{E}$-curve and $_2\overset{\circ}{A}$-curve. This fact lends weight to the view that the stock market may be a "link variable": if its idiosyncratic movements affect investment decisions, we may infer that the movements it shares with the F-ratio and the investment-decision variables may be transmitted to the latter via the stock market. Alternatively, we may suppose that the resemblances between the $_2\overset{\circ}{S}$-curve and the investment-decision curves show that all of these curves are reflecting a common cause in the shift of the climate of business expectations.

The hypothesis suggested above, that the free-reserve situation may act upon investment decisions by an expectational mechanism, seems to me to be strengthened by the relation between the stock-market variable and the other variables examined. Note that this hypothesis *requires* that the main features of the free-reserve curve should be found in the investment-decision curves, but *does not bar* the presence of features in the investment-decision curves which are absent from the F-curve. To say that monetary policy (via free reserves and bank information) is *a* major factor in shaping business expectations is not to say that it is the *only* important factor in shaping those expectations. I would argue that the case for considering changes in expectations as the carrier of monetary influences is strengthened by the observation that otherwise-induced changes in expectations (registered by the stock market) show themselves capable of moving the investment curves.

A CONSPECTUS

A summary view of the main variables considered in this paper is offered in Figure 5. In this figure, instead of marking off the time-scale into years to facilitate close comparison, I mark it off into tight-money and easy-money episodes as indicated by the shading of the F-curve. Housing starts (the $_2\overset{\circ}{H}$-curve) conform almost perfectly with the pattern of deceleration on tight money and accelera-

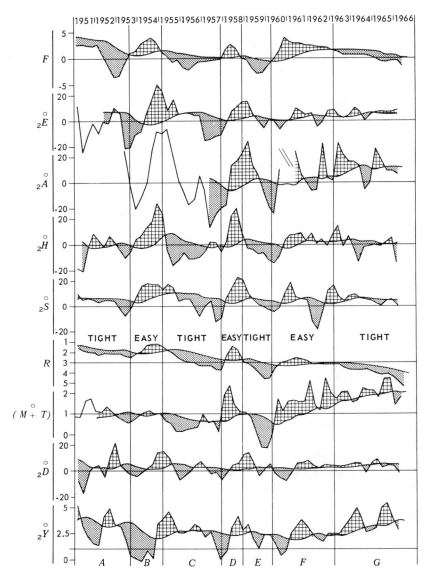

FIGURE 5. Conspectus of Relationships between Monetary Variables, Two-Quarter Changes in Investment Decisions and in Stock Prices, and Two-Quarter Changes in Disposable Income, Quarterly Figures 1951–1966.

Variables graphed

See account accompanying Charts I-IV

140

tion on easy money; and the same is true of the stock market ($_2\mathring{S}$-curve), except for the 1962 dip. The business-investment curves ($_2\mathring{E}$-curve and $_2\mathring{A}$-curve) conform with a lag which is fairly constant at about three quarters. The income-change curve ($_2\mathring{Y}$-curve at the foot of the chart) lags more—so much that its points of maximum acceleration and deceleration in the shorter swings are found in the ensuing phase of the monetary situation. The $_2\mathring{D}$-curve for durable goods conforms substantially to the timing of disposable income.

If we marked off our periods according to the R-curve for short-term interest, we would have essentially the same division of the time-span. However, the changes would be just great enough (deferring the opening of easy-money period B and tight-money period C) so that we would find the $_2\mathring{H}$-curve and $_2\mathring{S}$-curve moving in advance of the supposedly appropriate phase at times. Marking off the periods by the behavior of the $(M + T)$-curve would not alter things much *except* for the lack of a tight-money period G. Since the $_2\mathring{E}$-curve and $_2\mathring{A}$-curve fail to show deceleration on the whole in period G, this difference might seem to relieve us of an embarrassment. But we must remember that a monistic view of the determination of investment is not justified. During most of the period of observation, fiscal policy was sufficiently quiescent so that we should not expect a very intense effect on investment timing.[10] However the tax cuts effective at the beginning of 1954 were substantial, and were so publicized as to command a great deal of attention in connection with investment decisions. In 1965, there was a substantial acceleration of government expenditures. I would argue that to explain the *lack* of a strong 1964–1965 acceleration in investment decisions in this context requires us to suppose that monetary pressure introduced an offsetting force.

Agenda for Research

As I wrote at the opening of this paper, I am reporting here on an exploration rather than a definitive study. A quick graphical overview of this sort is suggestive of the lines along which a more rigorous study can be made—and is, I think sufficient to indicate the inadequacy of the conventional view of "monetary links"—but is no substitute for such a rigorous study. Hence the result of this

---

[10]Note however that there were important tax cuts effective in early 1954, which may have some bearing on the delayed-but-sharp acceleration of the $_2E$-curve.

investigation should be a research agenda rather than a set of findings.

The chief difference between a basic study and a quick exploration must lie in the careful consideration of interactions between monetary and other variables—taking account particularly of fiscal policy and of foreign trade. Monetary variables must be evaluated by their *partial* effects in a model which takes proper account of these other variables. Sorting out of autonomous as against induced effects in fiscal and foreign-trade variables, however, is a demanding task, without which the monetary-fiscal synthesis cannot be managed. In addition, much remains to be done in locating and making coherent further data that measure investment decisions rather than execution of past decisions—especially but not exclusively on the side of construction contracts. Furthermore, the interaction of monetary and other variables should be tested by further disaggregation of investment-decision variables where feasible, since such interacting variables as cash flow and new orders show interesting differences in pattern among different industries. I would urge that research along these lines is likely to prove highly productive, whereas exclusive attention to the traditional links may rule out essential expectational mechanisms in the action of monetary policy upon the goods-and-services economy.

Commentary

Deane Carson

Professor Hart's highly original paper on the linkage between monetary policy and investment provides a movable feast of ideas, and grist for the mills of all of us who harbor simpler notions concerning such matters.

Hart's centerpiece is the role of expectations flowing from

monetary policy decisions—not monetary changes—on fixed investment. He produces a substantial "chart show" to prove his point that something other than money, credit, or interest rates determines the flow of investment in fixed capital.

One's attention is called to the narrow confines of the question that Hart confronts: he is not concerned with aggregate expenditure, the business cycle, or total activity. Protagonists of various theories of the role of money, autonomous investment, and bank credit in the economy need not be disturbed.

On the other hand, the lack of a clearly stated hypothesis increases the difficulty of reviewing Hart's essay. At the risk of appearing presumptuous, and possibly wrong, one can derive at least one hypothesis, namely that the F-ratio determines bank lending and investment policies and is closely connected with investment expenditures. More specifically, the connection between bank policies and expectations is seen to involve the passing on of information which affect expectations. Falling below the "accustomed F-ratio," banks transmit this information in various ways to borrowers; rising above the accustomed F-ratio, they make it known that plentiful funds are available. The effect of these announcements cause investment to ebb and rise prior to any visible money, credit, and interest changes in the available statistical material.

From my own experience, the foregoing model—which I, not Hart, constructed—is unrealistic. Only at the latter end of a period of high interest rates and localized funds shortage do banks have to ration loans to their customary borrowers. Announcement effects of the kind suggested above, I suspect, are realized only in extreme cases.

Indeed, any generalized announcement of monetary policy change toward tightness should lead corporate treasurers to seek funds earlier than their schedules indicated as feasible before the change. If so, Hart's announcement effects should raise interest rates early in the business cycle, a movement that does not show up in the annals. This is not surprising. Changes in the F-ratio, contrary to Hart's assumption, do not measure "tightness" or "ease" in the banking markets. To give only one illustration, the computed F-ratio in several previous business cycles was smaller than in late 1966, but no one would say that money was "easier" in 1966. Yet, despite the fact of a falling F-ratio, the rate of bank loan expansion in 1965–1966 was 20 percent and the money stock grew 3.9 percent. In brief, I would question Hart's index of monetary policy based upon this statistic.

I also question Hart's implicit assumption that commercial banks supply a significant portion of fixed investment funds. Banks do provide long-term loans, but the major industrial borrowers consider bank financing as a stop-gap between excursions to other sources of funds. The charting of bank loans and investment conceals other, more important, capital market transactions.

However, all of these criticisms are superfluous, apparently, since Hart changes gears in mid-article, as adroitly as any Grand Prix driver at Le Mans. Admitting that he might wish to join the credit-availability school, he poses his main question: Do monetary linkages explain change in the flow of investment expenditures *ex ante?* The answer is a rather definite No: "The timing of changes in the rates of flow of such commitments casts serious doubt as to whether the conventional connecting links move early enough . . . as causes of changes in the flow of investment decisions."

This, I submit, is a breakthrough in our conventional wisdom. In effect, Hart asserts that fixed investment decisions are independent of current data concerning monetary conditions and are determined on the basis of their own expected conditions of cost and return. *Most* investment *is* independent of the monetary climate, the *average* rate of return being higher than the rate of interest. However, using aggregate data obscures the marginal affects of policy on investment.

My only quarrel with this aspect of Hart's paper is that it covers too much ground. Housing and state and local investment are certainly sensitive to current monetary conditions, a point to which he refers in a footnote. Finally, one might wish for a tighter statistical treatment of the data. Eyeball empiricism often leads to hypotheses, but almost never to accurate tests. The author correctly suggests that his work is an agenda for further exploration, and we are indebted to him for breaking the ground.

Chapter 5

Introduction

The problem of coordinating monetary and fiscal policies has disturbed relationships between central bank authorities and Treasury officials in virtually every free society. Central bankers, by their very experience and interests, are highly sensitive to maintaining a stable value of the monetary unit, while Treasury officials tend to be more sensitive to the goals of full employment and economic growth. Yet in the United States, we continue to have faith in independent agencies whose common concern is a healthy, expanding economy, hoping to reach reasonable compromises in policy decisions (even though it is not clear that in this policy area compromises yield optimum solutions).

To resolve such problems, Professor Arthur Smithies presents a technical primer on fiscal and monetary policy for those who would administer stabilization policy. He deals with the effects of alternative policy instruments upon actual output, full capacity output, and full employment output, in each of the following five situations:

1. maintaining full employment, once it has been achieved;
2. increasing or decreasing a steady rate of growth;
3. maintaining price stability with a steady growth rate;
4. maintaining balance-of-payment equilibrium under steady growth conditions;
5. returning to steady growth after departures from it have resulted in booms or depressions.

Smithies advocates utilizing monetary policy and profits taxation to influence investment while relying upon personal taxation or government expenditures to influence consumption. He adapts his growth model to illustrate the effects of alternative policy measures.

Finally, Smithies distinguishes between alternative types of booms which require control, because he accepts the proposition that booms are likely to be followed by depressions. Ideally, his desired result is to manipulate policy instruments so that actual output, capacity output, and full employment output grow at the same single, optimum rate. Use of Smithies' model is intended to prevent inconsistent monetary and fiscal policies, and to aid in the resolution of policy differences among those responsible for policy decisions.

FISCAL AND MONETARY POLICY: USES AND LIMITATIONS

Arthur Smithies

This paper is a primer on fiscal and monetary policy. Why, one may ask, is a primer needed at this late stage? The answer is that tradition and practice frequently seem to treat fiscal and monetary policies as separate compartments of economic life, as adversaries or competitors for attention.[1] This is not feasible in an economy that is pursuing a number of objectives at the same time. In contrast to earlier periods where some single objective, such as price stability or the current level of employment, was regarded as the dominant objective of policy, contemporary governments attempt in designing their policies, to achieve both these objectives and others as well. To achieve this range of objectives, the available fiscal and monetary instruments must be employed in a coordinated manner, and, even then, such measures are unlikely to be enough. One of the purposes of this paper is to point to the limitations as well as to the possibilities of fiscal and monetary policies.

As a minimum, one can say that governments are concerned with achieving full employment, price stability, a satisfactory rate of growth of total output, and external balance. Even at the over-all level, other objectives or constraints can easily be added. For instance, countries may aim at greater equality of income, or avoiding increased inequality. But the short list above is long enough for present purposes.

I shall assume to begin with that the instruments of policy consist of government expenditures, taxes on profits, taxes on personal incomes, transfer payments to individuals, and the

[1]Some of the few cases where the need for a mix of fiscal and monetary policy is explicitly discussed are the *Report of the Commission on Money and Credit* and the *Economic Report of the President* (in recent years, beginning January 1962), and James Tobin, "Economic Growth as an Object of Government Policy", *American Economic Review* Proceedings, May 1964, p. 1.

interest rate. I use the interest rate as a symbol to denote monetary policy in all its ramifications. Increased restrictiveness is accompanied by higher interest rates and vice versa, whether or not the operative factor is the interest rate, the quantity of money, the availability of credit, or some other aspect of the financial situation. It will appear that these instruments are insufficient. The possibilities of more refined fiscal and monetary instruments, and the use of other devices outside the fiscal and monetary area will then have to be considered.

The discussion can most conveniently be conducted in terms of a growth model that exhibits the influence of the policy variables, but is drastically simplified in other ways. It is an adaptation of a model I have used elsewhere.[2] The model is basically concerned with the behavior of three central variables, actual output, or GNP (Y), full capacity output (Y_F) and full employment output (Y_E). Y is the GNP to which the capital stock of the economy is adapted, while Y_E is the output required to give full employment to the labor force. Both of these concepts are defined on the *assumption* that there are adequate supplies of the other factor. Thus Y_F presupposes a supply of labor sufficient to permit operation with the "normal" capital-labor ratio, and Y_E presupposes an adequate supply of capital. However, I am not assuming rigidly fixed proportions. Y, for instance, can exceed Y_F or Y_E, but only under conditions of diminishing returns to capital or labor respectively. Thus, I am assuming a degree of substitutability between labor and capital that is intermediate between "fixed proportions" and full neo-classical substitutability.

The basic objective of policy is, then, to maintain substantial equality between these three variables and create a steady rate of growth over time—subject to the conditions of price stability and external balance. These concepts bear a close relationship to those of the Harrod model. If in a closed economy Y and Y_F are equal and growing at a steady rate, the "warranted rate of growth" is achieved, but not necessarily the natural rate. Where Y, Y_F, and Y_E are equal and growing together, the economy is growing at the Harrod natural rate. The term "natural," however, is unfortunate. It gives the impression that this rate is beyond policy control. A country that is concerned with raising *per capita* income in the long run must address itself to the task of increasing its natural

[2]"Economic Fluctuations and Growth," *Econometrica,* January 1957, and "The Control of Inflation," *Review of Economics and Statistics,* August 1957.

THE MODEL

The model is as follows:

SYMBOLS

All these variables are in constant prices

Y, Y_F, Y_E	already defined
E_C	consumers' expenditures
E_I	domestic net investment expenditures
E_G	government expenditures on goods and services
E_M	expenditures on imports
E_{FE}	expenditures for foreigners on exports
E_{FI}	net capital outflow
G	cost of government's program
S	annual loss of international reserves

t_1	personal taxes and transfer payments as proportion of Y
t_2	profits taxation as proportion of Y
p	index of the price level
r	interest rate
e	exchange rate
d	tariff rate
σ	marginal output-investment ratio
ρ	average productivity of labor
N	labor force

rate of growth. I say advisedly that the policy objective is to maintain *substantial* equality among the central variables. As we shall see, the attainment of other objectives may require that while the rate of growth of the variables should be the same, their levels should be different. For example, depending on circumstances, it may be desirable to run the economy with a permanent reserve of idle capacity. Other circumstances may suggest that the economy should operate with a permanent capacity shortage.

Without subscripts all symbols relate to the current year. The subscript $+1$ denotes next year and -1 last year. The subscript f on a variable such as Y or d signifies that the variable relates to "the rest of the world."

Equations

$$E_c = a' (1 - t_1 - t_2)Y - b'r + \epsilon_1 \tag{1}$$

$$E_{I+1} = a'' (1 - t_2)Y - b''r - c(Y_F - Y) + \epsilon_2 \tag{2}$$

$$E_G = G + \epsilon_3 \tag{3}$$

$$E_M = mY + np - qp_f e(1 + d) + h(Y_F - Y)_f + \epsilon_4 \tag{4}$$

$$E_{FE} \times p/ep_f = m_f Y_f + n_f p_f - q_f p(1 + d)/e + h_f(Y_F - Y) + \epsilon_5 \tag{5}$$

$$E_{FI} = h(r_f - r) + \epsilon_6 \tag{6}$$

$$E_c + E_I + E_G + E_{FE} - E_M = Y \tag{7}$$

$$E_M = E_{FL} - E_{FE} = S \tag{8}$$

$$p = p_{-1} + k(Y - \alpha Y_E) + l(Y - \beta Y_F) - s(\rho - \rho_{-1}) + \epsilon_7 \tag{9}$$

$$Y_{F+1} = Y_F + \sigma E_I + \epsilon_8 \tag{10}$$

$$Y_{E+1} = Y_E + \rho(N_{+1} - N) + N(\rho_{+1} - \rho) + \epsilon_9 \tag{11}$$

Equation (1) contains the hidden assumption that profits are a fixed proportion of GNP and dividends a fixed proportion of profits.[3] Personal taxation, assumed proportional to personal income can then be expressed as a fixed ratio of GNP. The equation then states that the *ratio* of consumers' expenditures to GNP depends negatively on tax rates and the interest rate. The interest

---

[3]The ratio of profits to GNP does, of course, fluctuate over the business cycle. But, I am using the present model mainly to discuss situations where the economy is reasonably close to full-capacity or full-employment operation.

rate may reflect consumer credit terms or other effects of monetary restrictiveness on consumer behavior.

Equation (2), based on the same assumptions as (1) states that private investment depends positively on profits and negatively on taxes and interest rates, and also negatively on the extent of excess capacity in the economy. A shortage of capacity will exert a positive influence. I assume, furthermore, that investment expenditures result from decisions made a year earlier. Thus current tax and monetary policies influence next year's investment rather than this year's.

Equation (3) assumes that government expenditures on goods and services are equal to the predetermined cost of what the government proposes to do. This implies that while such expenditures may be, and should be, determined in the light of economic conditions, they are not undertaken purely for stabilization purposes. To simplify the exposition and to indicate what would be desirable, I am assuming that the government can determine its expenditures on goods and services in the current year. To be realistic, lags should be included in this equation.

Equation (4) states that imports depend on the GNP of the importing country and on the relation between the domestic price level and the prices of imports on the domestic market. Those latter prices will be the foreign price multiplied by the exchange rate and increased by the tariff of the importing country. Excess capacity abroad is also added as a factor indicating the desire of foreign countries to supply exports. (Excess capacity at home could be added to indicate the extent of competition with imports.)

Equation (5) treats exports as imports by the rest of the world. The right-hand side of the equation is symmetrical with (4) and is intended to explain imports by the rest of the world in constant rest-of-the-world prices. E_{FE}, however, denotes exports in constant prices of the exporting country. To convert E_{FF} into imports in constant rest-of-the-world prices, it is necessary to multiply by the factor p/ep_f.

Equation (6) assumes that net capital outflow depends on differences between interest rates and profit rates abroad and at home. Differences in interest rates at least partially reflect differences in marginal profit rates. Differences in degree of capacity utilization could be included as further indicators of profit differences.

Equation (7) states that, in real terms, short-run equilibrium is achieved during the period, in the sense that expenditures as determined by the equation system are equal to output.

Equation (8) is the balance-of-payments equation. It states that the real loss of international reserves is equal to the difference between receipts from exports and payments on account of current imports *plus* net capital outflow. It represents the "official settlements balance," expressed in constant prices.

THE PRICE LEVEL. Equation (9) is intended to describe price determination. It assumes that wage and price increases depend on demand-and-supply conditions in the economy. The lower the level of unemployment, the more pressure for wage increases occurs. Employer resistance to wage increases depends on the degree of competitiveness in product markets (represented in the equation by the amount of excess capacity in the economy). Whatever the market structure, it can be assumed that increases in surplus capacity will intensify competition and increase resistance to wage demands.

The equation admits the possibilities that prices and wages may rise or fall together, and that the competition may narrow or widen profit margins. The addition of capacity use as a variable is, in my view, a necessary addition to the Phillips Curve treatment of the subject.

The equation indicates that prices will be stable if $Y = \alpha Y_E = \beta Y_F$. The effect of any degree of upward pressure on prices from labor shortage can be offset by a sufficient degree of excess capacity. In fact, however, there are bounds to the linear relationship. It may be realistic to assume that the price level can never be reduced and that there is an upper boundary to the influence of excess capacity in restraining price increases.

Finally, the rate of change in the productivity of labor has been included as a negative influence on the change in the price level. It is usually assumed that productivity increase is a factor that reduces wage-price inflation. This implies that money-wage demands result from efforts to increase the real income of labor, rather than to increase the labor share in the national income.

In a country heavily dependent on foreign trade, the influence of changes in import and export prices should be included as an additional factor.

CAPACITY INCREASES. Equation (10) shows the increase in Y_F, resulting from investment incentives of this year. Since investment occurs with a one-year lag, Y_F is given for the current year. The marginal output-investment ratio σ is provisionally assumed constant. However, it may change as a result of changes in the character of technological change or the age distribution of equipment. It may also change as a result of monetary and fiscal policies.

Equation (11) states that the increase in Y_E from one year to the next depends on the growth of the labor force, which we take as a given, and on the rate of increase in the productivity of labor. I am assuming that technological change is largely of the "embodied" variety and so depends on a sufficient rate of investment being undertaken. Y_E consequently cannot be affected until next year by policy measures taken this year.

THE OPERATION OF THE MODEL. The model describes a succession of short-run Keynesian equilibrium situations, and the exogenous or endogenous forces that impel the economy from one position to the next.

In any single year Y_F and Y_E are given; furthermore, investment expenditures E_I, are governed by decisions taken last year [in accord with (2)]. Ignoring price changes, the current level of Y is then determined by equations (1) to (7).

Next year's level of Y_F will be determined by this year's investment decisions which are dependent on this year's economic situation. Changes in the outside world and in government expenditures together with those investment decisions result in a new short-run equilibrium next year. Changes in the price level emerge from the "real" situation in any year, but in turn react on it.

With given fiscal and monetary policies, the model can yield a wide variety of economic situations. It can produce chronic tendencies for output to run ahead of, or behind, the creation of capacity, or persistent unemployment or over-employment. It can produce continuing tendencies or fluctuations in those directions. I have discussed such possibilities elsewhere.[4]

It is unlikely, however, that any given set of values of the policy variables can keep the economy on a path of steady growth for a considerable time. In the first place, none of the private

[4]"Economic Fluctuations and Growth," *Econometrica*, January 1957.

behavior equations is exact. Outside factors, included in the error terms, can affect the situation and have cumulative consequences. Second, private "propensities," particularly those relating to investment, are subject to change. Third, the behavior of the government and the outside world can and does preclude the possibility of steady growth without continuing policy adjustments.

PROBLEMS OF POLICY

— Both the long- and the short-run aspects of policy should be the objects of continuing attention. In principle, both long- and short-range objectives can most effectively be achieved if current policy is subjected to annual review and, if necessary, amendment. Adoption of fixed rules for the government's budget or the money supply may be warranted because of institutional difficulties and inadequacy of diagnostic and forecasting techniques. In this discussion, I shall assume that even though governments make mistakes and often fail to act in time, they are not helped by arbitrary restrictions on their freedom to act.

The year-to-year review and revision of policy is concerned with affecting the spending *decisions* of government and the private sector in the current year. Depending on the lag periods involved, these spending decisions will produce their expenditure effects in the current year or the next year (or beyond that in a fully realistic model).

The assumed objectives of employment — growth, provision for the public sector, price stability, and external balance — can be translated into year-to-year targets for the main variables of the model.

The current employment objective means that the current value of Y should be as close to Y_E as feasible.

The growth objective requires an annual increase in Y_F equal to that of Y_E if they are originally equal. If they are originally unequal, the growth of Y_F should be speeded up or slowed down.

The public sector objective requires government expenditures equal to the cost of necessary government programs.

Price stability means that the annual increase in prices should be zero, or, at any rate, confined within tolerable limits.

External balance means that the annual reserve loss should be held within a tolerable limit. The situation may, in fact, demand an accretion of reserves.

Denoting targets by bars on the variables, the government in any year then attempts to achieve

$$Y = \overline{Y}$$
$$Y_{F+1} = \overline{Y}_{F+1}$$
$$E_G = \overline{G}$$
$$\Delta P = 0$$
$$S = 0$$

With this framework, we can now consider the uses of fiscal and monetary policies in the following situations:

> Maintaining a steady full employment rate of growth, once it has been achieved in a closed economy;
> increasing or decreasing a steady rate of growth;
> maintaining price stability under conditions of steady growth;
> maintaining external balance under steady growth conditions;
> returning to a steady growth after departures from it have resulted in booms or depressions.

MAINTAINING STEADY GROWTH.   This is a desirable goal if the economy is growing steadily with full employment, $Y = Y_F = Y_E$, and if each of them is increasing at the desired rate. If we consider first the situation in a closed economy, and ignore the question of prices, fiscal and monetary measures should be equal to the task of keeping the economy on the path. The requirement that $Y_F = Y_E$ determines the desired rate of increase in Y_F. If the technological factors are given, the required rate of investment can be determined from equation (10). The rate of investment can be influenced by profits taxation, monetary policy, or some combination of the two. At the same time, government and private consumption can be adjusted, through personal taxation or government expenditures, to achieve in every period the desired level of Y. If government expenditures are to be used to finance government programs rather than to stabilize the economy, the burden of attaining the desired level of investment falls on taxation and monetary policy.

Suppose the government decides to increase its expenditures at the same rate as it desires the economy as a whole to grow. In those circumstances, according to our model, government expenditures, investment, and consumption must all remain the same proportions of GNP. Barring external disturbances, the fiscal and monetary policies adopted at the outset will keep the economy on its path of steady growth. The model, however, assumes that taxes are proportional. If the tax system is progressive with respect to GNP, tax rates must be continually reduced in order to keep both profits after taxes and disposable personal income at the same proportions of income. Otherwise, because of "fiscal drag," the desired growth rate will not be maintained.

If government expenditures increase less rapidly than the desired growth of GNP, personal tax rates must be continually reduced in order to keep consumption *plus* government expenditures at the same proportion of GNP. So far as the model is concerned, profits taxes and the interest rate should remain unchanged. If, however, political factors require that profits taxation should share in the tax reduction, increasing interest rates will be needed to keep investment at the required rate.

If, on the other hand, government expenditures increase faster than the desired growth of income, they must do so at the expense of personal consumption. The rate of personal taxation must consequently increase steadily, but the rate of profit taxation and the interest rate must not increase if the investment target is to be maintained. Politics, however, usually requires that personal and profits taxation increase together. In that event, interest rates must be continually reduced in order to maintain investment. If it is not feasible to lower them sufficiently, increasing government expenditures will mean reduction in the growth target. An increasing shortage of capacity may then preclude the attainment of full employment, or may permit it only at the price of inflation.

CHANGING THE RATE OF GROWTH.   Can fiscal and monetary policies achieve an increase in the rate of growth? The answer, in Harrod's terms, is that they can increase the warranted rate, but increasing the natural rate may be much more difficult.

A country may have a labor surplus in the sense that Y_F is less than Y_E, and consequently there is "classical" unemployment or underemployment. In that event, fiscal and monetary measures can increase the rate of saving and investment, and the rate of growth of Y and Y_F can be increased by an appropriate combination of tax and monetary policy, until the labor surplus is absorbed. At this point, however, the problem becomes one of increasing the growth rate of Y_E.

Leaving aside the possibility of increasing the rate of growth of the labor force in terms of sheer numbers, which is unlikely, an increased "natural" growth rate will depend on increasing the rate at which the average productivity of labor, ρ, increases. Labor productivity can be increased by increasing the capital intensity of production, which means decreasing σ, by accelerating the rate of technological change, which increases ρ while reducing or leaving σ unchanged, or by increasing the efficiency of the labor force itself.

I am taking the point of view, which is widely shared, that changes in interest rates are unlikely to have a pronounced effect on factor proportions, and that therefore an easy money policy is not an effective way to increase capital intensity. But fiscal and monetary policy may have indirect effects in that direction. If those policies are designed to keep Y and Y_F permanently in excess of Y_E, they may induce the continual introduction of labor-saving techniques and hence increase the rate of increase of ρ and Y_E. But it should be noted that such a policy will probably mean reduction in the real rate of return on investment, unless the rate of increase of real wages can be reduced. The likely result then is an inflationary scramble over distributive shares.

The most satisfactory way to increase the rate of growth of Y_E is to speed up the pace of technological change, if that can be done. I fail to see how any of the general fiscal and monetary instruments included in the model can be relied on to achieve the desired result. Special measures such as tax write-offs of obsolete equipment or tax allowances for research and development expenditures may be needed.

Measures to increase the quality of the labor force are likely to include government action to improve education and training.

Another possibility, not included in the model, is to take increased advantage of the possibilities of international trade. Productivity increases are not uniformly distributed among economic sectors. By giving up autarchic policies, a country may be able to specialize on those areas where its productivity trends are strongest.

A caveat to all these possibilities is that labor may prefer to realize its productivity gains by shortening the working week rather than by earning higher real wages.

I leave it to the reader to work out techniques for reducing the rate of growth, while still maintaining full employment. This has not yet emerged as a practical issue in any country but someday we may decide that everyone can lead a more congenial life with a slower rate of technological change.

PRICE STABILITY. Virtually all countries have come to the view that the creation of unemployment is not an appropriate way to achieve price stability. Consequently their governments are attempting to achieve price stability either through some type of "incomes policy" or through attempts to increase competitiveness in labor and product markets. Such measures, if successful, would help to reduce k and l in equation (9) and increase α and β. My purpose here is not to discuss these matters, but to discuss the role that monetary and fiscal policy can play in keeping prices stable.

Even though governments may eschew deflation as a remedy, I do not believe that they can go to the opposite extreme and assert or admit that monetary and fiscal policy will be used to attain "real" objectives, while the price question will be dealt with by other methods. If the monetary and fiscal authorities agreed to validate any price and wage increases that occurred, both wage pressure and employer resistance would diminish. Even if the use of deflation is given up as a regular expedient, the threat that it might be used must be preserved. The credibility of the threat may require the occasional use of the weapon.

Fiscal and monetary policy can also contribute to price stability by affecting the capacity level at which the economy regularly operates. I assume that the level of unemployment of labor that the country will tolerate is affected by political attitudes, the availability of unemployment compensation, and so forth. But the level of utilization of productive capacity at which it operates can be regarded as an economic matter. While steady growth requires that Y and Y_F should grow at the same rate, it does not mean that they should be equal — as I have hitherto assumed. By lowering profit taxes or interest rates, and thereby sustaining profit rates, the model could be made to run at, for example, 90 percent of capacity instead of 100 percent. The problem would be how to get the economy to the right starting point. In this way, fiscal and monetary policy could make a contribution to price stability.

However, I am not suggesting that other measures, outside the fiscal and monetary field, will not be needed.

THE BALANCE OF PAYMENTS.   Steady growth will continue without interruption from the international side if current exports and imports grow in the same proportion as GNP. If exports grow more rapidly or imports less rapidly, adjustments will be needed, but they will not be painful. The difficult problems arise when export income fails to grow at the desired rate. This may occur because the country wishes to grow more rapidly than the rest of the world, or because the world demand for its (primary) exports does not grow as rapidly as income abroad.

Suppose a country is confronted by the prospect of current account deficit. What can be done by fiscal and monetary measures to preserve balance and maintain the rate of steady growth?

One easy course suggested by the model is to allow the current deficit to occur but to reduce foreign lending or increase foreign borrowing and thus offset the loss of reserves. The technique for doing this is to raise interest rates in relation to rates abroad [according to equation (6)]. But other adjustments would then have to be made. Since monetary policy has now been pre-empted for international purposes, profits taxes must be reduced in order to maintain domestic inducements to invest. But domestic savings must also be reduced, since foreign investment has been reduced — because of the current-account deficit. This may call for reductions in personal taxes.

The same results may be attainable through the creation of additional instruments. For instance, the authorities may attempt to alter the structure of interest rates, using the long-term rate as an instrument for control of domestic investment, and the short-term rate for foreign lending. They may impose a tax on foreign lending, thus reducing the rate of return obtainable from foreign investment.

Whichever method is employed, the net result of these adjustments is that the desired rate of steady growth is maintained, but the country is relying less on domestic saving. Such a course of action is likely to provide an immediate solution at the cost of more serious difficulties in the future.

The other approach to the prospective deficit is to make adjustments on the foreign side that will permit domestic growth to continue while the current balance-of-payments is maintained at the desired level. The objective is to maintain the values of both exports and imports at the same proportion of domestic income. The effect will be achieved by lowering the prices of domestic goods in relation to those of internationally traded goods, producing the effects on exports and imports indicated by equations (4) and (5).

Fiscal and monetary measures can contribute to the desired result insofar as they help to maintain domestic price stability. If prices and wages at home can be kept from rising as fast as they do abroad, external balance may be preserved. If the authorities plan to run the economy at a lower level of capacity utilization, they will add to export incentives as well as contribute to price stability.

If a sufficient price differential between at home and abroad cannot be achieved by internal action, the remaining possibilities are direct import controls and tariff increases or exchange devaluation. All of these actions have direct effects on the relation between the prices of goods that enter into international trade and those of domestic goods and wage rates. Import controls, whether achieved through the tariff or by quantitative restriction, raise the domestic prices of imports and close import substitutes in relation to those of all other prices including those of exports. Devaluation raises the prices of exportables and importables in relation to domestic prices and wages.

In these cases, the task of fiscal and monetary policy is to help preserve the price differential rather than to achieve it. The problem again resolves itself into one of maintaining domestic price stability, or, rather, of confining the inevitable general price increase to the direct effects of the necessary relative price increase of international goods.

The task will be more difficult than it is when the price stabilizers merely have to contend with domestic factors. On the other hand, if the authorities do not act, the international action can be rendered largely or wholly ineffective, as has often happened to devaluations in the past.

Suppose the authorities feel compelled not merely to *preserve* the existing current-account balance, but to use import controls or devaluation to *reduce* the current deficit. If they are to succeed in doing this, their international action must be accompanied by action to restrict domestic consumption — presumably by increased taxation. If the growth objective is to be retained, the rate of domestic investment must continue unchanged, but increased domestic saving must balance reduced foreign borrowing. But the increased taxation needed to increase domestic saving may weaken investment incentives. Consequently, added incentives may be needed. If monetary policy is pre-empted to control capital movements, the incentive can be provided by a reduction in profits taxation. In that case, the fiscal policy needed to accompany a reduction of the current balance-of-payments deficit may consist of a reduction of profits taxation and an increase in personal taxation — a hard prescription for a democratic country to follow.

I have considered a number of situations in which the government has to deal with a potential or actual payments deficit. some countries, however, may be in the more fortunate position of having to contend with surpluses, arising from increasing world demand for their commodities or from the energy of their entrepreneurs in winning export markets. Such countries may, but rarely do, appreciate their currencies or reduce their tariffs so that international balance is again achieved. Their existing fiscal and monetary policies will then enable them to continue growth at the same rate, but at a higher lever than before.

Alternatively, the surplus country may wish to convert its increased export income into a permanent export surplus matched by corresponding foreign lending. The increased foreign lending will require reduction of domestic interest rates. To maintain the same rate of domestic investment, this reduction should be offset by increased profits taxes. Personal taxes should be raised to provide the additional savings needed to balance both domestic investment and increased foreign investment.

Countries frequently follow neither of these courses in response to an increase of export income, but prefer to let nature take its course. Increases in exports mean increased reserves of the banking system and hence lower interest rates. At the same time, increased export income directly raises spending at home. Expansion continues by familiar multiplier processes. If the country is already in a state of steady growth with full employment, the consequences will be inflationary. The outcome may be steady growth at a higher price level and a higher level of real income than before. On the other hand, the inflation may generate conditions that produce a subsequent depression.

BOOMS AND DEPRESSIONS.   Booms may have a number of config-
urations, depending on the structure of the economy, the disturbances to growth, and the government policy pursued. They
may occur when the government fails to correct departures from
the steady growth path, or they may occur as the consequence of
recovering from a previous depression. A boom may also occur
because the government itself undertakes large increases in
expenditures but fails to take the restraining fiscal and monetary
measures that the situation requires. In any case, I am assuming
that the objective of the government in controlling a boom is to
get the economy, as smoothly as possible, onto a steady growth
path. The fiscal and monetary action required will depend on the
diagnosis of the particular situation.

Possible boom situations can be described in terms of Y, Y_F,
and Y_E. At least three boom possibilities deserve attention.

> Y is greater than, and increasing more rapidly than, Y_F
> and Y_E.
> Y is greater than, and increasing more rapidly than, Y_F,
> but both are less than Y_E.
> Y_F is greater than, and increasing more rapidly than,
> Y_E, but Y is greater or less than Y_E.

The first situation represents a general state of excessive demand, and clearly the rate of growth Y should be reduced (to
attempt to reduce it absolutely can start a depression). The choice
of fiscal and monetary methods to be used depend on whether the
reduction should be borne by consumption or investment, and that
depends on the relationship between Y_F and Y_E. If there is a
tendency for Y_F to exceed Y_E, investment or its rate of growth
should be curtailed, whether or not consumption is restrained.
Otherwise, the restriction should fall on consumption.

In the second case, the economy is in a state of excess demand
with respect to capacity but not with respect to labor. In that case,
to slow down the growth of Y and still more, that of Y_F, would be
unsatisfactory, since it would prolong unemployment. The appropriate policy would be to allow both consumption and investment to continue to grow, but to speed up the growth of investment and slow down that of consumption. The end objective is to
have Y, Y_F, and Y_E growing at the same rate. The initial move in
the game is to reduce interest rates and raise taxes on consumption.

In the third case, the economy is sustaining current demand through the creation of capacity that is excessive from the point of view of full employment of labor. Such a situation is unlikely to be sustainable. It could be sustained for a time at the price of inflation, if the authorities were willing to allow demand to expand regardless of the labor shortage. If they were unwilling to do this, the growth of unused capacity would eventually depress investment no matter what fiscal or monetary inducements were employed to continue it. In such a situation, a tight money policy is clearly necessary to curtail investment. But at the same time, consumption should be stimulated by tax reduction to make up for the effects on demand of the restriction on investment.

To anyone engaged in the practical art of boom control, my policy conclusions are likely to appear fanciful. Indeed, in the present state of the art of diagnosis and prescription, they may be. But these cases may serve as a warning that simple monetary or fiscal rules for boom control may not be generally applicable. I am inclined to think that booms will be followed by recessions, and hope that they will be mild ones. A further moral of the story is that it is easier to stay on a steady path than to get back onto it.

A depression, on the other hand, almost invariably involves unused capacity and unemployed labor; that is, a level of Y below both Y_E and Y_F. Furthermore, the excess capacity may be such a powerful deterrent to investment that the direct stimulation of investment by fiscal and monetary measures may be ineffective. If profits are low and seem likely to remain low, neither tax reduction nor interest rate reductions are likely to produce large increases in investment. For similar reasons, tax reduction may not produce large increases in consumer demand when income is low.

In a severe depression, it is likely that a strong initial push is necessary to start expansion, after which tax policy and interest rates can become progressively effective. Unless the rest of the world comes to the rescue by increasing its import demands, increases in domestic government expenditures may be the only satisfactory way out of a depression impasse with large excess capacity. While government expenditure should be the main weapon, benefits that may be obtained from tax reduction and cheap money should be borne in mind.

Governments pursuing a policy of expenditures may encounter difficult problems in regard to the reversability or modification of their recovery measures. What is appropriate for rapid recovery may not be appropriate for continued growth at the desired rate. The government may be called on to tighten its expenditures or raise taxes at a time when revenues are increasing. The danger of an all-out recovery policy stimulated by government expenditures is that it may lead the way into a boom with shortages of capacity.

On the other hand, if energetic measures are taken to increase investment as part of a recovery program, other problems of reversability arise. If incentives are sufficient to stimulate investment under conditions of excess capacity, they can result in excessive investment when the impediment of excess capacity has disappeared. At the appropriate time, the authorities should begin to tighten up on monetary and fiscal incentives to investment. Analytically, the problems of recovery seem easier than those of the boom — but politically, they may be no easier.

Booms and depressions are still subjects worthy of study, even though we are assured that we have the knowledge and the techniques to keep prosperity forever.

Commentary

James Tobin

Are the conventional tools of monetary and fiscal policy numerous enough, and independent enough, to achieve simultaneously the usual economy-wide objectives of national economic policy? Professor Smithies answers this question in the negative. His answer, with which I substantially agree, opens the further question of whether the goals should be modified to accord with the realistic limitations of monetary and fiscal instruments or whether entirely different weapons should be added to the policy-maker's arsenal.

Smithies lists four goals: (G1) full employment of labor; (G2) price stability; (G3) a satisfactory rate of growth of output (which, for the most part, he translates into an appropriate ratio of investment to total output); and (G4), balance in external payments. To achieve these goals he allows the authorities normally only three instruments: (I1) the domestic profits tax rate; (I2) the ratio to national output of personal income taxes net of transfer payments; and (I3) the monetary interest rate, as an index of monetary policy. But he also considers offering them a fourth, (I4) the foreign exchange rate (or the tariff rate, which plays much the same role).

A possibly illuminating rearrangement of his four instruments is (I'1) fiscal-monetary influence on aggregate demand, combining I1, I2, and I3; (I'2) the structure of taxation, reflecting the combination of I2 and I3; (I3) the interest rate; and (I4) the effective exchange rate.

Note that fiscal policy is represented entirely by the two tax rates. Government expenditures on goods and services are assumed, quite properly, to be geared to another objective—the proper balance, in view of national priorities, between public and private uses of resources. This balance does not mean restriction on the strength of fiscal policy, since aggregate demand can be as well regulated by variation of taxes and transfers as by changes in public purchases.

It is scarcely surprising that three instruments do not suffice to achieve four targets. But the deficiency would not be remedied by adding the fourth instrument. The basic difficulty is that these monetary and fiscal policies can at best control aggregate demand relative to capital capacity and labor capacity. The price response of the economy at full employment is rooted in structural characteristics that are immune to monetary and fiscal manipulations. That is why wage-price guideposts and incomes policies are so much in the news. Their use, however, conflicts with other unlisted objectives: economic freedom and efficient allocation of resources. Yet unless the structural Phillips curve linkage of inflation and unemployment is broken by instruments of this kind, the best the monetary and fiscal authorities can do is trim their ambitions and aim at less than full employment and/or less than complete price stability.

Smithies' model does offer some small relief from this dilemma. He suggests that for given rates of utilization, prices will rise less rapidly the more rapid the growth of labor productivity. Thus, a capital-deepening program to accelerate growth will also moderate inflation.

I believe that this conclusion is correct, or at least consistent with the Phillips curve argument on which the linkage of unemployment and inflation is based. This may be seen as follows: Let η_w be the rate of change of money wages, η_p the rate of change of prices, η_ρ the rate of change of the (marginal) productivity of labor, and u the unemployment rate. There are then two equations:

$$\eta_w - \eta_p = \eta_\rho \tag{1}$$
$$\eta_w - \alpha\eta_p = f(u) \tag{2}$$

The first says that real wages advance with productivity. The second says that money wage increases depend on price increases and on the rate of unemployment. Clearly, if $\alpha = 1$, there is no dynamic money illusion and there is no solution. The advance of real wages is determined by (1); from (2), there is an unemployment rate in equilibrium with that advance; but money wages and prices are indeterminate. If α is less than 1, then the Phillips curve model applies. In that case $\eta_p = f(u) - \alpha\eta_\rho/1 - \alpha$, which shows that inflation will be retarded by increases in the rate of productivity advance η_ρ.

Smithies' equation (9) also suggests that prices can be kept from rising in a period of full employment if the economy is run with sufficient excess capital capacity. He seems, however, not to take this implication seriously, and his instinct is probably right. I find his two separate capacity output measures confusing. Smithies does not mean them to represent fixed-coefficient production relationships. If they were so interpreted, an excess of capital over labor capacity would not serve to police prices, and in any case investors would not long perpetuate such a capital surplus. But if Smithies allows variable proportions, even if only *ex ante*, then we should simply interpret $Y_F > Y_E$ to mean a high capital-labor ratio. So long as factor proportions accord with prevailing real wages and interest rates, there is no reason to believe that a high capital-output ratio leads to more price competition than a low one, or that full employment is less inflationary with one capital-labor ratio than with another.

Smithies finds the classical conflict of external and internal balance more manageable. In a fixed exchange rate régime, he finds it necessary to dedicate monetary policy to external balance. The interest rate must induce capital flows to offset whatever current account surplus or deficit arises from optimal aggregate demand at home. How, then, can the government meet its investment and growth objective? In the United States in the early 1960s, the promotion of economic growth seemed to indicate an easy money/tight budget combination. But the balance-of-payments deficit dictated the opposite mixture.

Smithies avoids this sort of dilemma by using the structure of taxation, instead of the interest rate, to control the composition of aggregate demand as between consumption and investment. In principle, fiscal policy can remain as loose or as tight as required to achieve full employment; at the same time, investment can be stimulated by low profits taxes and consumption be correspondingly restricted by relatively high personal income taxes. Meanwhile, the interest rate controls the external capital account. If the variation of the profits tax rate applied to profits from foreign operations as well as from domestic, the strategy would not work. Varying the tax on domestic profits alone is, in effect, a way of contriving a domestic interest rate appropriate to growth in conjunction with an international market interest rate appropriate for external balance.

Smithies acknowledges the narrow political limits to variation in the relative rates of taxation on profits and other incomes. Another way to make the same point is to add the objective of distributive equity to his list. There are economic objections too. Efficient international allocation of capital is prevented by measures which tax domestic and foreign profits differentially. If differential profit rates are inducing capital movements across borders, no basic adjustment will ever occur if the movements are prevented by differential taxation.

Smithies' equation for net capital inflow is too simple. International differences in profit rates are not adequately measured by differences in monetary interest rates. Expected movements in the real exchange rate are also relevant. For example, inflation is actually good for a country's external capital account if its exchange rate is regarded as stable. A foreigner can gain in his own currency by buying property in the inflating country, letting it appreciate with the inflation, then selling and repatriating the proceeds. This consideration calls into question the conventional wisdom, which Smithies repeats, that inflation leads to external deficit.

Perhaps Smithies' fourth instrument, the exchange rate, is

needed after all. If adjustment or fluctuation of the exchange rate maintains external balance, then monetary policy is free to serve the growth target.

In a closed economy, the interest rate is free to serve the objectives of growth and full employment. The world as a whole is a closed economy, and somehow the general world level of interest rates must be determined. In a fixed exchange rate system, the world level of interest rates is unsettled if every country follows Smithies' rule of adjusting its rate to rates abroad. If the world level of interest rates is high, the several countries are forced to maintain full employment by policy mixtures unfavorable to investment and growth. A deliberately coordinated international policy is needed; otherwise, the fiscal-monetary mix will be determined by default by whatever surplus country has the tightest monetary policy.

My comments have been confined mainly to the static relationships of instruments and goals. They do not do justice to Smithies' paper, which also discusses the complexities introduced by lags in policy decisions and in the economy's responses to them. Without further progress on these difficult dynamic problems and on the uncertainties associated with them, the theory of economic policy will be of limited practical use.

Chapter 6

Introduction

According to orthodox economic theory, the proper prescription for a balance-of-payments deficit is the introduction of the degree of internal deflation required to eliminate the deficit under the gold standard or its equivalent. The logic of this adjustment process runs as follows: Country A runs a deficit; after a point, this deficit must be paid for in gold; the outflow of gold leads, via pressure on bank reserves, to a monetary contraction. The internal monetary shortage imposes itself on the entire economy, causing a decline in the rate of growth or perhaps an actual decline in GNP. The impact on GNP has employment and price level effects, and the domestic price level continues to fall until international readjustments take place which correct the deficit. The logic of the theory is impeccable. There are, however, obvious problems associated with this remedy. No nation enjoys, and few governments can or will endure, internal deflation to correct imbalances in trade. In addition, the extended readjustments required within any economy to work through the entire process are clearly subject to a complex set of lags.

In his paper, Professor George N. Halm points out that these lags may be partially overcome by the introduction of flexible exchange rates. What Halm advocates is actually the so-called "band proposal," which would permit exchange rates to vary within an established range or prescribed limits. Technically, this permissiveness is in effect today; for example, the British pound may move between approximately $2.78 and $2.82. The significant difference in the band proposal is that the limits for fluctuation would rise from say 1 percent to 5 percent, and this would be regarded as only the first step toward even broader limits. Under flexible rates the value of a country's currency would be free to adjust with conditions in the market. A falling value for a currency would have an immediate effect of some degree on the ability to import, and so certain types of adjustments would take place much faster.

What is perhaps more important, however, is that we would know more about the current value of a currency than we do now. For example, the United States has run a deficit for almost a decade. Because of our swollen reserves at the start of this period, we have been able to avoid thus far any severe internal effects of the traditional kind. In these circumstances, what is the dollar really worth? If, following Halm, we permitted the exchange rates to fluctuate within fairly narrow limits, we would find out. If the dollar did not decline in value it would suggest the possibility that a revision in the traditional balance-of-payments theory was in order. Such a revision would continue to treat traditional theory as meaningful, but recognize it as a special case in a more general framework that would include the heterogeneous nature of balance-of-payments difficulties.

THE CASE FOR GREATER EXCHANGE-RATE FLEXIBILITY IN AN INTERDEPENDENT WORLD

George N. Halm

DOMESTIC MONEY AND THE FOREIGN EXCHANGES

The position of the rates of exchange in today's market economies is unique: they are the only prices which are more or less permanently fixed with the unanimous approval of businessmen and central bankers. In all other cases, price-fixing is, understandably, considered highly controversial, because a market economy cannot work without price variations as guidelines. If you stop these adjustments through price movements, you must introduce quantitative controls; and a consistent set of quantitative regulations implies some form of central planning.

Why should exchange rates be fixed when the logic of the market economy demands flexible prices? The reason is, I believe, that foreign currencies and their prices, the rates of exchange, play approximately the same role in international transactions that domestic money plays at home: they are used as means of payment, as liquidity reserves, and as units of account. Domestic money is generally accepted because it enjoys unquestionable price stability. The tautology that the dollar is always a dollar creates the illusion that the value or purchasing power of money is constant. This illusion is strong enough to make us accept and use money even in times of price inflation.

International transactions always involve at least two national monetary units whose purchasing powers do not always change in the same degree or even in the same direction. A rate of exchange, therefore, as link between two national monetary units and two national price structures, should be expected to vary together with the so-called purchasing-power parity, that is, with the ratio of change of the respective domestic values of the national currencies. Roughly, a ratio of 1:1 should become a ratio of 1:2 if the first country maintained price stability while the second permitted itself a 100 percent price increase. By fixing the rate of exchange, we impart to it price stability in terms of both currencies; and the general acceptability of domestic money becomes the free convertibility at the fixed rate in international transactions.

The desire to imitate the qualities of domestic money when dealing with the foreign exchanges ignores the fact that national monetary policies always differ, and that, assuming fixed exchange rates and free convertibility, the monetary authorities must stand ready to equalize disparities in demand and supply on the foreign exchange market (caused by disparities in monetary policies) by buying or selling foreign exchange (or gold) as the situation requires. However, only a surplus position can be maintained indefinitely through the creation of domestic money (that is, we can buy foreign exchange in unlimited amounts). Foreign money cannot be created and, accordingly, cannot be sold indefinitely. Out of the fixing of exchange rates, when national policies are less than perfectly integrated, arises the whole issue of international liquidity.

TRYING TO DO THE IMPOSSIBLE

In fixing the exchange rates, we try to combine four aims whose simultaneous achievement is impossible without infinitely large liquidity reserves. The four aims are:

1. fixed exchange rates;
2. free convertibility;
3. stable domestic prices;
4. full employment and economic growth.

Monopolistic arthritis has made it nearly impossible for us to combine price stability with full employment. When sufficient downward adjustability is lacking in the price system, the needed reallocations will have to take place via differentiated upward price changes with creeping inflation as the result. With varying degrees of inflation in different countries, fixed exchange rates can be maintained only by giving up convertibility through the introduction of controls (on capital flows, commodity movements, or international travel), or through very large foreign exchange reserves. When the reserves prove to be inadequate, the only choice left is between giving up convertibility or the fixed exchange rates. Of course, we can always argue for still higher reserves or a greater coordination of national economic policies (the Harrod and Rueff positions respectively). This is the spectrum of possibilities. I want to suggest that, under these conditions, it is unwise to rule out a thorough investigation of greater exchange-rate flexibility. It makes little sense to create problems by fixing a price when variations in price could help solve some of our problems.

THE RATE OF EXCHANGE
AND THE RATE OF INTEREST

In the good old days of the gold standard, the gold parity remained fixed but the gold flow led to conscious changes of the discount rates in the participating countries. In other words, the market economies paid for the fixing of one price by altering another price artificially, and thereby violated, strictly speaking, the domestic neutrality of money. Exchange-rate variations, had they been permitted, would have been the instant and automatic result of international payments disequilibria and would have led to instant adjustments. Fixed gold parities forced the central banks to transfer the adjustment function to interest-rate manipulations, that is, to a point at which price changes had to be induced artificially and where they interfered with domestic monetary policy. Interest rates affect the economy in its entirety (and not only in its international relations), and bring about international payments equilibrium indirectly for the most part, that is, via cumbersome changes in price and cost levels.

FIXED EXCHANGE RATES
AND CENTRAL BANK POLICIES

Before 1914, the maintenance of gold parities was not considered an unwelcome fetter upon domestic monetary policy. Employment and growth policies were unknown, and central-bank policy was guided by the simple fact that the gold reserves had to be defended to permit gold convertibility at permanently fixed parities. Domestically, the money supply was to follow the needs of trade through the rediscounting of prime commercial paper whose supply was evidence of the so-called legitimate credit demand of private business. The followers of this commercial-loan theory (among them were the architects of the Federal Reserve System) did not see that this so-called legitimate demand was a function of the rate of interest compared with anticipated rates of profit.

Had the central bankers been forced to consciously set a discount rate without the benefit of the gold-flow mechanism, the fiction of an automatic monetary policy which created an "ideal" amount of money would have collapsed. However, since the central banks had to defend their gold reserves through discount-rate changes, they were furnished with a most convenient device for determining the "correct" interest rates without being forced to think about domestic monetary policy.

Had somebody proposed flexible exchange rates on the grounds that they would permit a more neutral or a freer domestic monetary policy, he would have put the central bankers in the embarrassing position of having to find a substitute for the simple criteria of central bank policy which were the indirect result of permanently fixed gold parities.

The correctness of this interpretation is born out by Governor Strong's statement:

> "Until we get back to the automatic flow of gold which affects bank reserves and brings into play the automatic reactions from loss of reserves, I do not believe we are going to have all the satisfaction from the Federal Reserve System that we will have after that time comes. . . . I have great confidence that when the time comes to conduct these

things as they were in former years, a lot of the
need for the type of management which has to be
applied in the present situation will be eliminated.
It will be more automatic. We won't have to depend so much on judgment, and we can rely more
upon the play of natural forces and their reaction
on prices."[1]

It is amusing to note that a system which rests so much on the
fixing of a strategic price is recommended because it enables us
to rely more on the price mechanism.

Perhaps this is the best place to point out that the gold standard
system could never manage to avoid worldwide inflation and deflation because it automatically corrected only discrepancies in
national policies and not general deviations from price stability.
This weakness of the gold standard would equally be a weakness
of any system with fixed exchange rates and without conscious
integration of national economic policies. But let us remember
that the gold-standard mechanism had at least the virtue of producing some integration while some modern plans for fixed-rate
systems seem to be quite unaware of the central importance of the
adjustment problem.

THE ADJUSTABLE-PEG SYSTEM

The combined effects of price rigidities and of growing concern
with employment and growth have put an end to automatic
monetary integration but, inconsistently, not to the desire to
maintain currency convertibility at fixed exchange rates. We have
already seen that here lies the core of the liquidity problem.
Among the factors that determine the international demand for
liquidity, the degree of integration of national policies is far more
important than the growth of international trade.

The dilemma between adherence to fixed exchange rates and
to the new employment policy existed as far back as the Bretton
Woods conference. Since nobody argued for flexible exchange
rates and nobody was willing to return to the discipline of the

---

[1]Quoted by J. M. Keynes in *A Treatise on Money*, New York: Harcourt, Brace &
Co., 1930, Vol. 2, p. 305.

gold standard, the adjustable-peg system seemed to be the best compromise. The members of the International Monetary Fund were to adopt gold parities but could change these parities in case of "fundamental disequilibrium."

While it helped create the Fund, this compromise turned out to be rather disappointing. We have lost the discipline of unalterably fixed exchange rates without gaining a flexible connection between the national price systems. With insufficient coordination of national policies, fixed rates become wrong rates, they lead to a flow of reserves from deficit to surplus countries which advertise the deviation of the fixed rate from the equilibrium rate, and invite destabilizing speculations which are practically without risk. When peg adjustments are undertaken, they give a sudden shock to the whole economic system, which had operated far too long under wrong price signals.

Although these effects are now admitted, the admission has not led to greater exchange flexibility but rather to the attitude, now taken by the Fund and its more prominent members, that preferably, the exchange rates should remain permanently fixed. This attitude, however, will either have to be supported by greater international integration of domestic policies or by larger liquidity reserves if it is to become a workable policy.

POLICY MIX AS ESCAPE?

A combination of fixed rates of exchange and insufficiently integrated national policies has led to the attempt to try to do the impossible by a combination of monetary and fiscal policies that manages to reach both international payments equilibrium and full employment at stable prices.

Even within the domain of monetary policy, we can try to operate with two different interest rates. A high short-term rate, for instance, would attract foreign short-term funds to a deficit country (or prevent an outflow of domestic funds), while a low long-term rate of interest would induce domestic investment. But the fungibility of money capital is far too great to permit this easy escape. As Keynes pointed out: "Credit is like water; — whilst it may be used for a multiplicity of purposes, it is itself undifferentiated, can drip through crannies, and will remorselessly seek its own level over the whole field unless the parts of the field are rendered uncompromisingly watertight,—which in the case of credit is scarcely possible."[2] For the same reason, I do not believe that we shall be very successful in directing the flow of U.S. capital by moral suasion, unless the attempt deteriorates (or escalates) into the application of exchange controls (which would be the typical ending for any price-fixing policy).

The chances of a proper mix of monetary and fiscal policies are not much better. As proposed by Keynes, the combination of monetary and fiscal policies rested on the assumption that unemployment and balance-of-payments surplus (or, conversely, full employment and balance-of-payments deficit) would go together. In these cases, there was no conflict between monetary and fiscal policies because both could be employed in the same direction. But if we couple unemployment with balance-of-payments deficit (and full employment with balance-of-payments surplus), then monetary and fiscal policy are supposed to work in opposite directions or at cross purposes. We are now supposed to reach (or maintain) full employment and adequate growth rates through fiscal measures such as deficit spending or tax reduction programs, and at the same time to reach balance-of-payments equilibrium through increased interest rates to attract foreign capital and prevent the outflow of domestic capital. The opposite combination would have to be applied in a country which enjoys a high employment level but suffers from imported inflation: such a country is supposed to have low interest rates to attain international payments equilibrium while it would try to keep its inflation in check through restrictive tax policies.

However, an expansive fiscal policy in the unemployment country must be financed by money creation of some kind—which runs counter to the restrictive monetary policy of high interest rates. Similarly, the low-interest policy could not help but interfere with the anti-inflation policy of the surplus country. Again we have to cope with the extreme fungibility of loanable funds which will vitiate these policies and policy mixes. Mixing monetary and fiscal policies is difficult, even if the two are supposed to work in harmony, because monetary policies can be instantly applied and take effect slowly, while fiscal measures can only be modified

[2]J. M. Keynes, *Treatise*, Vol. 2, p. 319.

slowly but work much faster once they are introduced. This difficulty will prove to be even greater when the two policies work at cross purposes.

THE MAIN ARGUMENT
AGAINST FLEXIBLE EXCHANGE RATES

The main arguments against exchange-rate flexibility are well known: flexible rates, we are told, lead to competitive exchange depreciation, add a new and additional risk to international transactions, prevent the flow of capital, foster speculation, and, most importantly, are an invitation to disregard the balance-of-payments implications of domestic economic policies. Robert Triffin, for instance, accuses the advocates of flexible rates of making the exaggerated claim that "fluctuating exchange rates would automatically equalize cost disparities which derive from diverging national monetary policies, so that every country would be free to follow the most contradictory paths, without disturbing in the slightest the international payments equilibrium,"[3]

There is a grain of truth in this criticism. But we must also remember that the adjustable-peg system may be interpreted as an invitation to undisciplined behavior, or that even very large reserves could have that effect. On the other hand, the strongest argument for permanently fixed exchange rates is that they force the deficit countries to adjust their domestic policies to the average international behavior. However, this claim could never be extended to cover the surplus countries, and today, even the deficit countries refuse to play the game if it implies growing unemployment.

Since both flexible and fixed exchange rates have their good points (at least in the eyes of their advocates), but are mutually unacceptable in their pure form, a compromise must be found. Since the Bretton Woods compromise of the adjustable peg has not worked well, we meet with increasing frequency the proposal that the exchange rate be permitted to fluctuate — within a predetermined rate. This is the "band" proposal.

[3]Robert Triffin, "Die Währungsordnung des XX. Jahrhunderts" in *Inflation und Währungsordnung*, Erlenbach-Zürich und Stuttgart: Eugen Rentsch Verlag, 1963, p. 149.

THE BAND PROPOSAL

The band proposal need not be interpreted as a variation of the freely fluctuating exchange rate systems. It can just as well be classified as a proposal to widen the gold points in a gold standard system or the support points in any modern system with fixed exchange rates.

The proposal is old and was already known in 1819 when Robert Torrens recommended that "if a return were made to the gold standard, it would be desirable that the range between the gold points should not be too small." He opposed Ricardo's plan to substitute gold bullion for gold coin because "coin was a less eligible article for export," and permitted, therefore, a wider margin between gold points.[4] Jacob Viner[5] and Arthur Bloomfield[6] have shown that there always existed a desire to manipulate the gold points as alternatives or supplements to discount-rate changes. Their point is particularly interesting when we remember that the desire to widen the band existed at a time when the national price systems were still quite flexible, and rigid exchange rates accordingly much less problematic than they are today. Thus, it is not surprising that today's practitioners (though, as a rule, rejecting a widening of the band) are not unwilling to make use of exchange rate variations to the extent permitted by the Fund Agreement in Art. IV, Section 3.

Robert V. Roosa, for example, points out that "within the relatively narrow band which is, in any event, permitted under the rules of the International Monetary Fund, there must be room for market prices to demonstrate the basic strength or weakness of any currency."[7] He also states that "it is no part of our intention to disguise the basic sources of supply and demand or the various market evidences of changing needs and conditions in the international financial position of the United States or any other coun-

[4]See Jacob Viner, *Studies in the Theory of International Trade*, New York: Harper and Brothers, 1937, pp. 206–207.

[5]Viner, pp. 206–207.

[6]Arthur I. Bloomfield, *Monetary Policy under the International Gold Standard: 1880–1914*, Federal Reserve Bank of New York, October 1959, p. 52.

[7]Robert V. Roosa, "The Beginning of a New Policy," in *Factors Affecting the United States Balance of Payments,* Compilation of Studies Prepared for the Subcommittee on International Exchange and Payments. Joint Economic Committee, 87th Congress, 2d Session, Washington, 1962, p. 328.

try. We want and need the sensitive signals of changes in fundamental forces that are reflected in price fluctuations in free markets."[8]

This sounds to me like an excellent argument for the band proposal, though Roosa rejects the proposal in his recent book on the grounds that a widening of the margin would lead to competitive exchange depreciation.[9] But he may change his mind, as he recently did when he introduced exchange-value guarantees after having first rejected them as worse than useless.

There are a few encouraging signs. At one meeting of the Bellagio Conference,[10] for example, all economists present at that particular meeting favored the band proposal, though some accepted it only as a second-best choice; the recent Report of the Joint Economic Committee on *Guidelines for International Monetary Reform*[11] urges a study of the proposal; and recently the proposal was even favored by a member of the Board of Governors of the Federal Reserve System.[12]

A BRIEF SUMMARY
OF THE BAND PROPOSAL

Time does not permit a discussion of the several versions of the proposal. I shall, therefore, proceed on the basis of the following assumptions: the presently existing narrow band is to be broadened, possibly repeatedly, in a trial-and-error procedure; the par values or gold parities, however, remain fixed, that is, we assume the *de facto* abolition of the adjustable-peg system. The monetary authorities maintain perfectly elastic demand and supply conditions at the support points and are also permitted to influence the exchange rates within the band.

[8]Robert V. Roosa, "Banking and the Balance of Payments," p. 339.

[9]Robert V. Roosa, *Monetary Reform for the World Economy*, New York and Evanston, Ill.: Harper & Row, 1965, p. 27.

[10]See *International Monetary Arrangements: The Problem of Choice*. Report on the Deliberations of an International Study Group of 32 Economists, Princeton, N.J.: International Finance Section, Princeton University, 1964.

[11]*Guidelines for Improving the International Monetary System*, Report of the Subcommittee on International Exchange and Payments of the Joint Economic Committee, 89th Congress, 1st Session, Washington, 1965, pp. 19–21.

[12]Speech by Sherman J. Maisel to the Federal Reserve Bank directors in Dallas in November 1965.

It is obvious that in extreme cases of balance-of-payments disequilibria the parities may have to be changed. However, these cases should become rare exceptions, could be handled with the temporary imposition of exchange controls, and would, in any case, be no worse than the present system.

The broadening of the band works as follows:

1. It substitutes small but continuous variations around a permanently fixed parity for artificially delayed and abrupt changes. It acknowledges the present trend away from peg adjustments, but avoids rigidity.

2. The predetermined support points prevent wide exchange-rate fluctuations and serve as guideposts for a realistic amount of integration of national economic policies. The central banks will be strengthened in their difficult task of standing up against monopoly-induced inflation.

3. The band proposal does not permit countries to follow "most contradicting paths." On the contrary, it wants to achieve the greatest possible degree of exchange-rate stability compatible with reasonable domestic policies. Thus, it has the virtue of separating the proponents of flexible exchange rates into two groups: those who make unrealistic claims and want an unattainable degree of freedom for domestic policies, and flexibility. It also separates realists from dogmatists among the advocates of fixed par values.

4. Even modest exchange-rate variations will help adjust the trade balance. This adjustment process has the great virtue of being, like any market process, built-in and automatic. To the extent that it works, it avoids the difficult and often unsuccessful attempt to raise or to lower the national price levels through domestic monetary policies. We would then be able to avoid excessive unemployment in deficit countries and imported inflation in surplus countries.

5. We avoid unnecessary tampering with the short-term rate of interest. If exchange-rate variations can take care of the international equilibrium, bank-rate changes can serve domestic needs, and we do not have to employ monetary and fiscal policies at cross pur-

poses. However, Egon Sohmen goes too far when he suggests that a flexible exchange rate would strengthen domestic monetary policy to the extent that fiscal policy would become altogether unnecessary.[13]

6. Exchange-rate variations within a broadened band will lead to equilibrating capital movements. When the deficit country D has high, and the surplus country S low, interest rates, a flow of funds from S to D is equilibrating. This flow is strengthened by exchange-rate variations which are typical for this situation. D-currency will be bought by foreign creditors at a relatively cheap price in the expectation of an assured rebound.

7. Equally important is the protection against undesirable, disequilibrating capital movements. When interest rates are low in the deficit country D and high in the surplus country S, loanable funds may want to flow from D to S and increase the disequilibrium. We know from recent experience that this situation can exist. With fixed exchange rates and free convertibility, the central bank of S must acquire excessive amounts of D-currency and thus violate its own anti-inflation policy. In defending its reserves with high interest rates, country D violates its full employment policies. But the exchange-rate variations typical for this situation will counteract the disequilibrating capital flow, because the price of S-money will rise in terms of D-money and act as a counterweight to the profit from interest differentials.

8. Within the band, the exchange-rate variations can be influenced by the monetary authorities who will be able to manipulate them in such a way that, considering the given interest-rate differential, they help direct the right amount of capital flow in the right direction. The central banks gain (or strengthen) a valuable instrument of monetary policy.

9. Exchange-rate variations are a sensitive index of the momentary strength or weakness of a currency, a

[13]Egon Sohmen, *International Monetary Problems and the Foreign Exchanges,* Princeton, N.J.: International Finance Section, Princeton University, 1963.

better index than changes in liquidity reserves, and fully as effective as guidelines for monetary policy. They have the advantage of helping us avoid the need for defining a balance-of-payments deficit.

10. Use of exchange-rate variations for adjustment purposes and the correction of the flow of short-term funds would greatly reduce the need for international liquidity reserves.

CONCLUSION

The band proposal is not meant to be a panacea. But it offers a completely safe way to add flexibility to our international monetary system; it can be introduced so gradually that the central banks remain always in full control of the situation; it adds a valuable instrument to the arsenal of the monetary authority; it strengthens the adjustment mechanism in conformity with the basic principles of the market economy; its application can be adjusted to the prevailing degree of cooperation between countries or groups of countries; and its introduction would imply only minor changes of Art. IV, Section 3 of the Fund Agreement.

I do not propose a definite width for the band because I feel that only practical experience will tell us what it should be under given circumstances. But it seems to be quite obvious that a doubling of the present width (from 2 to 4 percent), introduced during a period of strength, could do no harm and might prove very useful.

As the Joint Economic Committee points out, the advantages of the band proposal "are so relevant to our present needs and the proposal [is] so evolutionary in character, that a careful exploration of offsetting disadvantages, if any, further implications, and practical problems of implementation, is called for. We must leave no stone unturned in search for improvements in the international monetary system which would permit greater freedom for international transactions, increase the ability of monetary and fiscal policies to focus on the achievement of domestic objectives, and at the same time strengthen the forces operating to restore international financial equilibrium.[14]

[14]*1965 Joint Economic Committee Report,* Washington, March 17, 1965, p. 15.

Commentary

Albert G. Hart

While it is possible to argue with Professor Halm about many details of his paper, I am bound to start off by stating my essential agreement. I agree with his diagnosis of the manner and degree in which rigidity of exchange rates may distort a country's economic policy—constituting one objective too many, which can be sought only at considerable cost measured by other objectives. I agree also with his prescription for adoption of the band proposal as a workable compromise between unbounded flexibility of exchange rates and a system of pegs. The comments which follow should therefore be taken as amplifications and amendments, not as root-and-branch criticism.

It is plain from the outset that the case for exchange flexibility could be pushed to absurd extremes. Halm does not go into the problem of the "optimum currency area." If he did, he would surely not contend that this area is so small that each household and firm should have its own monetary unit—nor even that such small geographical areas as cities, states, or Federal Reserve districts should have their own currencies with flexible rates. Hence the presumption for flexible exchange rates cannot be equated with the case for flexible prices in general, but must be limited in application; and the conditions under which exchange flexibility is desirable must be related more explicitly to policy proposals than it is in Halm's paper.

The case for flexible exchange rates has much in common with the case for protection—which should not be too surprising, since to a considerable extent, protection and exchange adjustment are measures that can be substituted for each other, as in 1965, when Britain adopted emergency import levies to stave off devaluation. Each case must rest on a demonstration that if a country trades with others on a basis of common currency (that is to say, a fixed exchange rate) and free trade, certain economic adjustments will miscarry. Given a certain inescapable mixture of competitive pressures and market imperfections, it can happen that *all* of the productive options available to a country in the short run are too costly (at the margin, when production is expanded to a full-employment level) to meet competition, and that the livelihood of a substantial proportion of the people is thus in danger. If a region within a country gets into this position, we can reject a regional solution of protection or devaluation because there are effective remedies for the underemployed labor of the region through migration within the country—and because in addition there is a national government which will take responsibility for helping the depressed area pending adjustment, and for helping to make the adjustment. Even where these remedies are strongly applied (witness Appalachia), problems may be formidable, and the adjustment may drag out so long as to blight the lives of a whole generation. Where cultural differences impede migration, and where no common government takes responsibility—where the depressed area is a country within a multinational common currency area—these problems may be completely intractable without protection or currency adjustment.[1]

Currency adjustment implies maintaining a reasonable cost relationship (whether figured in a country's own currency or in the currency of some other country) between that country's spread of products and closely competitive products of other countries. To say that a currency is overvalued is to say that the country's products are too costly relatively—or would be, at the margin, with any pattern of output-expansion to full employment. To devalue, in such circumstances, will enlarge sales both of exports and of import-substitutes. In addition, devaluation favors capital imports if it appears that the improved relationship will last long enough so that production with new capital will be at low enough operating costs to pay off an investment.

[1]It might be argued that the endangered workers could always find a livelihood by selling their personal services cheaper, and that in fact currency devaluation and protection are both indirect ways of reducing the price of labor services relative to that of products which laborers buy. But unless there is a government which (among its other responsibilities) undertakes to do all it can to prevent any avoidable redistribution of income to the disadvantage of sellers of labor services, it is socially disruptive to impose wage reductions, and the *process* of wage reduction is costly in itself. Even if protection and currency-adjustment are only to be regarded as indirect means of wage adjustment, (and I would argue they are more), they offer the advantages of "showing that the government is trying," and of adjusting wages by *resistance to increases,* with better prospects of demonstrating the necessities of the situation during the adjustment.

Extreme advocates of currency-flexibility tend to jump directly from the proposition just stated to the conclusion that if an exchange rate is left to find its own level, the level it finds will trace an optimum path through time. This jump is unwarranted; and the case for the band proposal hinges largely on the character of the logical steps left out in such a jump. In summary, the preceding argument is sufficient to show that subject to certain conditions, a rate *can* be found that will be reasonably satisfactory—though an *optimum* is hard to specify, since on examination its criteria hinge on medium-term and long-term expectations whose correctness can never be guaranteed.[2] But there is no *necessity* that market processes should yield such a reasonably satisfactory rate.

One of the implicit assumptions of the extreme advocates of flexibility is that appropriate market structures and bodies of speculative dealers either exist or will be called into existence by the announcement of a flexible-rate policy, so that governments and central banks can with confidence withdraw and leave the field to unregulated market forces. But it is conceivable, and even likely, if we think of small countries (and particularly of underdeveloped countries), that residents with enough sophistication and enough capital to be effective foreign-exchange speculators will be too few and too homogeneous in outlook to approximate the working of a free competitive market; while nonresidents who have large resources and are closely in touch with the country's currency will consist chiefly of giant companies in extractive industries. Governments and central banks will not be politically free to abdicate in favor of such forces; furthermore, if they declare their abdication, the private dealers will be unable to believe the central bank is permanently out of the market. Hence, we cannot realistically think of a market from which official intervention is permanently withdrawn—but, at most, of one from

---

[2]In the first place, if a currency is overvalued as of now, the reason may lie in what IMF calls a "temporary disequilibrium." Perhaps our country has had a crop failure, or competitive sellers of its export staples may have had a bumper crop. In such a case, the "signals" sent out by prices to producers in various countries will be falsified if the adjusted exchange rate does not give leeway for a more favorable relation of our country's costs to its wage rates in the medium-range future. In the second place, long-term prospects are crucial for capital imports (think of the case of Canada), which may have a large effect on the desirable balance of current flows of goods and services. History tells us that it is normal for both government agencies and astute businessmen to err in such judgments.

which it has been provisionally withdrawn. When we think of how dealers in such a market will learn to form their expectations, we must think of a series of drastic shocks, and of experiences which teach that the manner and level of resumption of official intervention is the most important single thing to forecast.

The problem just sketched will be particularly acute for the countries where the adjustable-peg system works worst — namely, underdeveloped countries in the numerous group where wage rates outpace the rise of productivity so strongly that prices (including the prices of foreign currencies) rise almost every year, and some years much more than others. Under the adjustable-peg system, governments of such countries tend to run overvalued currencies most of the time — presumably to avoid actions which notoriously accelerate the chronic rise in wages and living costs. Under a flexible-rate system where they cannot avoid intervening, such governments will probably move more rapidly along the one-way street of currency depreciation. But until they can overcome their fiscal weaknesses and cease to promise more than they can fulfil to a series of claimants for social programs and development projects, they will presumably still suffer the drawbacks of chronic overvaluation.[3]

However, for the countries with more disciplined internal economies which constitute the Organization for Economic Cooperation and Development, the band system of bounded exchange-flexibility offers substantial advantages, not only over a common currency or adjustable-peg system, but also over unlimited flexibility.

[3]A particularly antidevelopmental byproduct is the handicap that chronic overvaluation imposes on their export industries, except for those which have very inelastic export-supply schedules. Any manufactured export or specialty, such as wine, involves a program of market development over the years; but it is rare for such industries to have a long enough run of years when they are not priced out of export markets to carry out such market development. A related phenomenon is that import-competing industries are subject to a hazard of overwhelming price-competition from imports. Hence such import-competing industries seek forms of protection which not merely give them a price-margin but bar quantitative saturation of their markets by imports. These factors tend toward the compartmentalization of markets into one-country areas which are notoriously too small for efficiency — and toward the elimination of all competitive tests. I would urge that the common market, which is a genuine need of such areas as Latin America, does not require a common currency — but does require a currency system which avoids chronic overvaluation of currencies. Unfortunately, such a system requires internal reforms which are not yet in sight in Latin America.

To Halm's list of advantages of the band proposal, I would make one important addition regarding formation of expectations. I would argue that official intervention should take place only when the exchange rate was at one of the extremes of the band, and that firm intervention at such moments, and nonintervention when the rate was within the band, would generate experiences from which private speculators would learn that stabilizing speculation was more profitable than destabilizing speculation. Within the existing narrow-band system, a rather modest probability that devaluation may happen makes it attractive to transfer funds out of a country whose currency is endangered. If the devaluation does not take place, the loss is not painful. If it does take place, the necessity to place the new peg far enough below the old to make it clearly defensible guarantees a substantial gain. This asymmetry would be much mitigated with a wider band. Recovery of the endangered currency would entail a much greater loss prospect; while a movement to the lower border of the existing band would carry the rate a fair fraction of the way to the level likely to rule if the band is moved downward. The probability that a lower limit can be successfully defended would be enhanced by reducing the speculative bandwagon-effect against endangered currencies. Private speculators would have to pay more attention to long-term prospects — with the incidental result that their behavior would provide a more objective check of the official view of such prospects.

For underdeveloped countries with a chronic inflationary drift, as I indicated above, no currency system is apt to work well unless fiscal discipline and price-making machinery are much improved. But even in this case, the band system offers a framework within which the lessons of experience are more likely to generate helpful reactions. To break out of the pattern of chronic inflation and recurrent depreciations, such a country must some day give the bears on its currency a painful lesson. If it takes the stance of keeping exchange rates within a band rather than of defending a peg, the prospects of success are enhanced, because the incentives to transfer funds abroad on modest betting-odds of a depreciation are much reduced.

Chapter 7

Introduction

Among its other virtues, Professor Ira O. Scott, Jr.'s essay serves to readjust our historical image of the European capital market. It is difficult to reconcile our vision of the financial markets of London, Amsterdam, and Paris, the nineteenth century giants, with Scott's description of today's relatively small, highly segmented European markets. One more paradox of this comparison between the nineteenth and twentieth century is that the level of activity and the techniques employed in the European capital markets in the period since World War II represent real progress and development.

These changes are the financial counterpart of increased integration of production, for example, the coal and steel community, as well as the partial integration of the labor market. It is difficult to evaluate the many changes in widely different areas of the European economy since the war, but on Scott's evidence, it would seem that capital market integration has lagged behind the progress made elsewhere. There is no easy explanation of this phenomenon, but it is probably rooted in the desire to preserve national autonomy, with both business and national interests fearful of the effects on existing firms of a well developed, truly international capital market.

In spite of nationalistic restrictions, the European financial community has devised several ingenious ways to facilitate capital movement. The interest equalization tax imposed by the United States in 1963 has played, as Scott notes, an important role in these developments. The tax has served to drive the Europeans away from the New York financial markets and thereby forced a more rapid development of the purely European capital market. But by limiting the opportunity of using New York, the tax has restricted the development and distorted the character of the international capital market.

Scott classifies four types of debt instruments which have been developed to carry out European capital movements:

1. the single currency loan;
2. loans expressed in European units of account;
3. optional currency loans;
4. parallel loans.

Unfortunately, we have no quantitative estimates on the amounts of funds transferred by these and other techniques. Undoubtedly, they are small by the standards of the American capital market, but regardless of their amount, we hope that they mark the beginning of much larger capital flows.

RECENT INNOVATIONS
IN INTERNATIONAL
CAPITAL MARKETS

Ira O. Scott, Jr.

This paper is focused upon certain new instruments of international, long-term borrowing, and their role in the promotion of the integration of capital markets.[1] Background sections in the paper are devoted to a review of the forces leading to integration, the rationale of further liberalization, and prospects for its achievement. The central portion of the paper follows, with a description and analysis of the various instruments of indebtedness that provide alternative forms of international linkage. The paper is concluded with an evaluation of the potential role of these new security forms.

The Movement toward
Capital Market Freedom

Article 67 of the Treaty of Rome states:

> Member States shall, in the course of the transitional period and to the extent necessary for the proper functioning of the Common Market, progressively abolish as between themselves restrictions on the movement of capital belonging to persons resident in Member States and also any discriminatory treatment based on the nationality or place of residence of the parties or on the place in which such capital is invested.[2]

---

[1]This paper relies heavily on Ira O. Scott, Jr., *European Capital Markets*, Washington, D. C., Comptroller of the Currency, 1967.

[2]*Treaty Establishing the European Economic Community and Connected Documents*, Brussels: Publishing Services of the European Communities, 1958, p. 70.

The second of two directives leading to the partial implementation of Article 67 appeared in 1962.[3] The same year saw the publication of the de Voghel Report in Belgium.[4] During 1963, the Lorain Report[5] appeared in France and the Bank of Italy announced further capital market liberalization.[6] The years 1964 and 1965 saw important reforms affecting the German capital market.[7]

These manifestations within the Common Market of a sense of urgency regarding the need for the liberalization of capital movements early received the encouragement of U.S. officialdom striving to stem the outward flow of U.S. capital.[8] Such a need was felt even more sharply as the Interest Equalization Tax (IET) and the President's balance-of-payments program began to take hold.[9]

Additional stimuli to liberalization have been provided by the OECD[10] and by measures adopted in the United Kingdom as a means of increasing the attractiveness of London as a capital market center.[11]

Thus, the return to convertibility and the establishment of the European Economic Community in 1958 marked a new trend, and attempts to eliminate the remaining obstacles to full convertibility reflect to an important extent the momentum generated by

[3]"Deuxieme Directive du Conseil en date du 18 decembre 1962," *Journal Officiel des Communates Europeennes,* January 22, 1963, pp. 62–74.

[4]*Commission Gouvernementale pour L'Etude des Problemes de Financement de L'Expansion Economique, Rapport* and *Annexes Au Rapport,* Brussels: Banque Nationale de Belgique, March 31, 1962.

[5]*Rapport presente au Ministre des Finances et des Affaires Economiques par le Comite charge d'etudier le financement des investissements,* Paris: Ministere des Finances et des Affaires Economiques, May 1963.

[6]Banca d'Italia, abridged version of the *Report for the Year 1962,* Rome, May 31, 1963, p. 7,0.

[7]*International Monetary Fund Annual Report,* 1965, pp. 51–52.

[8]See also Remarks of the Honorable Douglas Dillon, Secretary of the Treasury, at the Ninth Annual Monetary Conference of the American Bankers Association, Rome, Italy, May 18, 1962.

[9]See also *Federal Reserve Bulletin,* March 1965, pp. 371–376, and July 1965, pp. 944–946; Model, Roland and Company, *Quarterly Review and Investment Survey,* Third Quarter 1965, and "Capital Outflows Slow," *Federal Reserve Bank of Chicago Business Conditions,* September 1965.

[10]Organization for Economic Cooperation and Development, *Code of Liberalization of Capital Movements,* Paris: June 1965.

[11]Bank of England, *Quarterly Bulletin,* Vol. 4, No. 4, December 1964, pp. 270–275.

those earlier moves. But the current revival of European interest in long-term lending has also been sparked by the IET and British measures taken to recapture for London its earlier role of entrepot for the world's capital flows. In addition, the urgency attached to national capital market reform within the EEC has been accentuated by developments affecting company finance. Thus, both a shifting income distribution in favor of wages and the growth in the size of individual companies increase the importance of developing the institutional paraphernalia that would facilitate external finance.

THE RATIONALE OF FURTHER LIBERALIZATION

Increased capital mobility is desirable in principle because it may promote the growth of real income. The free movement of capital, in other words, may lend to the equalization of expected real rates of return, and hence to the maximization of total output.

To some extent, the free movement of trade may serve as a substitute for the free movement of capital. For example, two countries having different factor endowments may form a customs union. The country which is rich in labor may specialize in products which are labor-intensive, while the capital-rich country may emphasize capital-intensive products. The resulting exchange of goods will raise the rates of return to those factors that are relatively abundant, and lower the rates of return to those factors which are relatively scarce. Thus, trade in commodities may tend to bring about an equalization of factor returns, even though the factors themselves are immobile.[12]

It is unlikely, however, that free trade will lead to the complete equalization of factor returns. The existence of transfer costs and

[12]See also Bertil Ohlin, *Interregional and International Trade*, Cambridge: Harvard University Press, 1935, pp. 35–37; Abba P. Lerner, "Factor Prices and International Trade," *Economica*, N. S., Vol. 19, No. 73, February 1952, pp. 1–18; J. E. Meade, *The Theory of International Economic Policy*, Vol. 2, *Trade and Welfare*, London: Oxford University Press, 1955, pp. 331–347; Richard E. Caves, *Trade and Economic Structure*, Cambridge, Mass.: Harvard University Press, 1963, pp. 76–92; and Paul A. Samuelson, *Collected Scientific Papers*, Cambridge, Mass.: Massachusetts Institute of Technology Press, 1966.

market imperfections will prevent such a result.[13] Consequently, since freedom of trade cannot be expected to eliminate differences in factor returns completely, freedom of factor movements may contribute to the achievement of this result.

It is conceivable that the free movement of capital could lead to a reduction in total output. This would be the case, for example, if social and private returns diverged because of differences in national tax, wage, or social policies.[14] However, given a coincidence of social and private returns, a movement of capital from a country where marginal returns to capital, after allowance for risks, are low, to a country where they are high will tend to increase the total output of the two countries combined.

Apart from its potential contribution to the growth of output, capital mobility may generate undesirable side effects. Short-term capital movements are notoriously subject to the whims of speculators, and to the more cautious operations of interest arbitragers who cover their exchange risk exposure. Such short-term movements are readily reversible, and, fortunately, may be controllable through the joint efforts of the monetary authorities involved. Eventually, it may be possible to eliminate them completely through the firm establishment of the fixed exchange rate system and the coordination of national monetary policies.

Long-term capital movements, to finance either direct invest-

[13]In addition to zero transfer costs and perfect competition, there are other highly restrictive conditions which must be met in order to assure factor price equalization. See also Bertil Ohlin, *Interregional and International Trade*, Cambridge, Mass.: Harvard University Press, 1935, pp. 37–39; Carl Iversen, *International Capital Movements*, London: Oxford University Press, 1935, pp. 152–156; James E. Meade, *Problems of Economic Union*, Chicago: University of Chicago Press, 1953, pp. 61–73; Bela Belassa, "The Factor-Price Equalization Controversy," *Weltwirtschaftliches Archiv*, Band 87, Heft 1, pp. 111–121; Gottfried Harberler, *A Survey of International Trade Theory*, Special Papers in International Economics, No. 1, Princeton, N.J.: International Finance Section, Princeton University, July 1961, pp. 17–19; Hans O. Lundstrom, *Capital Movements and Economic Intergration*, Leyden: A. W. Sythoff, 1961, pp. 52–53, 67–68; Bela Belassa, *The Theory of Economic Integration*, London: George Allen and Unwin, 1961, pp. 80–83; and W. M. Corden, *Recent Developments in the Theory of International Trade*, Special Papers in International Economics, No. 7, International Finance Section, Princeton, N.J.: Princeton University, March 1965, pp. 24–27.

[14]See also Bela Balassa, *The Theory of Economic Integration*, London: George Allen and Unwin, 1961, pp. 85–86; J. E. Meade, *The Theory of International Economic Policy*, Vol. 1, *The Balance of Payments*, London: Oxford University Press, 1951, p. 301; and James E. Meade, *Problems of Economic Union*, Chicago: University of Chicago Press, 1953, pp, 66, 74–83.

ment activities or portfolio acquisitions, are determined by a longer range evaluation of prospective earnings discounted for all relevant risks including devaluation. Such capital movements may generate external payments disequilibria for countries experiencing unemployment domestically. These capital flows reflect the relative unattractiveness of expected returns in these deficit countries. Monetary policies may be inappropriate in such countries. To some extent, the government of deficit countries may raise expected returns to foreign investors by financing antideflationary expenditures at home through flotations of securities abroad. However, limits attach to such a recourse.[15] And if surplus countries refuse to inflate and the deficit countries are denuded of their reserves before external equilibrium is achieved, emigration of the unemployed is the only solution—assuming that the gains from an over-all redistribution of capital are to be realized.

The principle of factor mobility has special application in the case of the Common Market. The system of fixed exchange rates within the EEC is possibly the forerunner of a single-currency system. But even within the latter, and especially within the former, disequilibrium system, the free movement of productive factors may actually facilitate the adjustment process and the simultaneous achievement of internal and external stabilization objectives. Although the Six may eventually be able to synchronize their respective monetary and fiscal policies,[16] the freedom of factor movements may still be necessary if unemployed resources are to be fully utilized in the face of rigid prices and demand shifts having a geographical dimension.[17]

The historical record of the achievement of economic freedom within the Common Market has conformed to an unusual pattern with regard to factor movements. Freedom of trade has come first; but freedom of labor movements has preceded the full

[15]See also Ira O. Scott, Jr. and Wilson E. Schmidt, "Imported Inflation and Monetary Policy," *Banca Nazionale del Lavoro Quarterly Review*, No. 71, December 1964, pp. 390–403.

[16]See also *Seventh Report on the Activities of the Monetary Committee*, European Economic Community, Brussels, February 12, 1965.

[17]See also J. E. Meade, "The Balance-of-Payments Problems of a European Free Trade Area," *Economic Journal*, Vol. 67, No. 267, September 1957, pp. 379–396; Robert A. Mundell, "A Theory of Optimum Currency Areas," *American Economic Review*, Vol. 51, No. 4, September 1961, pp. 657–665; and Ronald I. McKinnon, "Optimum Currency Areas," *American Economic Review*, Vol. 53, No. 4, September 1963, pp. 717–725.

acceptance of the freedom of capital movements. Normally, one would suppose that impediments to the movement of labor would be the last to be removed. In fact, these have been eliminated, while capital-movement freedom still awaits a closer alignment of social and economic policies.

PROSPECTS FOR INTEGRATION[18]

The rationale for integrating national capital markets—unlike the implementation of a program designed to achieve such integration—is relatively easy to delineate. The importance of the degree of freedom of currency convertibility achieved since World War II is not to be minimized. However, the fact is that full convertibility simply does not exist, except, perhaps, in the case of the German mark. One need only cite as evidence the continued surveillance of capital market flotations by Banks of Issue, increased reliance upon "cooperation" as an international adjustment mechanism, the IET, and so on.

Within the EEC, prospects for full integration are far from bright. Two directives drawn up by the Commission have received the approval of the Council of Ministers, but the provisions of a third and crucial "final" directive are still being debated. The first two directives freed direct investment, movements of personal capital, and short- and medium-term credits to finance trade. The third directive goes the whole way by calling for the abolition of

[18]On the prospects for integrating capital markets, see Claudio Segre, "Capital Movements in the European Economic Community," *Banca Nazionale del Lavoro Quarterly Review,* No. 60, March 1962, pp. 3–27; Charles P. Kindleberger, "European Economic Integration and the Development of a Single Financial Center for Long-Term Capital," *Weltwirtschaftliches Archiv,* Band 90, Heft 2, 1963, pp. 13–208; Peter B. Kenen, "Towards an Atlantic Capital Market," *Lloyds Bank Review,* No. 69, July 1963, pp. 15–30; "The International Role of Private Capital," *First National City Bank Monthly Economic Letter,* September 1963; Claudio Segre, "Financial Markets in the EEC.: Prospects for Integration," *Moorgate and Wall Street,* Autumn 1963, pp. 38–62; Claudio Segre, "Foreign Bond Issues in European Markets" *Banca Nazionale del Lavoro Quarterly Review,* No. 68, March 1964, pp. 3–47; J. S. G. Wilson, "The Internationalisation of Capital Markets," *Three Banks Review,* No. 62, June 1964, pp. 3–24; Karl Blessing, *Integration and its Monetary Problems,* an address before the European Convention of Chemical Engineering, June 27, 1964, Frankfurt; "As a Borrower Sees It," *The Economist,* September 19, 1964; and Oscar L. Altman, "The Integration of European Capital Markets," *Journal of Finance, Papers and Proceedings,* 20, No. 2, May 1965, pp. 209–221.

discriminatory laws and practices related to securities flotations, their quotation on national stock exchanges, and their purchase by financial institutions.

The chief obstacle to the achievement of full capital market freedom does not, as one might be led to believe, lie in the fear on the part of national monetary authorities that they will lose control of the balance of payments. Rather, there is a more subtle, yet more profound, problem which is actually inherent in the definition of discrimination. All involved are agreed that all discrimination of treatment on the basis of the nationality or place of residence of the security issuer should be removed. But would such removal impart true freedom to the capital market? Not at all. Take the French case. In France, domestic as well as foreign securities must be authorized by the government before they can be issued on the French market. The French could then readily accede to a Community rule for nondiscrimination, but at the same time reserve the right to ration capital to Frenchman and foreigner alike *according to the criterion that the proceeds of the issue should be consistent with the objectives of the French Plan.* Clearly, nondiscrimination in a quite literal sense does not really open up the French capital market to the foreigner.

ALTERNATIVE FORMS OF INTERNATIONAL LINKAGE

While De Gaulle sulks, the City remains an EFTA and Commonwealth preserve, and New York hides behind the IET barrier, enterprising investment bankers have attempted by various ingenious devices to make some progress toward bridging the gaps between the national capital markets of the world. These links have been forged through the creation of new kinds of foreign debt instruments, four of which will now be discussed.[19]

[19]General treatments of these new security forms may be found in Claudio Segre, "Foreign Bond Issues in European Markets," *Banca Nazionale del Lavoro Quarterly Review*, No. 68, March 1964, pp. 3–47; Jean O. M. van der Mensbrugghe, "Foreign Issues in Europe," *International Monetary Fund Staff Papers*, July 1964, pp. 327–334; "Start towards a European Capital Market," *Neue Zuricher Zeitung*, January 7, 1965; "Recent Innovations in European Capital Markets," *Federal Reserve Bank of New York Monthly Review*, January 1965; and David Williams, "The Development of Capital Markets in Europe," *International Monetary Fund Staff Papers*, 12, No. 1, March 1965, pp. 37–62.

Single currency loans

With the exception of a 20-year bond, denominated in Swiss francs, and offered in London by the City of Copenhagen, single currency loans have been denominated in U.S. dollars. These foreign dollar bonds were introduced in May 1963 with a private placing by the Belgian Government of $20 million in three-year bonds. It was the first loan not denominated in sterling placed in London since World War II. In the following year and a half, such borrowing countries or groups as Japan, Denmark, Norway, Italy, the European Coal and Steel Community, Austria, Finland, the European Investment Bank, Belgium, Portugal, the Council of Europe, and Israel raised over half a billion dollars in forty different loans denominated in U.S. dollars. These loans were arranged and placed, for the most part, through the London market. The dollar bond has generally been a 15–20 year maturity, and has carried a coupon of 5 1/2 to 6 1/2 percent. The major borrowers have been central governments, municipalities, and industrial firms of the Scandinavian countries, Finland, and Japan. Japanese issues alone have accounted for a quarter of the total.

The concept "market of issue" is vague in the case of these flotations, because the securities may actually be sold in several countries. It is said that they were issued in London because the issuing consortia were usually managed by London merchant banks. The securities are regularly listed on the London and Luxembourg stock exchanges. Subscriptions for the delivery of the securities would occur in Luxembourg. Service of the securities would be provided in major European financial centers and New York. The laws of the issuer's country governs the relationships among the issuer, the bondholders, and the underwriters. And, although issued in London, they would always be placed with residents of countries other than Great Britain because of the premium the U.K. residents must pay for investment dollars.

The characteristic of the single-currency loan that accounts for its feasibility and viability is the breadth of the appeal which the currency has for investors who are residents of different countries. This appeal is based on the anticipated long-term strength of the currency and upon its current marketability. Both of these factors facilitate its role as a medium for international lending. The position of the United States in the world power structure and the widespread use of its currency as a means of settling transactions in international commerce account for the popularity of the U.S. dollar. Similarly, the pivotal role of Switzerland in the structure of international financial relationships accounted for the use of the Swiss franc as a loan medium.

Shortcomings associated with the use of the single-currency loan stem from possible adverse repercussions upon the balance of payments of the country whose currency is being used. The effect may be unfavorable if interest rates are higher for the foreign loan than for domestic loans of comparable quality. On the other hand, the mechanism may tie up currency that would otherwise be presented by a foreign central bank for payment in gold. Swiss authorities were apparently pessimistic regarding the potential effect of the use of the Swiss franc, for they exerted sufficient pressure upon foreign central banks and underwriters to prevent a repetition of the one single-currency loan denominated in Swiss francs.

Loans Expressed in European Units of Account[20]

The search for ways to attract long-term funds has also led to the flotation of bonds denominated in European units of account. There have been several such issues, the first issue appearing in February 1961. These issues, with maturities ranging from fifteen to twenty years and with coupons between 5 1/2 and 6 percent, have usually been offered through Luxembourg and with a Belgian or Luxembourg bank heading the underwriting syndicate. U.S. underwriters have also participated in some of these issues.

Units of account were first used in the bookkeeping of the former European Payments Union (EPU).[21] The unit of account is composed of seventeen European currencies.[22] These currencies serve as a common denominator for issues floated in several

---

[20]Specific references to unit-of-account loans include Lombard, "European Unit of Account—the Big Question Mark," *The Economist,* November 6, 1963; Jean O. M. van der Mensbrugghe, "Bond Issues in European Units of Account," *International Monetary Fund Staff Papers,* November 1964, pp. 446–455; and Fernand Collin, *The Formation of a European Capital Market,* Brussels: The Kredietbank (no date).

[21]One UA = 0.88871 grams of fine gold = $1.00 US. The EPU Functioned until the advent of general convertibility in 1958.

[22]Austrian schillings, Belgian francs, British pounds, Danish kroner, German marks, French francs, Greek drachmas, Icelandic kronur, Irish pounds, Italian lire, Luxembourg francs, Netherlands guilders, Norwegian kroner, Portuguese escudos, Swedish kronor, Swiss francs, and Turkish liras.

markets and provide a limited guarantee against exchange rate fluctuations for debtors and creditors with liabilities and claims in foreign currencies.

The unit of account is an entirely artificial yardstick that is used solely to measure the value of contractual loan obligations — it is not a means of exchange. The unit-of-account formula has assumed several different forms. It has always provided that the value of the unit would change only if the values of all 17 reference currencies changed. However, under the terms of the more recent loan agreements, at least two-thirds of these changes must be in the same direction. Under these conditions, the value of the unit — and hence of the securities denominated in these units — would be adjusted, after a lapse of two years, in the same direction and proportion as the currency among the two-thirds (or more) that had changed the least. The protection afforded by this complex formula is, of course, not absolute. It does not cover the borrower if his currency is devalued, or the lender if his currency is revalued, vis-à-vis all the others. Nor is the lender insured against a uniform devaluation of all of the component currencies in terms of gold.[23]

In some cases, subscriptions could be made in any of the seventeen currencies. In other cases, subscriptions were restricted to a few of the more important currencies. The currency in which interest and amortization payments should be made could be chosen freely by the bondholder from among the seventeen currencies.

Designed to lure lenders into international lending, the unit-of-account formula suffers from the burden it places on the borrower. In other words, the presumption is that there is some risk that the borrower's currency will be devalued, and any protection afforded the lender clearly imposes costs on the borrower.

From the lender's point of view, the formula has been widely criticized as being unduly cumbersome and complex, thus failing to attract a broad investor base.

Optional Currency Loans

Another type of multiple-currency loan has provided the lender with an exchange option. That is, the lender may request pay-

---

[23]Such a guarantee would in any case be regarded as tantamount to a gold clause and therefore be illegal in many countries.

ment of interest and amortization—usually with only a few days notice—in one or more currencies, including or excluding the currency in which the issue is denominated, at an exchange rate based on the parity existing at the time of issue.

A few optional loans have been floated by international consortia in recent years. Thus, in 1960 and 1961, Banque Lambert managed syndicates underwriting Belgian issues denominated either in U.S. dollars or German marks. In 1964, the Government of Finland borrowed forty million marks in Germany, with investors being given the option of receiving payment in either German marks or U.S. dollars. In the same year, the city of Turin raised four million British pounds through London with a payment option in sterling or German marks. Sometimes dollar-mark issues have been extended to include other currencies such as the Dutch florin and the Belgian franc.

The optional currency formula is notably attractive to investors by virtue of the protection it extends against exchange risks. Moreover, institutional investors may regard such bonds as being in their national currency when this currency is included among the options.

By the same token, the exchange option may be extremely burdensome to borrowers. In effect, the exchange risk is multiplied by the number of optional currencies. For example, debtors with loans outstanding that were denominated in German marks and Dutch florins had to accept a 5-percent increase in their debt with the revaluation of these currencies in 1961.

Parallel Loans[24]

The most recent addition to the international investment banker's tool kit is the parallel loan. In this instance, an international loan is divided into tranches to be placed simultaneously in different markets at—if market conditions dictate—different rates of interest.

The first parallel loan was placed in 1965 for Ente Nazionale per l'Energia Elettrica (ENEL), the Italian electricity monopoly.

[24]See Herman J. Abs, *The European Security and New Issues Market with a View to International Financing*, a report presented to the Institut International d'Etudes Bancaires, Albert Plage, Knokke, Belgium, November 6, 1964; "Europe's Capital Markets, One Loan in Six Centres," *The Economist*, June 26, 1965; and "First European Parallel Loan," *International Financial News Survey*, Vol. 17, No. 27, July 9, 1965.

Separate tranches were offered in each of the six Common Market countries, all bonds carrying a 15 year maturity and a 6-percent coupon. Tranches of 100 million German marks ($25 million), 25 million Dutch guilders ($6.9 million), and 30 million Luxembourg francs ($0.6 million) were offered publicly at 95 for a 6.52 percent yield to maturity. The Belgian tranche of 100 million Belgian francs ($2 million) was placed privately on terms presumed to have been similar to those governing the German, Dutch, and Luxembourg tranches.

The Italian tranche of 100,000 million lire ($160 million) was issued at 96. However, the practice of Italian state enterprises, whereby lenders receive a 1.2 percent premium above par at redemption, brings this yield into line.

The only effective variation in issue price was for the French tranche of a hundred million French francs ($20.3 million), which was offered at 95 1/2 for a 6.475 yield to maturity. This yield differential made some allowance for the fact that interest rates in the French bond market were somewhat lower than in Belgium, Luxembourg, Germany, or Italy. On the other hand, no such allowance was made for the tranche issued in The Netherlands, where interest rates were the lowest among the Six.

The strength of the parallel loan technique lies precisely in the recognition it gives to investor bias in favor of the local currency. This bias is exploited at the same time that economics of scale are achieved through the flotation of a large loan through several capital markets, none of which could absorb the entire issue alone.

The most obvious potential defect in the parallel-loan proposal lies in the danger of a concentration of subscriptions in the highest yielding tranche. A related hazard involves the susceptibility of the arrangement to speculative attacks on a particular currency. Any speculative movement against one of the currencies would be thrown into prominence by the resulting price movements of the affected tranches.

CONCLUSION

Whenever societies place obstacles before a national economic process, someone will devise a means of circumventing those obstacles. Thus, recent innovations in European capital markets comprise the response of that economic region to the restrictions inherent in the continuation of nationalistic policies with respect to controls over capital movements. Much progress has been made in the pursuit of the goals of economic integration within the EEC. However, the area of intra-community capital movements will undoubtedly be the last to be freed. Moreover, the U.K., Switzerland, Sweden, and so on, are still outside the Common Market. Consequently, there has been a pressing need for alternative forms of linkage.

An evaluation of the potential role of these new financing techniques need not await a judgment as to which form or forms will eventually dominate the scene. Therefore, they will be considered as a totality.

To begin with, a caveat is in order; namely, that these new financing devices, whatever their merits, can never serve as fully effective substitutes for the freeing and strengthening of Europe's capital markets. Nevertheless, these financial innovations undoubtedly provide a net contribution to the mobilization of financial capital. Several factors account for this contribution. First, these flotations involve the marshalling of investment banking resources, providing an international network of distribution channels. Second, and related to the first factor, are the economies in flotations costs that these rather larger issues permit. Third, the introduction of these techniques probably contributes to the "freedom" of capital flows. Obviously, if none of these devices are used, an outright relaxation of capital market controls is implied.

Commentary

Wilson E. Schmidt

My comments are, by and large, concerned with a few small points. Obviously, Professor Scott has performed a useful service in his summary of recent innovations and I would not question his facts.

He does, however, hint that the Interest Equalization Tax has stimulated the integration of European capital markets. In this view he is joined by others. However, I would like to express a doubt about this tax. Before the tax, a substantial portion—some guesses run as high as 50 percent—of foreign dollar public issues sold in New York were bought by foreigners. In this way Europeans (and others) avoided their own inefficient markets and presumably shifted funds from low to high yields within Europe. Much of this traffic seems now lost or shifted to London. The loss of New York, once truly part of the European capital market, cannot be viewed as helping to integrate markets.

Scott might well have mentioned the role of multinational companies in improving the allocation of capital within Europe. As these firms widen their ties among countries and shift funds among their branches, much the same kind of integration takes place as he has in mind. Unfortunately, I cannot quantify the flows, but, at the margin, nothing is insignificant, so that this area might well bear future research.

He might have considered a brief discussion of the role of the Euro-dollar market in integrating capital markets in the Atlantic Community. So long as there is any communication between the short-, medium-, and long-term markets within countries, integrating any one of them tends to integrate the others. The last time that Oscar Altman of the IMF counted them, there were 400 commercial and private banks in the Euro-dollar market. The dollar deposits came from 25 countries and the final users resided in at least 35 countries. To be sure, much of the Euro-dollar business is concerned with the financing of international trade, but the development of the Euro-dollar market for the purpose of integration of markets probably eases pressure on domestic markets. Furthermore, large amounts of Euro-dollars have been employed for strictly domestic purposes in Germany, Italy, and the U.K., and smaller amounts have been so employed in Belgium. Finally, Euro-dollars are not necessary short-term dollars so the direct impact is not limited to the short-term market. This argument has an interesting parallel. Scott speaks of the achievement of integration in respect to movements of labor. All of the paraphernalia of the EEC in support of such integration is welcome, but quasi-clandestine movements of labor among European countries under the cover of tourist status have probably been a far more important factor in the integration of the labor markets.

I would also suggest, though far more tentatively, that it might be worthwhile to examine the accounts of the European Coal and Steel Community to determine if it has not served to integrate European capital markets both in its own flotations and in shifting its funds. Discussions with the ECSCS staff gave me this impression, but I have not tested the hypothesis.

While we are on the topic of integration of capital markets, the purpose of which is to achieve a better allocation of resources, it might be well to look at the operations of the European Development Fund and the European Investment Bank.

Scott suggests that short-term capital movements are "readily controllable," and he believes that it should be possible to eliminate them completely through the firm establishment of the fixed exchange rate system. I doubt this. I know of no chance, apart from political union with all the trappings implied, that can make the promise of fixed exchange rates credible.

Chapter 8

Introduction

With the demise of the gold standard in the 1920s and early 1930s, the nations of the world have struggled, in the words of William Jennings Bryan, to avoid being "crucified on a cross of gold." Currently, the world's central bankers are, through discussions, painfully attempting to forge a solution to the problem of insufficient sources of gold reserves to support an expanding volume of trade under conditions of fixed exchange parities among the world currencies. Most of the proposed solutions involve increasing the supply of monetary reserves by using various forms of supplemental reserve units. How to increase the supply of international currency and avoid the discipline of the discredited international gold standard is the topic of the day.

Professor Peter Kenen, in the paper that follows, urges a broader approach than one that simply involves increasing the supply of monetary reserves by advocating steps toward the creation of a supranational monetary system. He argues that a supranational monetary system must contain mechanisms for coordinating stabilization policies among deficit and surplus countries so that harsh internal adjustments within individual countries can be anticipated and avoided.

Kenen advocates the delegation of discretionary authority to managers of any supranational monetary system. He is convinced that any automatic system is doomed to failure because of the wide variety of forces causing payments disturbances which can only be adjusted in today's world by varied means. In some cases, labor and capital mobility may be counted upon to counter disturbances, while in others, particularly in countries whose trade is not widely diversified, adjustment is much more difficult. Fiscal and monetary measures or flexible exchange rates may suffice to achieve some solutions but alternative devices may be needed in other cases. To Kenen, discretion among alternative courses of action is an essential ingredient in any world monetary system.

In setting up guidelines for any future system, Kenen stresses the need to confront and reconcile national objectives, to coordinate national policies pertaining to domestic demand, and to offer sufficient resources to finance stubborn, persistent deficits. He rejects the conservative emphasis upon automatic discipline imposed by cutting off resources and substitutes a variety of alternative discretionary policies, backed up by authority, to provide the desired adjustments which can facilitate world trade and keep income growing steadily.

In short, Kenen argues that current approaches to payments equilibrium mismate "instruments and aims" to the detriment of the international monetary system. The realignment of aims and instruments under a managed world currency system could, hopefully, induce countries to pursue measures of adjustment which can be coordinated with policies of other countries.

TOWARD A SUPRANATIONAL MONETARY SYSTEM

Peter B. Kenen

After a decade of debate, academic and official, the leading governments are finally agreed on the need to create international reserves in a more orderly way. This agreement, to be sure, is still incomplete. The several official proposals for reform of the monetary system differ importantly, and the differences will not be easy to resolve. Yet the very decision to negotiate on rival plans is itself a major achievement. Less than five years ago, the principal American spokesman could argue that the reserve-creating capabilities of the present system "are clearly as promising as any of the more familiar proposals,"[1] and three years ago, the Group of Ten still believed that "there is no immediate need to reach a decision as to the introduction of a new type of reserve asset."[2]

Even now, however, the official dialogue on reform is too narrowly focused on technical questions — on the "backing" for the new reserve asset and its relationship to gold, on the size of the

[1]Robert V. Roosa, "Assuring the Free World's Liquidity," Federal Reserve Bank of Philadelphia, *Business Review, Supplement,* September 1962, p. 12.

[2]*Ministerial Statement of the Group of Ten: Annex Prepared by Deputies,* reprinted in the *Federal Reserve Bulletin,* August 1964, p. 988. The Group of Ten includes Belgium, Canada, France, Germany, Italy, Japan, the Netherlands, Sweden, the United Kingdom and the United States.

new fiduciary issue and its distribution. There has not been sufficient systematic discussion of basic aims or of the connection between new reserve creation and the evolution of the world economy. Too often, of course, a debate on first principles results in a rotund declaration devoid of operational content. But international reserves are, at most, time-buying aids to the execution of national policies, and decisions affecting the creation of reserves cannot be made wisely and harmoniously unless there is agreement regarding the proper deployment of national policies affecting international financial stability.

No such agreement prevails today, and none is in prospect.[3] Indeed, the disagreement on methods of reserve creation testifies to deep disarray on principles. The sharp cleavage between "anglo-saxon" and "continental" views arises because of a difference in policy aims and, in particular, because many Europeans hold that the United States and United Kingdom are dangerously tolerant of inflation.[4] Accordingly, the continental countries are determined to limit reserve creation very strictly, even among the industrial countries. They also oppose reserve creation by the International Monetary Fund, because they distrust the financial policies of the less-developed countries, who have a voice in IMF decisions. A second disagreement, concerning the interconvertibility of reserve assets and their relationship to gold, likewise reflects an imperfect faith in other countries' policies. The French demand that new reserves be closely linked to gold derives in part from a belief that every country should be empowered to veto an expansion of world reserves, by exchanging the new reserve asset for gold, so as to limit other countries' deficits.

My chief point is that the case for a reform of the monetary system and the mountain of monetary plans confronting us

[3]A detailed study of the "adjustment process" has been undertaken by the OECD. But the study of adjustment policies has been segregated from the planning of reform, as though the two problems were separate.

[4]The continental fear of inflation, may, in turn, reflect experience far more than dogma. One can, in fact, interpret much of the recent transatlantic dialogue on the U.S. payments problem in simple historical terms. The canons of central banking call upon deficit countries to deflate, accepting unemployment, and on surplus countries to inflate, accepting higher prices. The memories of those who make policy, however, cause them to rebel against this prescription. Twentieth-century American history has taught the United States to fear unemployment as the gravest economic evil, while twentieth-century European history has taught the continental countries to fear inflation above all.

should be appraised in the light of first principles.[5] Because the international monetary system must serve the international economy, its designers must pay painstaking attention to the strengths and weaknesses of that economy—and to the international political environment within which the monetary system has to function. Before writing a new constitution for the international monetary system, we must first identify the potential threats to international financial stability—to ask how payments problems can and may arise. Next, we must ask if those threats can be forestalled, whether by deliberate changes in national policies or by automatic adaptations in the market place. Finally, we must ask how the disturbances that actually emerge, as deficits or surpluses, can and should be met, and what role reserves should play in the insuing process of adjustment. In other words, we have to ask how the creation of international money is most apt to affect the speed and the quality of policy responses in the constituent national economies.

In order to answer these questions, we shall have to wander in a very arid wilderness. To identify the most important attributes of a supranational monetary system, we shall have to pick our way through the modern theory of the balance of payments, a desert no less dry or forbidding than Sinai itself.[6]

Modern balance-of-payments theory identifies several separate disturbances afflicting a nation's external transactions. It argues, moreover, that each such disturbance has to be met by a unique constellation of policies if the nation is to honor its domestic commitments to full employment, stable prices, and steady

[5]For compact summaries of the major plans, see R. G. Hawkins and S. E. Rolfe, "A Critical Survey of Plans for International Monetary Reform," C. J. Devine Institute of Finance, New York University, *Bulletin*, November 1965, and F. Machlup, *Plans for Reform of the Monetary System*, Princeton, N.J.: International Finance Section, 1964; also, *Report of the Study Group on the Creation of Reserve Assets*, Rome: Banca d'Italia, 1965.

[6]The exposition that follows will draw heavily on the writings of J. E. Meade, *The Balance of Payments*, London: Oxford University Press, 1961, and H. G. Johnson (especially his "Toward a General Theory of the Balance of Payments," in *International Trade and Economic Growth*, London: George Allen & Unwin, 1958). It will also borrow from recent work on the theory of optimum currency areas (see especially, R. A. Mundell, "A Theory of Optimum Currency Areas," *American Economic Review*, Vol. 51, No. 4, September 1961, pp. 657–664, and R. I. McKinnon, "Comment," *American Economic Review*, Vol, 53, No. 4, September 1963, pp. 717–725, and on Richard Cooper's study of Atlantic economic policy, soon to be published by the Council on Foreign Relations.

growth. To illustrate this principle, I shall ask you to contemplate a simple two-country world in which there are no international movements of labor or capital, and in which money wage rates cannot be reduced except by raising unemployment to intolerable heights.

These suppositions can be stated formally, using the familiar identities of national-income accounting:

$$Y = E + X - M$$
$$B = X - M$$

where Y is national income, E is national expenditure (including its import content), X and M are exports and imports, respectively, and B is the balance of trade in goods and services.[7] To start, let

$$Y = Y*$$
$$B = B* = 0$$

where $Y*$ is the full-employment or "target" level of national income and $B*$ is the "target" balance of foreign trade. Next, write out changes in E, X and M as:

$$dE = dE^a + (1 - s)\, dY$$
$$dX = dX^a$$
$$dM = dM^a + m(dY)$$

where s is the "marginal propensity to save," m is the "marginal propensity to import," and the arguments dE^a, dX^a and dM^a are income-autonomous disturbances affecting domestic expenditure, exports, and imports. Combining these three statements with the definitions of Y and B, one obtains the conventional Keynesian multipliers for an open economy:[8]

[7]If there are no international movements of capital, balanced foreign trade implies balanced foreign payments.

[8]These formulae ignore "foreign repercussions" because they treat changes in each country's exports as if they were fully autonomous rather than dependent on changes in the other country's income. But the formulae with foreign repercussions, though much more complicated, convey the same messages as those in the text. The more important defect of these formulae, to which I shall return in a subsequent note, pertains to their application at full employment. If labor is fully employed, an increase in money income will be fully dissipated in rising prices, not manifest in rising real output and income, dY. Price and real-income changes will, of course, have similar effects on the trade balance (albeit by different routes), but may call for somewhat different policy responses.

$$dY = \frac{dE^a + dX^a - dM^a}{m + s}$$

$$\frac{dE^a + dB^a}{m + s}$$

$$dB = \frac{-m(dE^a) + s(dB^a)}{m + s}$$

If $Y = Y^*$ and $B = B^*$ to start, any autonomous change in domestic spending, dE^a, or in foreign trade, dB^a, will bring about an unwanted change in Y or B, and any such departure from the target values will require a change in national policies.

Notice, however, that the two disturbances lead to dissimilar changes in the trade balance. An autonomous decline in domestic spending ($dE^a < 0$), occasioned perhaps by a change in monetary policy, government spending, or tax rates, will depress national income ($dY < 0$) and will cause a surplus in the trade balance ($dB > 0$). An autonomous decrease of exports or increase of imports ($dB^a < 0$), occasioned by a change in tastes or costs of production, will also depress national income, but will cause a deficit in the trade balance ($dB < 0$). The two types of disturbance will consequently call for somewhat different changes in national policies.

A country confronting a decline in domestic expenditure can always prevent an unwanted fall in its national output and income by deliberately inducing a shift in the trade balance — by devaluing its currency to stimulate exports and reduce imports or by erecting new trade barriers. Indeed, a shift in the trade balance, dB^a, equal in absolute size to the shortfall of domestic spending, dE^a, would precisely suffice to stabilize national income. Following these policies, however, the country would drive its trade balance further into surplus, and the other country's balance further into deficit, for dE^a and dB^a take opposite signs in the trade-balance equation.[9] The efficient response to a decline in expenditure is, then, directly to combat that decline by cutting interest rates or tax rates, or raising government expenditure, for these actions would prevent or reverse the change in national income and in the trade balance.

---

[9]The course of action described here, often described as a "beggar-my-neighbor" policy, was frequently pursued and roundly condemned during the inter-war period.

A country confronting an autonomous decrease of exports or increase of imports can prevent a fall in national income by inducing an expansion of domestic expenditure—by adjusting its interest rates or fiscal policies to foster a countervailing dE^a. Doing so, however, the country would compound its external problem by driving the trade balance further into deficit. In this case, the most efficient policy response is to offset the trade-balance disturbance directly by changing the exchange rate or altering trade controls. If successful in correcting the trade balance, these policies would also stabilize national income and employment, for the initial dB^a would be cancelled from both multipliers.[10]

These simple principles of economic policy are not new or controversial, and are applied, with occasional lapses, by most major countries. But if they are relevant to national conduct, they should also influence the design and appraisal of monetary plans. If, for example, trade-balance disturbances are frequent or severe, and countries abjure the use of trade controls, the monetary system should surely countenance changes in exchange rates. Yet devaluations and revaluations are not regarded as normal policy measures. On the contrary, they are treated as remedies of last resort, not to be used unless all other policies fail.[11] What is worse, an emerging official consensus strongly favors the rapid correction of deficits and corresponding limitations on reserve creation, so that deficit countries will be compelled to take early action. This prescription would make sense if deficits were always due to excess demand, but when deficits are due to trade-balance dis-

---

[10]A change in the exchange rate would be equally efficient in two other cases: (1) As suggested in an earlier note, an autonomous increase in domestic expenditure will increase wages and prices when the economy is fully employed to start, and once they are raised, prices are not cut back easily. In consequence, a temporary rise in domestic expenditure may leave in its wake an enduring deterioration in the trade balance, requiring a change in the exchange rate. (2) An autonomous outflow of capital, hitherto excluded by the assumption that there are no international factor movements, requires an improvement in the trade balance to prevent an imbalance in over-all payments, and this can be accomplished by devaluation. In this second case, however, devaluation is an efficient response but is not sufficient; it must be accompanied by a reduction of domestic expenditure to stabilize income as the trade balance improves. Alternatively, the monetary authorities may choose to stem the capital outflow by raising interest rates, but must then relax their fiscal policies to offset the effects of higher interest rates on domestic spending and national income; on this point, see R. A. Mundell, "The Appropriate Use of Monetary and Fiscal Policy for Internal and External Stability," International Monetary Fund, *Staff Papers,* Vol. 9, No. 1, March 1962 pp. 70 ff.

[11]See, for example, *Ministerial Statement,* paragraph (7), pp. 978–979.

turbances, and exchange rates are fixed, the deficit countries may have to reduce their internal wages and prices relative to those abroad, thereby generating a countervailing increase of exports and decrease of imports. Such a reduction in wages and prices calls for a restriction of domestic demand. The prompt elimination of a payments deficit caused by a trade-balance disturbance may therefore require the creation of more unemployment than prudence or conscience can allow. The process of adjustment to a trade-balance change has instead to be spread out, and an ample financing of the intervening deficit will be required, even by the manufacture of new reserves. In brief, the international monetary system has to deal differently with different disturbances—to foster efficient national policies.

To amplify and qualify this proposition, I should like to draw an extended analogy between international payments adjustment and interregional payments adjustment. The separate regions of a single country will, at times, run deficits in their external trade and cannot resort to devaluation or to trade controls. In these ways, they resemble the members of an "integrated" international economy committed to the maintenance of fixed exchange rates and freely flowing trade. Countries, however, are different from regions in important respects, so that a supranational monetary system has to differ in design and operation from a national monetary system.

To pursue this analogy, I shall use the same simple model as before, treating dY, dB, dB^a, and dE^a as changes in national or regional income, trade, and expenditure. I shall also extend the model to take fleeting account of the labor and capital movements that may result from various disturbances.

If payments experience were dominated by expenditure changes, dE^a's rather than dB^a's, there would be a unique relationship between the internal and external problems of countries or regions. Assuming, once again, that those countries or regions begin with full employment and balanced trade, those that experience inflation will display trade-balance deficits, while those that experience deflation will experience trade-balance surpluses. In such a world, moreover, labor and capital mobility cannot substantially mitigate the internal and external problems caused by the disturbances. If expenditure were increased in one country or region, the corresponding shortage of labor could be fully satisfied by an inflow of labor, but other countries or regions would then experience labor shortages (a decrease of supply with unchanged demand). Labor mobility, much like trade itself, serves merely to diffuse an expenditure disturbance. An inflow of capital, by contrast, would be quite helpful from the external standpoint, but would exacerbate the internal problem. An autonomous increase of spending in one country or region, driving up interest rates, would attract outside funds and finance all or part of the trade-balance deficit. The inflow, however, would also sustain bank liquidity in the deficit country or region, short-circuiting the automatic monetary processes that would otherwise serve to curb the increase of expenditure.[12]

The combinations inflation-*cum*-deficit and deflation-*cum*-surplus are common occurences in international monetary annals. They are, indeed, so familiar that central bankers are apt to recommend restrictive policies whenever a country lapses into deficit. But one would not expect to encounter these combinations as frequently in interregional payments experience. The regions of a single country are subject to a common national monetary policy and, in substantial degree, to a common fiscal policy, leaving little scope for disparate changes in regional expenditure.

There are twelve Federal Reserve Banks in the United States, but their separate powers are sharply circumscribed by law and practice. They cannot run the monetary printing press at will to generate independent trends in expenditure. The several states have somewhat more fiscal autonomy; they can tax and spend on their own initiative. Yet this autonomy is also circumscribed, partly by legal and market constraints on the states' ability to borrow, partly by the internal mobility of American capital and labor which threatens to punish any community whose tax rate or spending on public services moves far out of line. Furthermore, Federal taxes and spending, being much larger, tend to swamp state-by-state differences,[13] while the Federal tax system tends also

[12]The capital movement would likewise work to raise interest rates in the outside world, but this would be salutary, not harmful, because it would compress effective demand, thereby offsetting the increase in demand for the outside world's goods occasioned by the increase of import demand in the deficit country or region.

[13]The geographic distribution of Federal expenditures is, of course, subject to change, but these variations are best regarded as autonomous changes in the governmental demand for regional exports, so as to separate the macroeconomic and microeconomic aspects of fiscal policy. For a more detailed discussion of these and related issues, see G. H. Borts and J. L. Stein, *Economic Growth in a Free Market*, New York: Columbia University Press, 1964; and J. T. Romans, *Capital Exports and Growth among U.S. Regions*, Middletown, Conn.: Wesleyan University Press, 1965.

to average out regional differences in effective tax rates by allowing the deduction of state and local taxes from income subject to Federal tax.

A supranational monetary system would also have to align expenditure trends in its constituent national economies in order to combat the combinations of inflation-*cum*-deficit and deflation-*cum*-surplus. It would have to accomplish a coordination of monetary and fiscal policies to simulate the centralization of policies characteristic of a national economy. But if it were constructed for this task alone, a supranational system might damage some of its members, and in the absence of a supranational political system empowered to prevent or punish defection, it might not last for long. If its operations prevented member countries from achieving important domestic objectives, it would evoke insistent demands for secession or, at the very least, for the application of trade controls amounting to *de facto* secession. To see why an unswerving alignment of policies could get in the way of national goals, we have again to study trade-balance disturbances.[14]

If payments experience were dominated by trade-balance disturbances, dB^a's rather than dE^a's, there would be a different and more difficult relationship between the internal and external problems confronting national and regional economies. When a country or region suffers an autonomous decline in the demand

[14]Differences in rates of economic growth and in its character could also engender serious tensions. If population, investment, and technology advance at different rates in constituent countries or regions, output targets, Y^*, will also change at different rates. In this case, an alignment of actual expenditure trends may lead to cumulative gaps between potential and actual performance, and the economies with the highest growth rates may come to experience overt unemployment. If, further, economic growth leads to a systematic change in the composition of production costs, or demand patterns, calling for adjustments in the terms of trade, payments problems will arise despite the alignment of trends in expenditure. This class of problems is more apt to arise between countries than regions, because knowledge, capital, and labor move less freely between countries than within them. A substantial mobility of knowledge and capital serves, *ex ante*, to even out regional growth rates; a substantial mobility of labor serves, *ex post*, to reduce the differences in unemployment rates resulting from the residual differences in growth rates. In general, resource mobility is an efficient response to any disturbance that would, in its absence, require a change in the terms of trade. For a more rigorous treatment of these growth problems, with a formal statement of the conditions for external and internal balance, see my "*Déséquilibres des Paiements et Etalon Monétaire International*," Banque Nationale de Belgique, *Bulletin d'Information et de Documentation*, January 1965.

for its exports, it will display deflation-*cum*-deficit; when it enjoys an autonomous increase, it will display inflation-*cum*-surplus. These changes in demand, moreover, happen quite frequently in export and import markets alike; they are the inevitable counterparts of product substitution, the advent of new competitors, and changes in relative costs of production due to different rates of change in money wages and in man-hour output. They have struck at whole countries and at regions inside countries. Consider, as examples, Britain's experience in the 1920s, when a deep depression was combined with a payments deficit, and the similar but less severe American experience in the late 1950s.[15] Consider, too, the current plight of Appalachia due to the substitution of oil for coal as an industrial and household fuel, and the stagnation of New England in the late 1940s and early 1950s due to the growth of Southern textile production.[16]

An adjustment of monetary and fiscal policies cannot fully answer a trade-balance disturbance. A decrease of spending by the deficit country and an increase by the surplus country will, of course, restore external balance, but will also aggravate each country's domestic problem. An increase of spending by the deficit country and a decrease by the surplus country will restore internal balance all around, but will work to aggravate the payments problem. When, therefore, trade flows are disturbed, the countries or regions affected either have to reallocate resources, between or within them, or foster a change in the pattern of world demand favoring the products of the deficit country.

Here, then, factor mobility can help. When consumers in one of two countries switch from home to foreign goods, that country will experience deflation-*cum*-deficit, and the other will experience inflation-*cum*-surplus. If labor moves freely between them, however, responding to differences in market conditions, both countries may be able to regain full employment without any change in

[15]It is commonly agreed that Britain's depression was due to the sluggish evolution of her export industries before the First World War and was then compounded by the decision, in 1925, to reestablish convertibility at the pre-war exchange rate. The American balance-of-payments problem first emerged in 1958 with a sharp deterioration in the U.S. trade balance, and was associated with a stagnation of exports and a sharp increase of manufactured imports. At one point in 1959, the United States even displayed a merchandise-trade deficit. The prolongation of the U.S. payments problem, however, must be ascribed to different causes, notably the increase in capital exports during and after 1960.

[16]One might also associate the prolonged expansion of the West Coast economy with a trade-balance disturbance — the growth of demand for its defense-related exports.

national policies; the deficit country will have a labor surplus, the surplus country will have a labor shortage, and an exodus of labor from the deficit country can resolve each country's problem.[17] This same transfer of labor, moreover, will work to relieve the imbalance in their external trade; the shrinkage of employment, output, and income in the deficit country will reduce its demand for imports, and a corresponding expansion in the surplus country will augment its imports. It is, indeed, conceivable that the migration required to eliminate each country's employment problem will exactly suffice to erase the imbalance in foreign trade.[18]

Extending this same argument, several authors have maintained that a perfect mobility of labor between countries or regions is the necessary and sufficient condition for participation in a monetary union—for maintaining a fixed exchange rate between their currencies.[19] But though it may suffice in certain circumstances, mobility may not be required for a fixed-rate regime to function efficiently. When labor does not move between countries or regions, a trade-balance disturbance will call for a change in the terms of trade; prices must fall in the deficit country or rise in the surplus country so as to induce a countervailing shift in the pattern of world demand—an increase in spending on the products of the country with the deflation-*cum*-deficit. But the size of the requisite change in prices and the terms of trade depends upon consumer and producer responses to changes in relative prices. If a country or region is wholly dependent on a single export, actually and potentially, and the demand for its export declines, it must accept a deterioration in its terms of trade and real wage rates sufficient to restore fully the global demand for that single export. If, instead, it can export a variety of products, its terms of trade and real wage rates do not have to fall so far. Producer substitution inside the country will be joined to consumer substitution, inside and outside, restoring full employment and the trade balance at a smaller sacrifice, transitional and permanent.

A diversification of output and internal labor mobility, geo-

---

[17]But if there is a difference in the two countries' labor requirements per unit of output, migration may not fully solve both countries' problems.

[18]A corresponding mobility of capital, however, could exacerbate the two countries' problems. The decline of economic activity in the deficit country, reducing its interest rates, could increase its foreign lending and enlarge its payments deficit.

[19]See, for example, Mundell. "A Theory of Optimum Currency Areas," *American Economic Review*, September 1961, pp. 657 ff.

graphic and occupational, may consequently serve as effective substitutes for the international or interregional labor mobility that has been so much emphasized by recent writers. This same diversification of output may serve a related purpose. If output and exports are thoroughly diversified and the disturbances affecting foreign trade are independent of one another, a country or region may count on the law of large numbers to keep its foreign trade in balance and also to protect its domestic economy from external perturbations. This possibility is sometimes acknowledged, but has not attracted sufficient attention. It is, I submit, precisely because of this internal diversification that major industrial countries do not often display the painful combinations of deflation-*cum*-deficit and inflation-*cum*-surplus: the many disturbances affecting their foreign trade tend to average out rather than accumulate.[20] For the same reason, smaller less-developed countries and regions of a single country, being less diversified, display these combinations frequently and painfully. It is, finally, for this reason that economists who favor fixed exchange rates are often willing to exempt the less-developed countries. Because the economies of the latter are not well diversified, there is insufficient averaging of trade-balance disturbances, and when those disturbances appear, large changes in the terms of trade are sometimes needed to reestablish external and internal balance. The less-developed countries must be allowed to alter their exchange rates.

Although regions may experience deflation-*cum*-deficit more often than countries, they may be more fortunate in other respects. As labor moves more freely between regions than countries, regions need not always accept major changes in their terms of trade and real wage rates when they encounter trade-balance disturbances. Workers may begin to leave a depressed region when wage rates start to fall, reducing the region's labor surplus and limiting the decline, requisite and actual, in the terms of trade. In addition, regions derive several advantages from participation in a national economy. When, for example, an American community suffers deflation-*cum*-deficit, its Federal tax payments diminish at once, slowing the decline in its purchasing power and compressing the cash outflow on its balance of payments. There is also an inflow of Federal money—of unemployment benefits.

[20]When, indeed, these combinations do occur, they are apt to come from the capital account (where large disturbances can bunch up quite readily), or to result from general changes in wage rates or productivity; they may also represent the cumulative growth effects mentioned in a previous note.

Furthermore, regions can borrow (or sell off securities) in the national capital market more easily than countries can borrow abroad.[21] Finally, regions afflicted by deflation-*cum*-deficit can often obtain discretionary aid from the central government; special programs of financial and technical assistance to depressed areas have been enacted by a number of countries, including the United States.

Lacking comparable powers and instruments to compensate its member countries, a supranational monetary system perhaps has to function somewhat differently from a national monetary system.[22] As we have not yet developed efficient machinery for making international transfer payments and cannot count on private capital transactions to finance obdurate payments problems, a supranational monetary system must be able to bestow large amounts of credit on countries afflicted by trade-balance disturbances (or variations in capital flows). It must be empowered to pay a high bribe price for the maintenance of stable exchange rates and for compliance with its rules—to dissuade deficit countries from restricting international trade and investment, and to encourage the gradual changes in domestic costs and prices required to offset autonomous shifts in exports, imports, and capital flows.[23]

By implication, the managers of such a system must seek to discriminate between disturbances. They must require a prompt

[21]This point has been emphasized by J. C. Ingram; see especially his contribution to *Factors Affecting the United States Balance of Payments*, Washington D. C.: Government Printing Office, 1962.

[22]One can, of course, cite instances in which countries have obtained similar external aid. The Marshall Plan effected massive transfers to countries with difficult payments problems; more recently, the IMF has granted special drawing rights to less-developed countries dependent on exports of primary products. But these international arrangements operate sporadically and are primitive compared to the machinery for regional transfers that has been built into advanced national economies.

[23]From time to time, moreover, the system must be willing to finance a deficit country that is not making any change in domestic costs or prices but is, instead, attempting institutional reforms. It is sometimes said that adaptations of this sort are not legitimate substitutes for conventional cost-price adjustments, precisely because they should be made even in the absence of a payments deficit. But this argument forgets that once they have been made, there will be no need for cost-price adjustments (and if these are made too, they will have to be reversed). It also ignores a pervasive fact of economic and political life—that some things which should be done will not be attempted until the onset of a crisis. Sometimes, indeed, a crisis is required merely to identify the need for adaptation, let alone to galvanize those who must make the changes, be they in government or in the private sector.

response to deficits resulting from excess domestic demand and, correspondingly, should not grant much credit to the deficit country; but they must allow a slow response to deficits resulting from external disturbances and should grant ample credit to the deficit country. Failing to make this distinction, they will either be too tolerant of deficits due to excess demand or too intolerant of deficits due to trade-balance shifts and changes in capital flows. If too tolerant of the former, they will permit individual countries to export their policy errors; if too intolerant of the latter, they will impose undue hardship on countries already suffering the painful domestic consequences of shifts in world demand or production. In either case, they are bound to provoke international dissension, and in a world that does not yet possess supranational political institutions with coercive powers over national policy, they will witness a renewed disintegration of the international economy, rather than the further integration that is—or ought to be—the ultimate aim of international financial arrangements.[24]

It is the further implication of my analysis that any supranational monetary system designed to function automatically—to be proof against the fallibility of man—is also apt to fail. A system of fully flexible exchange rates, favored by many economists, would make speedy changes in the terms of trade, correcting trade-balance disturbances whenever they arose. It would also protect the world at large from errors in national policy, inflationary or deflationary, but would do so by "bottling up" the errors in the countries committing them, and punishing those countries' citizens. A country restricting domestic demand would experience an appreciation of its own currency, and this would compound the consequences of its mistake by creating additional slack in its economy.[25] Flexible exchange rates, then, are not fully efficient at coping with disturbances in national expenditure.

[24]It is regrettably easy to document this gloomy forecast. One has only to list the succession of measures taken by the United States during the past few years —the tying of foreign aid, the increase of "Buy-American" preferences governing Federal procurement, the taxation of capital outflows, and most recently, the resort to quantitative restrictions on foreign investment, called "guidelines" for the sake of form, but no less damaging to an integrated international economy.

[25]There is a further problem with flexible exchange rates: When international capital movements are sensitive to differences in national interest rates, an increase in one country's interest rate, attracting foreign capital, will cause that country's currency to appreciate and will thereby shift global spending onto other countries' goods, causing those countries to experience inflation. Full flexibility, then, may actually sensitize—not immunize—the world economy to errors in national monetary policies.

A full-fledged gold standard would also function automatically,[26] but might not be sufficiently generous in dealing with trade-balance shifts. Under a gold standard, a deficit country would be compelled to cut back its money stock as it lost reserves; it would be obliged to reinforce the deflationary pressures that emanate directly from external disturbances. With the passage of time, wages and prices would begin to fall in the deficit country (and would also rise in the surplus country), accomplishing the change in relative prices needed to neutralize external disturbances. But this would be a costly way to combat imbalances — and one that most governments sought to avoid long before they acknowledged an explicit commitment to maintain full employment.[27]

This is, perhaps, the point at which to recapitulate and offer some suggestions regarding the design of a supranational monetary system. Such a system, it is clear, cannot apply the same standards and sanctions to all the countries of the world. The major industrial nations may be ready to refrain from restricting their trade; they may also be able to maintain stable exchange rates — though this is far from certain and may not be desirable. The less-developed economies, by contrast, lack the resilience and flexibility that diversified production confers; they are exposed to external disturbances. They also lack a large armory of policy instruments and the internal political cohesion required to master external disturbances by adjusting domestic wages and prices. They must be encouraged to change their exchange rates to resolve their payments problems.[28]

Furthermore, the major industrial countries have still to foster a sufficient international mobility of capital, knowledge, and labor among themselves. International transfers of capital and technical knowledge can generate more uniform rates of growth in output and demand. International transfers of labor can cut down the costs of trade-balance adjustment. It is, incidentally, the chief function of private direct investment to redistribute capital and knowledge among the industrial countries, because transfers of

---

[26]I have in mind a textbook gold standard, under which the national money supply would be governed by the central bank's holdings of gold, not De Gaulle's gold standard, under which central banks would hold their reserves in gold but would retain autonomy in monetary policy.

[27]See, for example, R. Nurkse, *International Currency Experience*, Geneva: League of Nations, 1944, Chap. 4; and A. I. Bloomfield, *The International Gold Standard, 1880–1914*, New York: Federal Reserve Bank of New York, 1959.

[28]They should, indeed, be urged to alter their exchange rates in lieu of using trade controls to foster development by further import substitution.

this sort occur much more freely among the far-flung branches of a single firm than between competing firms. And it is for this reason, if no other, that restrictions on private direct investment may damage the world economy. These restrictions may be quite effective in correcting payments deficits, but are correspondingly destructive of a vital equilibrating mechanism, which would be beneficial to the whole international economy over the longer run.

A supranational monetary system encompassing these same industrial countries should, in turn, display three separate attributes:

1. It should provide for a continuous confrontation and reconciliation of national objectives. All countries cannot run trade-balances surpluses at once; nor can they all achieve over-all surpluses unless international reserves are made to grow at the corresponding rate. No country, moreover, can enlarge its foreign lending unless some other country is willing to borrow more (and also enlarge domestic expenditure relative to output). Going one step further, it is important to formulate and ratify the domestic aims of each constituent national economy. The international community cannot censure any country for failing to restore external balance without weighing the domestic opportunity cost of faster or larger external adjustment. More generally, one cannot define an "optimum policy mix" for a single country or group of countries without first articulating a consistent constellation of national and international objectives; the very concept of optimality implies a correspondence between instruments and aims.

2. The system should provide for a close coordination of national policies pertaining to domestic demand. This is the necessary substitute for a supranational financial policy to standardize trends in national expenditure and thereby to forestall the emergence of inflation-*cum*-surplus or deflation-*cum*-deficit anywhere within the system. A partial coordination of national policies has already been achieved among the industrial countries; frank and wide-ranging discussions in Working Party Three of the OECD have begun to exert a significant influence on national policies, especially monetary policies. But a closer coordination is needed, and it should be extended to fiscal policies.

3. The system should be capable of financing obdurate deficits, whether by the transfer of existing reserves from one country to another or by the creation of new reserves. It should, of course, be able to insist that countries making use of its credit facilities give evidence of progress toward external balance. It should even be able to withhold assistance from countries that misbehave — those that permit domestic inflation or resort to trade controls. But if it is forbidden to finance long-lasting deficits, it cannot expect deficit countries to obey its injunctions against the use of trade restrictions and to accomplish painful changes in domestic costs and prices.

These three activities, and notably the last two, also have to be linked in a special way. The connections among them, moreover, are often misunderstood.

Much of what is written on the monetary system proposes that national policies be "disciplined" by limiting reserve creation — that rationing reserves will force an alignment of trends in expenditure. This prescription assumes that most imbalances arise from divergent expenditure trends, and implies that the remaining imbalances can be handled by modest adjustments in the policy mix (such as countervailing changes in monetary and fiscal policies) arranged by consultation and negotiation.

If my own analysis is correct, the conventional prescription mismates instruments and aims, and may be destructive of the monetary system. It would be more logical — and very much easier — to seek the required alignment of national policies through multilateral consultation, then to gear reserve creation for the financing of residual deficits. It is, in fact, necessary to proceed this way if, at this juncture, the monetary system is obliged to operate by purchasing compliance, rather than by punishing aberrant policies. If it were forbidden to finance the most difficult adjustments, it could not provide meaningful incentives. Put differently, any attempt to regulate the quality of payments policies by negotiation would not succeed if, by reining-in on credit creation, the system had already required a rapid suppression of every imbalance.[29]

---

[29]There is the further difficulty that a deflationary departure from accepted standards of national policy cannot be punished by restricting reserve creation; in this instance, limitations on access to credit would damage the innocent (who would be in deficit) rather than the guilty (who would be in surplus).

Some will surely object that adherence to any such monetary system calls for a considerable sacrifice of national sovereignty. But the sacrifice of sovereignty took place long ago. It occurred when the major industrial countries opted for stable exchange rates and pledged themselves to work for freer international trade and investment. To honor these commitments, nations must behave much as if they were the regions of a single country, and the international monetary system should be designed to reward them when they act that way.

Commentary

Robert Triffin

I find myself in the embarrassing and most unusual position of being unable to offer any comments on Professor Kenen's paper other than complete agreement and sincere admiration, with no "but" or other qualifications. My only regret is that it was not presented at the 1966 meeting in Zürich between academics and the main officials of the Group of Ten. It should have received top billing there, and steered in a most useful and operational direction our discussion of the "adjustment process" and its relation to the international liquidity problem.

I particularly welcome: (1) the distinction so lucidly drawn by Kenen between imbalances resulting from excesses (or shortages) of aggregate expenditures in relation to productive capacity and those arising from disturbances in international competitiveness; (2) his suggested diagnosis of the first case as one evidenced by inflation-*cum*-deficit (or deflation-*cum*-surplus) and of the second as evidenced by inflation-*cum*-surplus (or deflation-*cum*-deficit); and (3) his cogent argument for appropriate policy prescriptions discriminating between these major sources of national, as well as international, maladjustments.

I had stressed the same distinction myself, many years ago, in a brief paper for the Joint Economic Committee,[1] and highlighted it in the statistical framework for income and monetary analysis applied in *Statistics of Sources and Uses of Finance: 1948–1958*.[2] Kenen goes much further, however, in developing the policy implications of this analytic and statistical framework.

The radically different types of disequilibria revealed by his suggested diagnosis obviously call for radically different policy prescriptions, rather than for any single panacea, whether it be the current academic fad for flexible exchange rates or the traditional bias for automatic—and predominantly deflationary—responses to all balance-of-payments disturbances. Exchange-rate readjustments may be an appropriate cure for uncompetitiveness, but not for excesses—or shortages—of aggregate demand. Conversely, policies directed at changing aggregate demand fit the second of these two cases, but not the first.

The flexible rates school and the disciplinarian school both tend to underestimate, moreover, the role that "financing" should play in avoiding unnecessary—and, indeed, disequilibrating in the long run—readjustment of temporary imbalance, or in encouraging the adoption of desirable, but often slow-working, methods of readjustment in preference to faster, but "beggar-my-neighbor" policies.

The most novel parts of Kenen's paper, however, are:

1. his discussion of internal and external mobility (reallocation) of factors of production and consumption patterns in the adjustment process, and of the greater obstacles faced in this respect by the typically undiversified economies of the less developed countries;

2. the parallel and contrasts which he draws between the problem of *interregional* adjustment within a national economy and *international* adjustment between differ-

---

[1]"Adjusting Features in the Mechanism of the Balance of Payments and Exchange Rates" in *Foreign Economic Policy* (Hearings before Subcommittee on Foreign Economic Policy), Washington, D.C., 1955, pp. 134–142, reproduced in *The World Money Maze: National Currencies in International Payments*, New Haven, Conn.: Yale University Press, 1966.

[2]OEEC, Paris, 1960; see particularly the breakdown of the "Total Expenditure Gap" and "Total Monetary Financing," in Tables 1 and 1a, between "Production Increases" on the one hand, and "Expenditure in Excess of Production" (grouping together "Price Increases" and "Import Surpluses"), on the other.

ent countries, with separate, theoretically independent and sovereign monetary and fiscal authorities. Realistic aims of international monetary policy should, in the latter case, be tailored down to the degree of cooperation that can practically be elicited from the participating national authorities, but should also grow rapidly over time *pari passu* with a keener understanding of the real problems and opportunity-costs of alternative policies, or lack of policies. The rate of progress that is likely to prove achievable will differ greatly, however, for world-wide cooperation and for more limited *regional groups*, such as the European Economic Community, the OECD, the Central American Monetary Union, and so forth. Kenen's previous remarks about the role of factor mobility would also suggest that developed countries, with a more diversified economy, can assign themselves more ambitious goals in this respect than less-developed countries, with a less diversified economy.

I fully agree with these perceptive and imaginative views of the true nature of the "adjustment problem" which looms so large today in the marathon negotiations of the IMF, the Group of Ten, and UNCTAD about international monetary reform. Policy decisions regarding the financing or elimination of balance-of-payments surpluses or deficits cannot be handled rationally by each surplus or deficit country, in utter disregard of their mutually supporting, or mutually defeating, impact upon the country's partners. International surpluses and deficits are the two sides of the same coin. The adjustment problem is an *international* problem rather than a conglomerate of separate *national* problems, and calls for *joint*, rather than isolated, decisions by the countries concerned.

In brief, Kenen has viewed the adjustment problem in the international perspective in which it properly belongs, and set forth boldly the inescapable political and institutional implications of this radical recasting of the anachronistic approach still enshrined in most academic textbooks as well as in official negotiations.

Adjustment, financing, and liquidity creation constitute three different, but inseparable, facets of international monetary reform. Let us hope that Kenen's paper will help demonstrate their interrelationship to the Group of Ten negotiators and dispel the fog of nonsense accumulated by the advocates of an automatic CRU system of "earned," "owned," "unconditional" reserves "to hold" rather than "to spend," totally divorced from the financing of future balance-of-payments surpluses and deficits, as well as from desirable pressures and incentives to readjustment policies.

Index